DESIGNING YOUR
FASHION PORTFOLIO

FAIRCHILD
BOOKS

DESIGNING YOUR FASHION PORTFOLIO

FROM CONCEPT TO PRESENTATION

Joanne Ciresi Barrett

FAIRCHILD BOOKS

NEW YORK

Fairchild Books

An imprint of Bloomsbury Publishing Inc

175 Fifth Avenue
New York
NY 10010
USA

50 Bedford Square
London
WC1B 3DP
UK

www.fairchildbooks.com

Library of Congress Cataloging-in-Publication Data
Barrett, Joanne Ciresi
Designing Your Fashion Portfolio: From Concept to Presentation
2012937632

ISBN: 978-1-60901-0072

Text design and typesetting by Alicia Freile, Tango Media
Cover Design by Sarah Silberg
Cover Art: Tommy Ton/Trunk Archive
Printed and bound in the United States of America

TABLE OF CONTENTS

EXTENDED TABLE OF CONTENTS

PREFACE

The goal of *Designing Your Fashion Portfolio: From Concept to Presentation* is to free your mind of the question, "what makes a portfolio stand out as exceptional, and how can I create one?"

The ultimate goal of the text is to give you, the designer, a tangible set of skills and a visual imprint of the process and completion of a job placement portfolio. The skills and techniques can be put into practice throughout your student and professional career. The fashion design portfolio (FDP) method is motivational. The teachings encourage you to increase your inner drive, enabling your creative level to reach high standards. The approach is to demonstrate how to become systematic while being creative. The text walks the you through exercises, self-evaluation critiques, goal-setting lists, commercial refinement research, and applied techniques, and shows you how to do these tasks while simultaneously maintaining the creative design process.

Unlike a typical refinement application being the very end of the process, FDP teaches you to visualize your finest portfolio contents at the outset of the project and then guides you through the exercises that lead to the realization of your ideal portfolio.

FDP presents you with direction and choices that best match your skill level. The exercises teach you to understand how your skill level affects your goal planning to produce your best image package. Proven techniques help you determine how far to go out of your comfort zone with your current skills set, as well as how to acquire and hone stronger skills. The system enables you to fuel your individual creative engine throughout the design process. It intends to maintain the flow of your creative thoughts balanced by extreme reality checks for portfolio betterment.

Based upon my years of teaching on the college level, the book presents real-life questions by current-day students, which are answered by example and brought into the process of portfolio development. Professional designers' experiences are presented for reference and motivation. The sequence of the chapters is based on in-class development of portfolios in the senior-level exit portfolio courses. The chapters can be referenced throughout your professional career in fashion design, as well as during college.

The visual examples in the text are meant to show diversity in skill level and segments of the fashion market to encourage you to work at the level that best showcases your strengths and understanding of not just who you are as a designer, but what you can bring to the company or design studio job. The exercises, boxes, and visuals aid you in executing the portfolio project.

ORGANIZATION OF THE TEXT

The chapters of *Designing Your Fashion Portfolio* are sequenced to take readers step by step through the process of creating a portfolio to present as a primary way to market themselves to potential employers. The first five chapters discuss the initial steps of collecting one's work and selecting the contents of a portfolio focused on a particular market segment. Chapter 6 is a pivotal chapter that provides options for organizing a portfolio geared to promoting the designer's qualifications for a job with a specific company. The remaining three chapters discuss how to revise the contents of the portfolio to market the designer to other potential employers and how to present the portfolio in an interview.

In Chapter 1, the contents of the portfolio are defined and illustrated by examples of each element. This chapter outlines collection size, number of collections, and sequencing of the portfolio pages. An explanation of the different end uses of a portfolio and the importance of the sketchbook are emphasized. Students set up an initial portfolio of past and current work for immediate interviews and to serve as a catalyst for launching the final portfolio project. They preview steps in portfolio building that will be studied in more detail in later chapters.

Chapter 2 serves to organize the building process of designing the portfolio collection. The conceptual design of the portfolio layout is planned at the same time the collection is designed. Activities performed within and outside of the studio are segmented for the purposes of creating clarity, but designers can worked on these tasks as they see fit. The basic steps of the design process are used as a map for collection building. The chapter includes the basic guides to organizational techniques, retail shopping, forecast and color trend services, fashion and trade shows, and the textile and print markets. Icons of the compile, edit, finalize, and designer filter formulas serve as visual cues for steps in portfolio building. Exercises ask the designer to outline the process of a designer project, to research category specializations, and to apply a "hit this mark" method of designing a market-right collection.

Chapter 3 sharpens the designer's portfolio marketing strategies by focusing on retail channels of distribution and considering a market specialization. The exercises walk the designer through how to identify the target consumer, the designer's own taste, price points, and designing for age groups and size ranges. In addition, the exercises tap the designer's motivations for portfolio direction and ask the designer to idealize the final portfolio through visualization techniques. The final exercise is the preparation of the designer grid to position all the design aspects of mood, color, textiles, and silhouettes of the portfolio collections.

Chapter 4 defines the market-focused portfolio through viewing, planning, and technique. Portfolios focused on gender, children's wear,

maternity, and large sizes are discussed. Attention is also given to key category influences, general sportswear portfolios, specialized portfolios, and attitudinizing the fashion figure for a specific market. The exercises ask the designer to compare sizes in retail stores to better understand the consumer's fit and function requirements, and to study influential fashion illustrators for inspiration in portraying appropriate figure attitudes in their own portfolio collections.

The specialized portfolio is defined in explicit detail in Chapter 5. Categories of design are described verbally and shown in illustrations. The boxes itemize the types of specializations, inform the readers about how the specialized designer works to meet the client's needs, and give further in-depth descriptions of the activewear, bridal, and millinery categories. The exercises enforce the need to get to know one's specialized client and to evaluate one's own design and problem-solving capabilities for a specialized category.

In Chapter 6, students undertake the Portfolio Project. The portfolio pages are described and illustrated in terms of the segments of mood, color, textiles, and silhouettes/flats pages, and each segment is designed through the steps of concept development, editing, and finalization. The building blocks of the previously completed materials are utilized: The designer grid, the idealized final portfolio exercise, the sketchbook, retail market reports, illustrations, layout and finalization evaluations, and art supplies and CAD programs are all brought together as tools for creating the final portfolio story.

Chapter 7 walks the designer through the completion of all collections being shown in the portfolio. The portfolio project is reviewed for adherence to the idealized portfolio goals, the layout goals, and the page sequencing to tell the story of the designer's collections. The designer considers options for further refinement of the layout details, page-turning dramatic effects, branding/packaging, and possibilities of including past collections in the portfolio. Keeping fluid in portfolio building and refinement is presented as a lifetime endeavor. Exercises help readers evaluate whether their portfolio goals are actualized, train them to become more objective in their critiques of their work, and guide them to make changes in their portfolio projects to present themselves effectively with a portfolio tailored to each new interview throughout their careers. A sequencing exercise tasks designers with evaluating the drama created in the order of the portfolio pages.

Chapter 8 introduces the designer to the basic language, formats, and visual presentations of digital and Web-based portfolios. "Old school" presentations are blended with "new school" portfolio combinations for designers to decide how much technology to apply to their books. This chapter surveys programs and devices that can enhance designers' portfolios through modern technology.

Chapter 9 prepares the designer for interviews for entry-level, design-related jobs in the apparel industry. Preparation for the interview, expectation of the designer and interviewer, and interview follow-up methods are outlined in the text and practiced in an in-class role-play exercise. In a series of interviews, design professionals share their insights and inform and inspire student designers as they take their portfolios on the road for their first job interviews.

An epilogue reviews what was accomplished in each chapter; it can be used as a reference during portfolio building throughout a designer's career.

Finally, this book is about learning to be open to new challenges in designing a portfolio that best suits the client and the designer's specific career goals.

ACKNOWLEDGEMENTS

This book is dedicated to all of my former and future students. I am sincerely grateful to all of the students I have had the privilege to teach in my classroom at Massachusetts College of Art and Design. I've learned so much from each of you. My experiences working with you have shown me where there was need for a textbook to help you learn the process of creating a design portfolio; and thanks to you, I learned how to teach my craft.

I am eternally grateful to the incredible designers who contributed to this book with their work and their insights, including Joseph Abboud, Amsale Aberra, Doranne Westerhouse Awad, David Bermingham, Katie Choquette, Christos, Bissie Clover, Cat Craig, Mary-Frances Cusick, Carole D'Arconte, Jerry Dellova, Virginia Fretto, Annie Kee Gaia, Pavlina Gilson, Kerrin Marie Griffin, Jane Henry, Ithwa Huq-Jones, Maya Luz, Margee Minier, Kelly Moore, Alexandra Palmisano, Peter Morrone, Plugg Jeans, Shawn Reddy, Miri Rooney, Jeury Rosario, Lindsey Rogue Russell, Jamie Sadock, Rebecca Sheehan, Nooree Suh, Katherine Waddell, Jenn Webb, and Cheryl Zarcone. These talented designers contributed their work to this book without hesitation. It is because of them that the book can show you a range of work styles to use as a benchmark for your designs. This is the principle premise of the book: each designer works differently and needs to find his or her voice in a final portfolio form. Their design visuals drive this textbook. Thank you for your generous support—your work will inspire students for years to come!

Thanks to my friends and former colleagues at Massachusetts College of Art and Design, Boston Massachusetts, without whom this book would not be possible. I've learned so much from each of you, especially Sondra Grace, chair of the Fashion Design department, and Elizabeth Resnick, chair of the Graphic Design department.

A special thank you to the wonderful professors and instructors that I had the honor to work with at MassArt: Jayne Avery, Anne Bernays-Trevenen, John DiStefano, Renee Harding, Yelena Piliavsky, Jennifer Varekamp, and Meg Young. Thank you to Velma Johnson for her administrative support, smile, and genuine friendship while I was at MassArt.

Thank you to all of the professors and instructors at the Fashion Institute of Technology, New York, New York, who taught me how to be a fashion designer. The college was and is my professional backbone. The quality of high-level mentoring and hands-on instruction that I received at FIT make me the designer I am today.

Thank you all of the great fashion professionals I've had the pleasure to work with in the industry since 1980; you've taught me so much. Your support and belief in me throughout my career have been incredible and are greatly appreciated.

The following reviewers, selected by the publisher, provided many helpful recommendations: Abra Berman, Art Institute of San Francisco; Catherine Darlington, IADT, Chicago; Kelly De Melo, Art Institute of Dallas; Barbara Gutenberg, FIDM; Monica Klos, formerly of IADT, Pittsburgh; Van Dyk Lewis, Cornell University; Jeanie Lisenby, Miami International University of Art and Design; Tania Pazelsky, Wood Tobé Coburn School; Nancy L. Strickler, Purdue University; and Theresa M. Winge, Indiana University.

To the staff of Fairchild Books I extend my thanks for educating me in the textbook publishing process and helping me translate my strategies for portfolio design from my classroom presentation into a printed format that other instructors can share with their students. Specifically, I thank my editors: Jaclyn Bergeron for supporting this project from the outset, Sylvia Weber for helping me organize and revise the text, Jessica Katz for shepherding the manuscript through copyediting and production, and Amy Butler for her assistance with the preparation of ancillary materials for the instructor. I appreciate the guidance of Sarah Silberg in communicating my vision for the layout and design and the help of Avital Aronowitz with photo research.

Finally, I owe my family and friends a big thank you for their support, especially Anna Marie Ciresi; Michael DeCuollo; Scott Miller; Mary Wolff; my wonderful husband of 26 years, Kevin; and my loving children Dylan and Alana. You made this book possible each time you encouraged me to keep on writing! Thanks for the "go Joey" and the "go Mommy" love.

DESIGNING YOUR FASHION PORTFOLIO

Chapter 1

INTRODUCTION TO PORTFOLIO BUILDING FOR FASHION DESIGNERS

OBJECTIVES

+ Describe the contents of a fashion portfolio.

+ Maintain a sketchbook that reflects your creative process.

+ Complete a temporary portfolio of student work to be ready for self-critique and on-the-spot job interviews.

+ Purchase a portfolio case based upon your ideals for a final portfolio.

Regardless of your strengths in 2D (illustration) or 3D (making your garments work on the runway) design, what lands you a job is a dynamic portfolio. Your portfolio is your selling tool, your visual communication device. It is your designer message presented in a strong illustrated package.

The portfolio is always presented by the designer in the first interview for an assistant, associate, or designer position. You will edit your portfolio throughout your career to represent yourself in your best light for each interview. This textbook will help you prepare the portfolio for your exit interview from school and adapt the portfolio you prepare for that purpose for later use.

THE USES OF A FASHION DESIGN PORTFOLIO

Fashion design portfolios have different end uses depending on the market for particular talents and skills. Different end uses lead to different expectations on the part of the person or people reviewing a portfolio.

Your student portfolio, where you assemble your work for different courses, will be different from your exit portfolio from college. As you enter each stage of advancement in your career, you will update your portfolio. It will become an ongoing process.

Different end uses for portfolios include the following:

+ Placement into college or graduate school.
+ National or international design competitions.
+ Exit interview from college.
+ Interview with a job placement counselor.
+ Interview with a head hunter.
+ Assistant design internship (paying or non-paying) while in college or after graduation.
+ Entry-level position in the industry: assistant designer or assistant tech designer.
+ Entry-level position in the industry as a first patternmaker or an assistant draper: sometimes a designer will interview for a position as a first pattern maker or assistant draper as an option to building a career in patternmaking or draping instead of design or as a foot in the door to become an assistant designer.
+ Presentation for the next levels of design after your first job: associate designer, associate tech designer, tech designer, designer, head designer, design director, creative director.
+ Interview with a specific company—designing a collection just for the interview.
+ Follow-up interview with presentation board.

DIFFERENT EXPECTATIONS

During your college years, keep all of your final fashion plates in acetate portfolio sleeves. Keep a temporary portfolio with the pages inserted in the portfolio case. Review your work periodically, and have the case ready to go for an internship or related opportunity. Itoya-brand cases are fine for very temporary or short-term use.

Also keep your design competition collections in your portfolio, along with any credentials or awards and press releases regarding the nature of the competition.

The exit portfolio and the entry-level portfolio you will be developing using this textbook will be the same and will follow the contents listed in Table 1.1. Your design portfolio is your foot in the door to an entry-level design job. The portfolio needed for the job interview is inherently more refined than a basic student portfolio, which is traditionally a compilation of your student assignments in college. More advanced levels and specialized versions of portfolio development are presented in Chapters 4 through 7, and interviews are detailed at length in Chapter 9.

When you are on a first interview, whether for your first full-time position or later in your career, you may be asked to come back for a second or third interview with a completed board presentation of a collection that the interviewer asks you to design for the company or design firm.

Itoya is a brand name for inexpensive portfolio cases in which to store and organize unedited work before selecting the content of the portfolio to be used for presentation. It is not recommended for a final, professional portfolio. Itoya portfolio cases allow designers to slide their fashion plate into the clear pocket pages, which are acid and PVC free. The book is made of lightweight polypropylene, which protects artwork from damaging environmental elements. The book is designed to lie completely flat when opened. There is a pocket on the spine for a label. Sizes, in inches, suitable for designer portfolio work are: 8½ x 11, 9 x 12, 11 x 14, and 14 x 17. *(Image courtesy of ITOYA of America, Ltd.)*

COMMON EXPECTATIONS

As you review this evolution, try to understand the complexities within the industry that put increasing demand on the designer's portfolio to be more than a library of fashion plates. A story needs to be told, and you are charged with creating the narrative, illustrations, plot, character development, beginning, and end—all the while luring the viewer into your design statement and your design world.

Over the last few years, dramatic industry changes have stretched the role of the designer, requiring a multitude of demanding skills. In addition to telling your design story, your portfolio must show your instructors—and, later, potential employers—your capabilities as a designer, including the following:

+ Forecasting and displaying mood, texture, and color statements to buyers
+ Ability to design for multiple seasons and quick-turn merchandise
+ Understanding of retail distribution
+ Hand-rendering as well as computer-aided skills (CAD systems, Adobe Photoshop and Illustrator programs)
+ Ability to execute flat drawings with exacting spec calculations
+ Production and factory communication

In the past, designers' presentations were much simpler than the portfolios needed to advance in today's global fashion industry. Single-figure **fashion plates** (one page of a fashion illustration that a designer or an illustrator creates) were standard projections of image and style for the designer. Hand-rendered, frozen in time, posing in her Sunday-best; she stood awaiting next season's fashions. Some designers use their favorite **croquis** (a template of the fashion figure that can serve as the foundation for an illustration of a design) and simply redress it in the next season's ensemble collections. The **flat** sketch intended to show the specifications of the garment was minimally represented in a thumbnail sketch. The frayed swatch of fabric was hastily pasted onto the plate, and the designer original would be created through direct contact with the pattern maker, draper, samplehand (the sample sewer), and finally the production team. (*Author's collection*)

Today's portfolios incorporate intricate manipulation skills both with hand-rendering and computer drawing. The 2D page can be treated in a multilayer format, creating dimension, depth, and texture that extend beyond the garment collections. It has become a theatrical stage, backdrop, or added marketing element that is more in keeping with today's fully loaded sensory media projections. Hired designers get their jobs from these modern portfolios because the book can sell the designers' looks to the interviewer. Today's designers are hired for their ability to communicate with their potential audiences—internal corporate merchandisers and selling teams, the retail buyer, and eventually the consumer. *(Courtesy of Nooree Suh)*

Conversely, many modern designers have been hired because of a portfolio that stands out in its simplicity of presentation. Pure designers with a dynamic ability to capture their images with the stroke of a pen or brush are encouraged to continue doing so, after they have evaluated the market and their own goals. *(Courtesy of Jeury Rosario)*

TYPICAL PORTFOLIO CONTENTS

The typical fashion design portfolio case consists of the items described in Table 1.1. As a designer, you will not just present your apparel collection story, but you will *design* your portfolio presentation in a story format to project a marketing or style image with a forward-thinking message. This is an opportunity to showcase your unique talents.

To protect the pages of your portfolio, use only *polypropylene or acetate sleeves*. This material is an archival-quality plastic that can preserve all artwork for a lifetime and prevent damage, with the exception of a flood or fire. Clear plastic sleeves that are *not* designated as archival will allow permanent damage to your artwork by fading, yellowing, and/or "lifting" your illustrations off of the page.

Follow the checklist in Exercise 1.1 as you go through the book to check off your portfolio contents.

The basic leather zip-case portfolio with the multi-ring binder system. This style case is available from different manufacturers in vinyl, leather, and premium leather. The handle is mounted on the spine of the case, keeping the pages hanging straight and preventing them from bending. Some cases are sold with 10–25 super-clear archival pages, which are sealed on three sides or open on three sides (depending on the brand) and include acid-free black paper inserts. Sizes, in inches, for designers are 8½ x 11, 11 x 14, and 14 x 17. *(Courtesy of Portfolios-and-art-cases.com)*

Archival page protectors are sold as refills that fit all multi-ring portfolio cases and are made of archival-grade polypropylene for transparency and chemical stability. The binders shown here are sealed on three sides and load from the open top. Page protectors are also available with three open sides. The fashion plate is inserted from the top, bottom, or binder side. This style is recommended, as the page lies more smoothly and is less disruptive to the viewer. Each page comes with an acid-free black paper insert, and it should be marked as meeting requirements for archival storage. *(Courtesy of Portfolios-and-art-cases.com)*

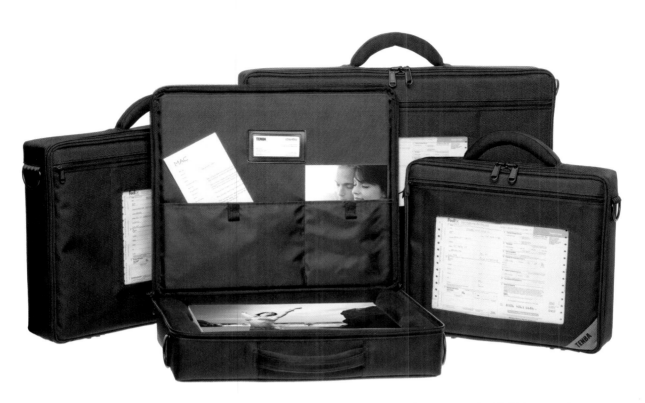

Designer's identification label with name, address, phone number, and e-mail address on inside page cover. This label is important in case you lose your portfolio. *(Courtesy of Portfolios-and-art-cases.com)*

TABLE 1.1. | **Typical Portfolio Contents**

Item	Description	Presentation Options and Purpose
Portfolio case	A formal book or carrying case (not an informal Itoya case with plastic sleeves), typically ring bound, or a box containing individual pages. Can be leather or vinyl bound or a metal box covered in leather or vinyl. Construction can include a zipper closure, open edges, or a lid. May have a shoulder strap or handle. Standard industry sizes : 9" x 12", 11" x 14", or 14" x 17"	Attractive container to show designs during an interview.
Identification label	Plain white paper or specialty paper, approximately 3 ¼" x 2" (size of a business card) printed with designer's name, address, phone number(s) (land line and/or cell), and e-mail address.	Affixed to the inside front cover of the portfolio to identify the owner so that it can be returned if it is left with an interviewer or accidentally lost.
Résumé	One-page chronological description of one's work, educational experience, and other qualifications. Printed on business-quality paper.	10 copies in a folder inserted in the front sleeve or pocket of the portfolio case to be available to present during interviews.
Polypropylene sleeves	Sleeves of thermoplastic substance. May be punched with holes to insert into a ring-bound portfolio. Sometimes called acetate or plastic pages, but must be of archival quality.	Protects pages of the portfolio collection from moisture, fading from sunlight, tearing, and other causes of damage.
Title page or intro page	Optional first page of a portfolio. Either a full-page or business-card size. May include a designer's statement.	An introduction to the collection(s) presented, creating a brand image or a setting for viewing the contents of the portfolio.
Mood or concept pages	1 to 2 pages per collection of images cut and pasted from various sources and/or computer-generated images that set the mood for the collection or suggest sources of inspiration.	Establish a concept or mood for the collection, giving it a unifying theme or identity. May be combined with other pages or shown separately. Pages should be all portrait or all landscape orientation, with few exceptions if needed, to allow for easy viewing by interviewers.
Color presentation pages	1 to 2 pages per collection of colors, presented as 1"–3" skeins of yarn, swatches of fabric, paint chips, hand-rendered or computer-generated squares of color, typically 2" or 5" or other shapes.	Presentation of the colorways for the collection(s) shown in the portfolio. May be combined with other pages or shown separately. Pages should be all portrait or all landscape orientation, with few exceptions if needed, to allow for easy viewing by interviewers.

Item	Description	Presentation Options and Purpose
Textile presentation pages	1 to 2 pages per collection of fabric swatches, cleanly mounted on paper or neatly folded. Edges of swatches may be cut straight or with pinking shears. Usually 1" x 2" or 4" x 5" rectangles or similarly sized squares. Swatches are usually of uniform size for each collection.	Presentation of the fabrics selected for a collection. May be combined with other pages or shown separately. Pages should be all portrait or all landscape orientation, with just a few exceptions if needed, to allow for easy viewing by interviewers.
Fashion plates	6 to 8 pages per collection of full or cropped figures, 1–8 figures on a page. May be hand-drawn and hand-rendered, computer generated, or a combination.	Presentation of the silhouettes of designs within a collection. May be combined with other pages or shown separately. Pages should be all portrait or all landscape orientation, with only a few exceptions if needed, to allow for easy viewing by interviewers.
Flat drawings	Technical drawing of garments as they would appear if lying flat on a surface rather than being worn. Show front and back views; back view may be 5–10% smaller than front view. Drawn to exact proportions of the cut and sewn garment. Outline may be thicker than lines showing stitching or details. Typically not shaded. May be hand-drawn or computer-generated, or a combination.	In production, used to communicate measurements to sample makers; in portfolios, used to demonstrate ability to communicate technical information visually for production. May be combined with other pages, especially fashion plates, or shown separately. Pages should be all portrait or all landscape orientation, with a few exceptions if needed, to allow for easy viewing by interviewers.
CAD pages	Computer-generated mood, color, textile, fashion plate, and flat drawing pages, as separate pages or in combinations.	Demonstrate the designer's skills with CAD programs. Pages should be all portrait or all landscape orientation, with a few exceptions if needed, to allow for easy viewing by interviewers.
Sketchbook (journal)	A bound or spiral bound notebook, 3" x 5", 8 ½" x 11", 11" x 14", or 14" x 17" with pages showing rough sketches, doodles, notes, colorings, cutouts, and other images in an unorganized format.	Carried with the designer at all times to record ideas and inspirations. Taken to interviews in the back-cover pocket of the portfolio or carried separately, if necessary, to demonstrate to interviewers the designer's thought processes and trend-tracking skills.
Leave-behind piece	Optional flash drive, CD-ROM, DVD, or page printed in full color that serves as a reminder of the designer's style, brand, or identity. Includes same information as on the identification label in the portfolio case; for electronic leave-behind pieces, identification information is on the covering as well as within the electronic files.	A condensed presentation of the portfolio images to leave an impression of the designer's work after the interview and serve as a reminder of the designer's brand or image.
Computer-based presentation	An optional item; a flash drive carried in the front or back sleeve of the portfolio case. Can be a PowerPoint presentation. Shows entire portfolio.	Makes portfolio available for the interviewer to view on his or her computer or share with co-workers who may have a voice in the hiring decision.

Two-page spread of a designer mood board. *(Courtesy of Kelly Moore)*

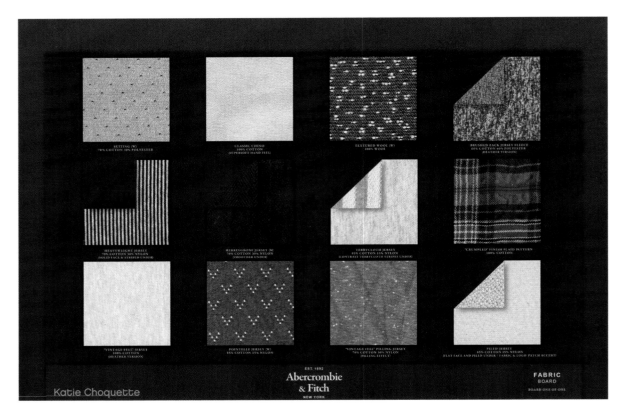

Textile presentation page for an interview with Abercrombie & Fitch. *(Courtesy of Katie Choquette)*

Color presentation spread with additional pages of title, mood, and textile presentation. *(Courtesy of Lindsey Russell)*

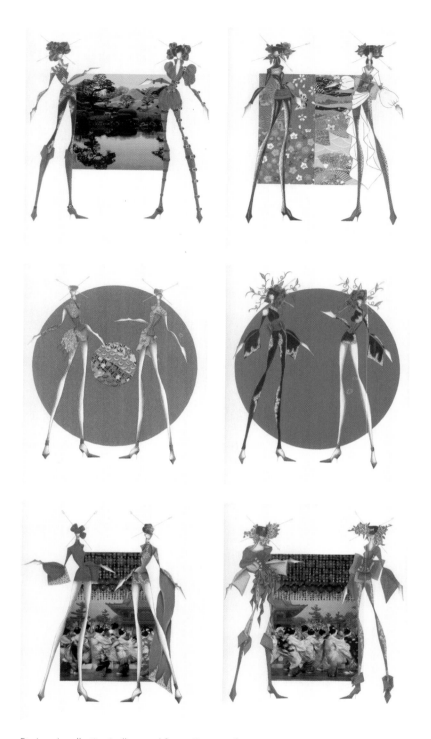

Designer's collection in illustrated form. *(Courtesy of Jeury Rosario)*

Flats presentation page. *(Courtesy of Jeury Rosario)*

New Casual-Jumper,Casual Jacket, Military

CAD portfolio page. The designer chose an illustration, layout, and presentation style to support the military design message of the garment collection. The fashion illustrations are intentionally rigid and without movement to support this military look. The monotone skin color, hand gesture, leg stance, and proportions are deliberate to accentuate the look of a soldier. The designer rendered a display case for her background to add structure to the garment presentation. The typeface, heading, and spec information are simply rendered to give the facts in a straightforward manner. The color palette is depicted at the top right corner. The garment details are clearly and precisely drawn, and the flats match the proportions depicted on the fashion figure. She states her fabric and lining fiber contents. The suggestion of linear striping in the background structure mimics stripes on a military uniform. While not all CAD pages show illustrations, flats, and designer specs, this page is an example of a designer's choice for this collection. *(Courtesy of Nooree Suh)*

Sketchbook pages. *(Courtesy of Rebecca Sheehan)*

OBJECTIVE: To ensure that your portfolio is completed on schedule.

USE: To track your progress in preparing a portfolio.

Copy this chart and complete it every time you prepare a portfolio for a class critique or an interview.

Item	Completion/Interview		Concepts Formulated		Edited Versions 1, 2, 3, etc.	
	DUE	ACTUAL	DUE	ACTUAL	DUE	ACTUAL
Portfolio case						
ID label						
Résumé						
Archival-quality sleeves						
Title page						
Mood page(s)						
Color page(s)						
Textile page(s)						
Illustrations/ fashion plates						
Flats						
CAD page(s)						
Sketchbook						
Leave-behind piece (optional)						
Computer-based presentation (optional)						

SKETCHBOOK BASICS: THE STEPPING STONES OF CREATIVITY

Your fashion design experience in college will most likely start with the use of the fashion design journal or sketchbook. Sketchbooks for designers are available in various sizes and configurations. The cover of the book is usually black, but specialty sketchbooks can be purchased in different colors. The hardbound sketchbook style is most traditionally used in an interview; it is available in the sizes (in inches) 4 x 6, 5½ x 8, 8½ x 11, and 11 x 14. The downside of the hardbound book is that it does not lie flat very easily, and some designers may find sketching in it cumbersome.

The second choice is the wire-bound sketchbook, which usually has a thick black cover and comes in the sizes (in inches): 5 x 7, 6 x 4, 7 x 10, 9 x 12, and 11 x 14. The plus side of the wire-bound sketchbook is that the wire bindings allow the book to lie flat easily for sketching. The downside of the wire-bound book is it is not as professional in appearance as the more formal hardbound sketchbook, and it may be more difficult to pack into a portfolio case. The spiral rings might press into the portfolio archive pages, making impression marks and causing damage. The third and less traditional configuration is the balloon field sketchbook, with the wire binding on the shortest side of the book. It comes in sizes 7 x 10 and 8½ x 11.

Examples of hard cover sketchbooks
(Image courtesy of DickBlick.com, Blick Art Materials)

Try different sizes, even after you are comfortable with one particular size. This can shake up your creativity and allow you to find the best approach for layout ideas for the page. Be sure to sketch vertically, horizontally, and/or diagonally—all orientations are acceptable and welcomed. The chaotic jumble of images is how you should work, without thought or care to organization or finishing touches. This is a document of your thoughts, inspirations, and doodles. You need to work contrary to what your teachers may have lectured about the messy doodles and notes in your notebook. This design journal is for your personal expression of creative ideas, intended to be a messy mish-mash of disjointed, disconnected conceptual thoughts.

Take your sketchbook with you wherever you go and whatever you do—bus, plane, car, class, watching TV, doing homework, or anywhere else. Jot down any thought of design, color, silhouette, trend, texture, written word, advertisement, music inspiration, facial expression, and so on that you might want to use in a design. You can use pencil, pen, marker, or any other medium to record these thoughts in your sketchbook. If you don't have your sketchbook with you, use a napkin at a restaurant, a scrap piece of paper, a digital tablet or smartphone to scribble down your idea. You can later insert the loose paper into your sketchbook or sketch the idea directly into your book.

Many designers prefer to work routinely with separate sheets of paper rather than in a bound book or spiral-bound sketchbook. The industry does not require that you work with a formal sketchbook. However, as a designer, you place your initial design thoughts onto the page *somewhere*, whether it is in a sketchbook, on a table napkin, on pattern making paper on a drafting table, or in your smartphone, digital tablet, netbook, or computer. As a student, compile all of this information in a sketchbook for creating and sifting through the chaos of design ideas. Many of your first interviewers will ask to look at your design process, and these professionals will not want to look at a scattered presentation.

Keep it all in one book by using Scotch tape or glue, affixing the images to the page as cleanly as possible. Keep the taping and gluing neat, but the sketches need not be neat or organized. They should be chaotic-looking thoughts or sketches, and the interviewers expect to see some disorder.

A designer's sketchbook featuring her inspirational notes, sketches, colors, silhouettes, and mood images. *(Courtesy of Maya Luz)*

You should bring your sketchbook with you on every interview. Not every potential employer will ask to see your sketchbook. Some might not even have time to look through your entire portfolio contents and your sketchbook, but others might want to see both.

Most designers, potential employers, under-graduate/graduate department heads, and professors will want to see your *design process*, which is clearly spelled out in your sketchbook. This journal shows how you arrive at your final design conclusions, and *how you get there* is sometimes more important than the portfolio itself. If the interviewer sees potential in your portfolio but is questioning some of your sketching skills, the sketchbook will address the issue. Seeing how you think in the creative, chaotic stage of first development is critical to the hiring process. Most designers or merchandisers interviewing you are looking for someone who "gets it,"—someone who understands what's happening in the market and how to make it happen with a dynamic design collection. The sketchbook shows how well you do this.

A basic sketchbook consists of all or some of the items listed in the next section and may include many more exciting elements. It is your journal, and, much like a diary, it is up to you to personalize it. Some designers like to cover their sketchbooks in a collage, fabric, or textured paper; others leave it with its original cover. All choices are right—there is no set rule for the cover or the inside contents. The only rule is disorder. This is your little place to collect or try on your different ideas, to log a fleeting thought before you forget something you saw or dreamed of.

SKETCHBOOK CONTENTS

This is a condensed list of some of the usual or expected contents found in a designer sketchbook. Use your creativity and allow yourself to add, embellish, edit, or delete in an unabashed and bold fashion based on your personal design plan. Don't hold back by old thoughts of self-judgment and condemnation as you begin to draw. Think of each page as a fresh start. Discard your old habits of holding back for fear that an idea or observation is not accurate or is too far-fetched.

This is how trends start, with visual observations and recording at the moment the thought enters your mind. As you review and read through your sketchbook, you can begin to step back and observe how you perceive things. You can look back on your work year after year and check your thoughts for accuracy, validating what you thought and what is then shown on the runway or at retail. This is your personal document about what you think drives fashion and how you would like to translate that information. In its most crude or primitive state, the first thought or gut reaction to a street scene or garment that you record in your sketchbook can be used as a base platform of information for an entire season, a year, or a decade of trend-setting style.

Attempt to draw in bold, quick strokes without a plan. Discard any studied approaches to sketching a figure or a garment detail. Be prolific and collect, draw, and document as much as possible as expediently as possible.

Often in an interview with a young designer, a clean portfolio looks very promising and will showcase many new-looking thoughts. The interviewer is very interested in seeing how you got there. Upon looking at the sketchbook, the interviewer looks at how you see trends and formulate designs. Sometimes, the portfolio may not show well-executed designs, but the sketchbook does show tremendous potential of basic design-plotting skills, and this can make or break the interview. Other interviewers are simply not interested or they do not have the time to look through your journal.

In the industry, when you work with a design team, creative director, and/or merchandiser, the meetings take place with your pencil sketch ideas. Then, after brain-storming through your conceptual drawings, the team can decide the direction the designer should go in. The designer has shared the initial thoughts and is now freed to go off and design a line. This way, the designer is not just working in a vacuum, completing a line, and then springing it on the group too late in the development process to go back and make changes or to start all over.

Many designers draw free-hand, and just as many will use the croquis method for their sketchbook and their illustrations. The croquis flat or croquis of the figure can be drawn in a very dark Sharpie marker on a Bristol board or piece of paper and carried with the sketchbook. The croquis drawn with a dark outline will be readable through the opacity of the sketchbook page, so the designer can sketch the garments right over the template of the figure or flat sketch. This frees the mind to design the garments without worrying about anatomical or realistic proportions, which become the job of the underlay template.

Most importantly, keep sketching, documenting and interpreting information, and designing in your sketchbook.

For a student or a professional designer, the sketchbook could be documenting trends, color ideas, yarn samples, swatches of fabric and color, silhouette sketches, marker renderings, notes, and so on, as shown on page 23.

The designer builds her ideas for two separate collections by sketching in her book and adding layers of ideas via cutting/ pasting/taping magazine images, ink/tint colors, fabric swatches, and so on develop her concepts to the fullest potential before the editing and finalization stages of putting her portfolio images together. *(Courtesy of Jenn Webb)*

Sketches

The sketches in your journal can be rough pencil sketches; they are studies and should not look like final drawings. They may include the following:

Doodles
Garment details
Design collections on croquis
Design collections drawn on the flat
Design collections drawn freehand

Observational Documentation

By observing the world around you (either passively or actively), your thoughts should be documented in your journal either in sketch or written form. Thoughts that come to your mind at any time of the day or night should be added to the sketchbook. Make an active effort to study and conduct research by using this checklist:

In-store shopping
Street scenes
Theater
Movies
Television
Videos
Concerts
Museums
Magazine or runway fashions
Go doodle!

Cut and Paste into Your Journal

Adding items into your journal that inspire you is part of the process of building the conceptual base of the collections. These might include the following:

+ Fabric or yarn swatches
+ Inspirational images from periodicals or the Internet
+ Written articles from periodicals or the Internet
+ Blurbs or inspirational portions or words from articles from periodicals or the Internet
+ Color ideas or swatch references

Practice Sketching

As a designer, you must continuously hone your drawing skills. Concentrate on sketching the following:

Faces, facial features
Hand or body gestures
Figures freehand, and/or use magazine references

Have friends pose for you to practice drawing figures, faces, and gestures.

Draw and Sketch Accessories

Many trends and influences can be garnered by making segmented observations and studies of accessories, including hats, belts, handbags, luggage, leashes, jewelry, socks, gloves, hairstyles, shoes, pets, and in some celebrity circles, children and babies. Observe accessories people are carrying and make notes. Draw the accessories for future fashion plates, or accessory designs.

Tips and Techniques

Experiment with different types of pencils (See Appendix D):

+ No. 2 graphite pencil (Same as HB in drawing pencil)
+ 2B graphite pencil (soft)
+ 4H graphite pencil (hard)
+ Mechanical pencil with different leads (HB, 2H, 4H, 2B, 4B, etc.)
+ Color pencils, watercolor pencils

Experiment with different types of markers (fine line, medium, and wide nibs). You might try the following:

Use just pencil, or try drawing the initial idea with pencil, then going over the pencil line with markers to bring out the details. Sometimes the darker line of the marker can add another expression to your pencil work.

Drawing

Use a croquis underneath your sketchpad paper to help you sketch quickly. Having this reusable template will let you focus on your design ideas rather than on getting the proportions of the figure to be correct for each new drawing. If you draw the croquis figure in a heavy black Sharpie marker, you will be able to see the figure through your sketchpad well enough to help you draw your designs faster.

Use a flat template underneath your sketch paper to help you sketch quickly. As in the croquis technique, use a heavy black Sharpie marker to draw the flat template.

Taking Notes in Retail Stores

Take the garments into the dressing room with you. Use the dressing room for your drawing or writing room. Document the silhouette in a drawing and the fabric content from the label, draw the surface texture, document the price, and note other details.

Use tracing paper to trace ideas from magazines, and then reference the details as you design in your sketchbook. This is not knocking off, as long as you are just referencing the ideas to formulate your own ideas.

Use a section of your illustration textbook about how to sketch faces, hands, gestures, shoes, and other details to practice sketching these features in your sketchbook.

Example of a stylized croquis figure template for use under pages of a sketchbook.

SHOWCASING YOUR COLLECTION

Keep in mind that the presentation sequence follows some basic guidelines, but individual designers show mood, concept, color, textiles, fashion plates, and flats separately on individual pages, and others combine one or more of these features on the same page. Each time you add or change a collection presentation, the sequence of presentation can change, based on your story-telling goals for each collection. The book needs to read as a cohesive statement from start to finish, but the formula can be rearranged to add interest to the flow and to show off your varied presentation abilities.

Use this contents page count to get a rough estimate of the number of pages that an entry-level portfolio should contain:

Intro page	1
Mood pages	2
Color pages	2
Textile pages	2
Collection illustrations	6–8
Flats	2
CAD	2-4
Totals	17–21 for each collection

It is good to show two collections in your entry-level portfolio, taking your total page count to 34 to 38 pages. Again, there are exceptions and variables within this estimate. As noted, you may condense your intro, mood, color, and textiles pages into one or two pages, and/or blend the mood, color, and textiles into the illustration pages. This could mean each collection could be as few as 10 to 12 pages. You must take into account all these considerations when designing your first student portfolio and each time you update it.

As your portfolio building is critiqued during the class exercises, you will learn to strike the correct balance between "simple" or "pure" fashion plates and the bells-and-whistles approach. There are many different levels in between, and the text exercises will help you answer the question, how much is too much?

YOUR TEMPORARY PORTFOLIO

Throughout your college career, you should have been saving work from a variety of classes in a student portfolio. These images are the resource for setting up a temporary portfolio, which will serve you in two ways: (1) as a portfolio for immediate, or on-the-fly, interviews, and (2) as a catalyst for launching your final, refined portfolio.

The temporary portfolio houses the visual reference for your current (and past) level of accomplishment. By viewing your work in a portfolio case, you start to see what you want your dream portfolio to look like. The temporary portfolio also helps you conceptualize what your next accomplishment levels need to be to work toward your dream portfolio.

+ *Set up* the temporary portfolio of your student work to be used as a demonstration for evaluation, critique, and self-awareness, and one that can be used for an interview if necessary.
+ *Explore* portfolio case styles. Resolve size, function, and style by research shopping. Then commit by purchasing a portfolio case.
+ *Gather* research on historic portfolio presentations and portfolio influencers. Learn to stay informed of ongoing trends in illustration and page and layout style.
+ *Establish* key ingredients you would like to assimilate into your image-making process.
+ *Ascertain* your current skill level by deciding which artistic skills need improving, then gauge the time it will take to make the improvements with consideration for completion deadlines.
+ *Define* the design direction for your portfolio presentation by examining which fashion market you want to design for.

SETUP

Follow Exercises 1.2, 1.3, and 1.4 to create a basic skeleton portfolio. Reference the skeleton portfolio for your final portfolio. Your final portfolio may, in fact, be composed of many illustration pages from this basic skeleton portfolio.

You have produced many fashion plates during your student career. From the outset, it is important that you keep each fashion plate stored in a cool, dry, flat place. The fashion plates can initially be stored on a shelf with sheets of tracing paper in between each plate to preserve each from rub-off or transfer of color or lines from one plate to another.

You can also purchase, initially, the polypropylene replacement sheets to store your work, which will protect the fashion plates from sun, water, moisture, and damage due to aging.

To set up a portfolio of your fashion plates, follow Exercise 1.2

As the student portfolios demonstrate, there is now an organized flow to the work you have produced. Use Exercise 1.3 to evaluate and assess your work.

Gather work from different assignments and instructors. Student work can naturally appear to be scattered in theme, because you have created work from varied academic courses, as well as different semesters or years of work. Place your work on a table or wall, view your pieces, and track your progress. It should prove to be a visual representation of the strides you have made in your design, rendering, layout, and collection building. Careful review of your work should prove your consequent design advancement. Use this as a stepping stone. You can browse through the temporary portfolio, which will enhance your confidence.

The Basics

Textured Wovens

Embellishments

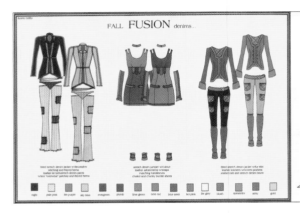

Student work should be shown in the temporary portfolio chosen in Exercise 1.1. Here are examples of student work shown in a portfolio case. The student organized her work by including her illustrations from class projects. *(Courtesy of Kerrin Griffin)*

OBJECTIVE: To create a tangible book for self-evaluation and preparation for the final portfolio. USE: For a last-minute interview, as well as for the objective critique.

1. Purchase an ITOYA portfolio (or similar brand) in the largest size that will hold all of your best work.

2. Gather all of your past fashion plates. Use this portfolio exclusively for fashion plates. You can include pre-college work if you feel it serves a valid purpose for an interview or for tracking your growth. Remember to look through the fashion plates you have produced for different classes, not just your illustration courses.

3. Lay out your best work on a tabletop. You can eliminate from here, but it's best to have edited out the pieces you feel don't add to the objectives outlined above.

4. The tabletop, floor, or a bulletin board will work for further viewing. If you are using a bulletin board, use tape on the *back* of the fashion plates, *not push pins*. Work in your portfolio should not have push pin holes in the corners.

5. You can arrange your fashion plates on the surface of your choice in chronological order and in collection or theme subcategories.

   Mount your work on white Bristol board if it is not rendered on it to give the fashion plates the stability they need within a portfolio. This ensures that the pages don't become wrinkled or pinched, that they are opaque, as some marker papers have a translucent surface. If you put the fashion plate rendered on marker paper into your portfolio, you will see the black paper from below coming through; this effect is not professional.

   If you have worked on watercolor paper, which is stiff, be sure that the bubble or wrinkle effect is eliminated. This can best be accomplished by laying the fashion plate on a flat surface, putting a piece of tracing paper on top of the plate to protect your work, and placing very heavy books on top for a few days. Multiple plates can be flattened in between three to four layers of books.

6. For mounting fashion plates on Bristol board, use only Scotch Magic Tape by 3M. Cellophane-based tape or masking tape is not archival. It will cast a shadow and eventually yellow, marring your original artwork. Fold a 1"–1½" length of Magic Tape in half with the adhesive side out, and attach it to the back of the fashion plate at the upper left and right corners. Carefully affix the Bristol board to the back of the fashion plate.

7. Next, see whether the sequence you have chosen works in a story format as a "page turner; that is, is the story you are telling compelling." Determine this by putting the plates in between the page sheets in the portfolio or laying the plates on top of each page and then turning the pages.

8. If a fashion plate is not representative of the designs you would want to show in an interview, then it is best not to include in your book. Your illustrations, layouts, and designs should tell you a story of who you are as a designer *at the current time*.

9. The current time story will serve to allow you to step away from your work. Look at your work as objectively as possible. Pretend you are presented the book from another designer. What would you see? The book should put distance between you and your work. This gives you:

a. A clearer objective perspective to evaluate your work for design validity.

b. The ability to concentrate on where you are now and where you would like to be.

c. A formality and a structure to your fashions. This is a little composite of you, the designer brand.

OBJECTIVE: To brand your story.

USE: To strengthen your presentation for interviews.

1. Look at the pages as you have arranged them in your temporary portfolio. The story you tell should unfold at a pace with which you would want to explain yourself to an interviewer, visually rather than verbally.
2. Arrange your work in an order that represents your style in the best light for showing to a teacher, friend, client, or interviewer.

Your choices are as follows:

a. *Open and close with a bang*. That is, is the story you are telling compelling. Put your best collections at the front and at the back of the book. The pages in the middle might be all solidly "average" representations of your work.
b. *Open, middle, and close*. Same as above, just put a third collection in the very middle that is as dynamic as the open and close collections. In between, place the "average" presentations.
c. *Good, better, best*. Open with your with a soft impact, build to the better collections, and then end with the best.

3. Experiment with all of these choices, as well as combinations. Step back and look at each of the versions with a few hours between each change. You will see something different each time.
4. Ask a friend or a group of people to review your work with you. Consider and weigh their opinions against your own assessments. Make a final decision based on the process of considering all layout options, your critical opinion, and those of trusted others. Hint: When asking friends, you will need to consider the source, and learn to pick and choose the information that you want to apply. The more times you elicit opinions, the better skilled you will become at sorting through the opinions to see whose judgment you value and whose advice is less useful. You will make the final decision that brands your merchandise presentation.
7. Pick the strongest layout presentation for "The 'Over Time Critique'" (Exercise 1.4).

Follow the list in Exercise 1.4 to track your progress and to apply to your dream of an advanced portfolio. This list is best called "the Over Time Critique," as all of the criteria are based on the improvement you can spot in your work over a period of time.

Look through your fashion plates and discover how many of these details have changed for the better over time. The period of time can be 2 months through 10 years! You should always see improvement in your work, and there should always be room for further improvement. The object is not to critique each and every point listed; you can pick and choose which details you want to zero in on or those that you can readily see when you critique your fashion plates.

Use Exercise 1.4 as proof of advancement when critiquing your work. Take notes as you go through your critique of the improvements you see. Decide what points you would like to improve upon. Take notes of these points.

OBJECTIVE: Assess the level of your illustration development and determine the direction in which you would like your 2D presentations to progress.

USE: To forecast and go forward with realistic goals for the completion of the final portfolio.

1. Use your portfolio and any fashion plates that will help you track your progress over the period of time that you have been designing. You can also look at the work in your designer sketchbook to help you evaluate your progress. Look for advancement in the categories listed below, and focus on areas you consider your weakest points. Discover your strengths, and, as in Exercise 1.3, "Layout Critique," ask friends or associates their opinions. Remember to process your own and outside opinions carefully.

2. Take notes on your evaluation, considering the following questions:

▶ Regarding figures, over time:

  ▶ Do your figures show improvement in size and adherence to the elongated, nine-heads proportions of the fashion figure?

  ▶ Does your fashion figure look more stylized or exaggerated/elongated?

  ▶ Is the figure less static?

  ▶ Is the figure showing different poses, not just the same pose?

  ▶ Is the figure walking or moving? Does it appear to be captured while walking on a runway?

  ▶ Is there an attitude to the figure that reflects your attitude toward the fashion muse?

  ▶ Are gestures being added to the figures? Are the hands gesturing? Are the hands/fingers reflecting the same attitude as the figure gesture/posture represents?

  ▶ Are the heads used in profile, straight on, and in three-quarter views?

  ▶ Are the figures shown in profile, straight on, and in three-quarter views?

  ▶ Details on hands, feet, shoes: Is drawing getting better or closer to the stylized version you would like them to have?

  ▶ Are the feet drawn in proportion to the body? Are they deliberately becoming larger or smaller as part of an effect you want to have on the clothing and on the viewer?

  ▶ Are the shoes shown with the level of importance that you need for your head-to-toe look?

  ▶ Are multiple figures being shown on one page?

  ▶ Are multiple figures being shown on facing pages in a continuum?

  ▶ Do your figures represent diverse populations of culture and gender? Do skin colors reflect diverse populations?

  ▶ Are your hair styles representative of the era and feeling of the clothing?

  ▶ Are your hair styles appropriate for the age group for which your collection is designed?

▶ Regarding garment drawing and garment rendering, over time:

  ▶ Do your drawings show more detail on each garment silhouette?

  ▶ Do your garments show off your designs? Do you need to exaggerate the details more for the viewer to get the impact that you desire?

  ▶ Is the garment moving in the correct direction based on the figure's stance?

  ▶ Do the gathers, pleats, folds, darts, top-stitching, bends, etc. accurately represent the thoughts in your head and the garments that you constructed based on these designs?

  ▶ Are your garments detailed more accurately?

  ▶ Are your garments rendered with shadows and source-of-light considerations?

- Do your garments show the body moving underneath the clothing?
- Regarding fabric and fabric rendering, over time:
  - Does your fabric rendered emulate the fabric swatch?
  - Is the fabric moving with the body?
  - Is the fabric showing the correct volume or exaggerated volume you need to show off your design silhouette?
  - Is the surface texture of the fabric represented accurately as crisp, smooth, tight-fitting, sheer, opaque, translucent, stiff, flowing, soft, rough, course weave, slub weave, shiney, dull, matte, reflective, shimmering, wrinkled, or pleated?
  - Is the silhouette created by the drawing the same as what the fabric on the body would create?
  - Is the print or pattern shown to best represent your overall style or attitude? Did you play with different scales of print rendering?
  - Have you tried different media to achieve the effects that best represent the fabric?
- Regarding line quality, over time, does your line quality:
  - Vary from page to page?
  - Vary within one page?
  - Evolve to better explain your designs and details?
  - Appear too light, too dark, too crisp, too blurry, or too varied, for the effect you wanted?
  - Demonstrate that you have tried different outline qualities, and different pens, markers, paints, brushes, pencils, CAD programs, or other media?
- Regarding layout, over time, do your individual page layouts and your sequenced paged collections demonstrate:
  - Effective use of negative and positive space?
  - A clean approach to the page (no wrinkles, smudges, eraser marks—unless intentionally place for effect)?
- Experimentation with horizontal and vertical orientations on the page?
- That you have begun to establish your most effective size of page?
- Interaction among the figures?
- Proper scale of your figures on each page?
- Experimentation with cropped figures?
- Figures on different planes in some plates?
- Experimentation with different layouts to see which you prefer: the fabric swatch on the page, the fabric swatches on a separate page? The flats on a separate page, the flats on the same page as the figures?
- Combinations of your fabric swatches, color tabs, and mood references within the fashion plates?
- Growing facility with changing your hand-rendered layouts with a computer program?
- A consistent aspect ratio as you manipulate the details on the computer?
- A relationship of pages to one another within a collection?
- Regarding backgrounds, effects, and use of varied media, over time, do you have layouts that incorporate:
  - Background: Shadows, brushstrokes of color, back-lighting, extreme reflection of light, faded images in halftones from hand rendering, or CAD effects?
  - Effects: Work with different mood-setting or image-making effects, including fading or gradation of color, use of varied tones of colored and textured background paper and/or scanned-in colors and textures, and deconstructed or deliberately destroyed paper effects?
  - Experimentation with borders, letters, logos, or words, in varied widths and proportions?
  - Many different media throughout your book? If you have decided to stay with just one effect, does it show enough range?

EXPLORE AND COMMIT TO A PORTFOLIO STYLE

It is important to purchase a portfolio case for your final portfolio. Take ownership of your work with a formal case. Hold yourself accountable to each self-improvement exercise you complete in this text.

The case and its contents are all part of your marketing package and the first image that a potential interviewer has of you. Viewing your work inside the case helps you to (1) view your work objectively, (2) take your student work seriously, (3) view your work as an interviewer would, and (4) detach yourself personally from the illustration and view it as a commercial product. The case represents a committed designer with a purpose and a goal.

If you are having difficulty with size and layout, keep your student portfolio in the temporary case and work with your instructors to make your final decision.

You can go through all the exercises in Chapter 1, and then make your final purchase, or purchase it at any point during your reading of this chapter when you are ready. Some students will be working on size selection of their artwork as they go through the entire book. If you are one of those students, consider purchasing a portfolio that would best showcase your current student work, and if necessary, purchase a different-size case if you discover that you work better in a larger or smaller size.

Use Appendix E, "Art Supply Sources," to find sources for purchasing your portfolio. The "Do's and Don'ts of Portfolio Shopping" (page 36) and the shopping chart described in the following section will help you determine the right case to purchase.

THE PORTFOLIO SHOPPING CHART

Portfolios are made from different materials such as leather, vinyl, or metal. The cases can be zippered shut, without a zipper closure, or encased in a box. The bindings can be aluminum multi-ring bindings or screwpost bindings.

The portfolio case is meant to protect your work, help you carry your work, and help you present your work to the client. Explore the gamut of portfolio cases to see which style works best for you by in-store shopping and by searching the Internet sites of art supply stores. Keep in mind that viewing the actual portfolios is preferred for your final selection. You should see in person how the portfolio looks, how it feels to the touch, and how it feels to carry it. Specifically, check the following:

+ Cover texture: Hard or soft, vinyl or leather.
+ Style: Case, cover case, box, carrying case, handles and/or strap.
+ Color: Black, brown, white, red, or custom color.
+ Closures: Open edge, zipper closure, boxed book.

+ Type: Ready-made or custom-designed.
+ Size: Industry standard for page sizes 9" x 12", 11" x 14", and 14" x 17".
+ Weight: Pick up the portfolio to see what feels best to you in your hands, or on your shoulder if there is a shoulder strap.
+ Page inserts: Purchase only archival-quality polypropylene or acetate sleeves.

As you go through the different choices of portfolios, remember that the most important part of your portfolio is the *contents*, not the cover. Your design presentation is impressive *if* the designs *inside* your book are innovative and fashion-forward when encased in a sophisticated portfolio purchased at an opening price point. This is just as impressive as the customized, over-the-top portfolio case. Nothing could be less fortunate for a young designer than to present a smashing, expensive portfolio showcasing mediocre or, worse yet, stale, boring, or poorly executed fashion designs. The case cannot mask what is inside.

Commit by purchasing your portfolio and page inserts *now*.

DO'S AND DON'TS OF PORTFOLIO SHOPPING

Do's

▶ Keep it simple. The portfolio cover does not need to be fancy.

▶ Concentrate on the contents, not the cover.

▶ Look at custom portfolios for choices.

▶ If you have a design style, and you can find a cover that mirrors that style, by all means choose that portfolio style.

▶ Choose the right size. As mentioned in the text, experiment and evaluate which size works best to show your work and which size you prefer for illustrator/rendering/designing. Sometimes, designers purchase their portfolio case and realize they need to work in another size. You can always have your first portfolio case in one size and a newer version in a different size. You can fit smaller-sized work into a larger portfolio by adding borders to fill the page or resizing in a CAD program.

▶ Keep in mind the city or terrain where you will be interviewing or visiting for interviews. If you will be traveling by subway or bus, be sure the portfolio has a shoulder strap attachment, or you can get a cover bag with a shoulder strap for those long subway rides and walks through the streets.

▶ If you are planning on traveling by plane with your portfolio, keep in mind the dimensions for the overhead compartments.

▶ Purchase archival replacement sheets for your book, if the book does not come with enough pages.

▶ Look for landscape portfolio presentation books if this is your style.

▶ Know your style of handling precious materials. If you are naturally rough on your luggage and handbags, you will need to purchase a rugged material-covered case. If you are delicate and careful, and can live with the consequences of scratches or nicks, then do buy a metal portfolio case. Know your style: rough—more practical case, careful—more delicate case.

▶ Check that the portfolio is the correct weight for you to carry in the environment in which you will be using it.

▶ Purchase a soft-sided or weather-proof cover for your book if it is especially delicate.

Don'ts

▶ Don't use a temporary plastic portfolio case for your final portfolio.

▶ Don't use cheap plastic sheet protectors.

▶ Don't look for a gimmicky portfolio cover, or have a gimmicky portfolio custom made. This is not professional; it is amateurish.

▶ Don't plan for horizontal and landscape presentation pages in your book—pick one orientation and stick to it as best you can (one or two pages in the opposite orientation is fine).

▶ Don't overlook the "zipper closure" portfolio cases. They provide supreme protection from weather conditions and from dust and dirt.

The landscape aluminum portfolio is appropriate for designers who wish to showcase their work in the horizontal orientation. These cases are crafted of satin-finish aluminum for the front and back covers, with a ¾" screwpost mechanism. Archival page protectors, adhesive hinge strips, black zippered nylon jacket, or a padded transport jacket are available at an extra cost, as well as screwpost extension packs at ½" or ¼" widths. The book will hold up to 15 pages with the included screwpost hardware and up to 40 pages with the extension pack. Portfolio size, in inches: 11 x 14. *(Courtesy of Portfolios-and-art-cases.com)*

The screwpost portfolio, which is available in aluminum, acrylic, synthetic leather, frost semi-opaque, bookbinder's cloth, nylon-backed PVC, clear flexible PVC, and hardboard. Screwpost extension packs are sold separately to increase the width of the portfolio for extra pages to be added. Sizes, in inches, for designers are 8½ x 11, 11 x 14, and 14 x 17. *(Courtesy of Portfolios-and-art-cases.com)*

Display easel binder portfolio, for designers that want to show their work propped up on a table to their client. For landscape/horizontal display only (see example). Sizes are: 8½ x 11, 11 x 14, and 14 x 17. *(Image courtesy of DickBlick.com, Blick Art Materials)*

GATHER HISTORIC REFERENCES

Fashion illustrations from the past should greatly influence your planning for a portfolio presentation. By reviewing past and present illustrations, you can better plan your future portfolio, which will need to have a shelf life of approximately 6 months to 1 year. There are trends within the annals of (for instance) *Vogue* back issues, which can be used to jump-start your ideas for layout, concepts, and design. This passive research of browsing and *leisurely enjoying* the old periodicals will aid in the creative flow of thoughts. Remember, in the past (not that long ago—this would include the 1990s), most reading was done using hard-copy materials, not the Internet. This allowed the reader to sit and enjoy reading a magazine or browsing through the newspaper, permitting the relaxed mind to soak up the magazine visuals. By browsing hard-copy materials, you will have the same sensory experience, which will imbue your work with a sense of history.

Using Appendix B for research sources, spend at least 2 hours in the school library browsing through the periodicals suggested among the resources. Remember to take notes and/or trace or draw the ideas that inspire you most.

For current portfolios, review the online portfolios listed in Appendix C. Remember to review these online portfolios throughout your career for current trends.

ESTABLISH KEY INGREDIENTS

Take the key ingredients from your historic and current trends and establish a list of features you think are important for your portfolio to contain or portray.

ASCERTAIN YOUR SKILL LEVEL

Follow next by completing Exercises 1.5, 1.6, and 1.7. It is necessary to be aware of your current skill level of rendering, illustration, layout, and design. Knowing your strengths and weaknesses will help you establish a realistic timeline for applying new techniques, and how far to go with these ideas to meet the deadline for completion.

OBJECTIVE: Assess all aspects of your portfolio and collection building work.

USE: To make changes before, during, and after you put together your final portfolio based upon your observations of your temporary portfolio.

DIRECTIONS: For each segment listed below, rate yourself 1–10. (1 being the lowest, 10 being the highest). How do you think you perform the task or execute the final product? Also rate yourself on how your processed the information from the initial concept. Do you need to work harder on the steps of each task or how you process the information you gained from performing the task?

Concepts

Rate your conceptual development on each of these steps listed below.

Media research

Historical research

General ideas: Are they varied and eclectic?

Theme/mood: Am I consistent with my message from silhouette, fabric, color, and theme?

Consistency from concept to completion:

Do I follow through with my ideas on a consistent basis, or do I waiver and confuse or muddle my message to the consumer?

Are my original ideas actualized?

Editing: Did I put in too much or too little?

Overall rating (average of scores of all points)

Trend Tracking

Rate your level of trend research and follow-through on each step listed below.

Observation skills: Observation; logging in journal

Developing trends from concept to finalization

Sources: Too few or too many?

Accuracy: Am I on track, too late, or too early with trends? Do I know how to spot trends in a timely manner?

Overall rating (average score of all points)

Color Development

Rate your level of color research and follow-through on each step listed below.

Research: Too much or too little?

Editing: Too much or too little?

Do I make a distinct color presentation for each collection?

Overall rating (average score of all points)

Textiles

Rate your level of textile research and follow-through on each step listed below.

Research: Too much or too little?

Do I need to expand or reduce the number of sources?

Do I focus my research for specific apparel categories?

Editing: Too much or too little?

Do my fabrics allow my silhouettes to function?

Can my garments be cut in this cloth in an efficient manner to be manufactured?

Overall rating (average score of all points)

Silhouettes

Rate your level of silhouette design and follow-through on each step listed below.

Are my shapes drawn accurately for the chosen fabric?

Are my silhouettes working in synch with my colors, fabric, and theme?

Overall rating (average score of all points)

Layout

Rate your general level of layout skills and follow-through.

CAD Skills

Rate your general level of skills using CAD programs.

Hand-Rendering Skills

Rate your general level of hand-rendering skills and follow-through.

Fashion Design Skills

Rate your general level of the following categories, from concept to follow-through:

Construction

Draping

Patternmaking

Technical design/specs

Overall rating (average score of all points)

OBJECTIVE: To achieve a higher level of rendering style and skill.

USE: For creating the final portfolio fashion illustration and layout pages.

1. Track and rate your rendering skills.
2. Determine techniques you want to apply or improve upon.
3. Determine what, if any, techniques or methods you decide are not worth exploring.

Rate your work 1 to 10 (1 being the lowest, 10 being the highest) on each of the points listed below. Decide what has worked best for you in your current work, and make a list of the techniques or materials you need to add to your repertoire.

Media: Be sure to evaluate whether you have used or experimented with a wide range of suppliers. If not, you will need to purchase more materials to expand your range. See Appendix F for suppliers of the various media listed below.

Rate the work you have completed in each medium.

Pencil—HB through H, 1 to 9, mechanical or regular pencil

Colored pencils

Markers

Paints

Paper Size: Have you worked with 9" x 12", 11" x 14", and 14" x 17" pages?

Combining media: Have you combined all of the media on one page on occasion?

Layering of media: Have you layered different media to achieve textural results?

Rendering Communication Skills

Rate your work based upon your evaluation of how well you are conveying these details.

Flat surfaces

Shiny surfaces

Thick, thin, stretch, knit, flowing, stiff, wrinkles, pleats, linings

Surface patterns

Texture

Topstitching

Buttons

Buttonholes

Seams

Leathers

Suedes

Knobby textures

Line Quality

Rate your work based upon your evaluation of how well you convey these details or use the media to achieve the best possible outcome. For example, if you think your use of outlines in pencils is not strong enough, and you haven't experimented with markers or inks; then you would rate yourself a "5" and make a note in the margin to experiment with marker and inks for outlines to better stylize your fashion plate illustrations.

Does your outline quality convey the stylization you desire?

Are you making the best use of assorted mediums for your outlines?

Conclusions

1. After you have rated yourself, make a list of improvements that you want to make.
2. Look through your work in general terms, and write the answers to the questions listed below.
3. Determine what (if anything) you can add to your list based on the answers to Question 2.
4. Create your additional questions to evaluate other needs or goals not previously covered
5. Amend your list of improvements to include the findings in points 2–4.
6. Review your list and begin to formulate a plan for your work style for the portfolio project.

Do you need to be less sketchy, more defined, crisper, freer, more structured?

Do you desire an edgier look to your work?

Do you need to look at other illustrators' work to help define your style?

OBJECTIVE: To meet a deadline for completion of the final portfolio project.

USE: To set goals and deadlines based on an objective evaluation of your work.

1. Using the list you created in Exercise 1.6, choose the top ten rendering skills you wish to work on.

2. Assign an approximate number of hours it will take you to refine each individual skill.

3. Assign the "due date" for completion of your final collection and the new portfolio you will be creating. Subtract 2 weeks from the due date for final completion. Use this date as your final date. The extra 2 weeks will give you a cushion of time for mistakes, breakdown of printers or scanners, markers that are out of stock, and other unforeseeable problems.

4. Factor in the amount of time you will have to work on refinement of skills with the hours it will take you to complete your final collection for your new portfolio in the given time frame.

5. As you look at the "big picture" of completing your portfolio, you may need to edit down your refinement goals from ten to five, or even one skill that you decide to work on.

6. Post the edited list on your bulletin board over your work area to remind you of your goals and your time frame.

DEFINE YOUR
DESIGN DIRECTION

Your portfolio, with a focused collection or series of collections, should have an easily noticeable direction. Browse through Chapters 4 and 5 for a visual example of the different categories of manufacturers and designers. This chapter introduce you to the basic fundamentals of design categories. Your instructors may have had you illustrate collections in these categories. Evaluate your interest in these specific areas with Exercise 1.7.

Begin sketching in your journal ideas for the categories you are interested in. Consider market segments—are you trained to design women's, men's, or children's clothing? Have you specialized in tailoring or knit fabrics? You may choose to draw on your experience or successes in any of these fields, or you may want to expand your designs into different categories.

Keep in mind that you may choose to present your collections for men and for women, perhaps as a unisex collection.

You will focus your collection further with market research, which you will conduct in Chapter 3.

Expand your critical thinking skills by working through the self-evaluation Exercise 1.8.

Your portfolio will most likely be suited for the country you are living in, but you can also reach the global market by researching many countries or a country where you have spent a semester or internship. Your research should help you determine whether your style and interests are likely to make a focus on a particular culture appropriate.

OBJECTIVE: Using the visual cues in your fashion illustrations, consider specializing or focusing your final portfolio collection or career path in a given market.

USE: Apply the findings to the storyline of your portfolio in a focused direction or specialized fashion category.

Review all of your student work that you have deemed important for your temporary portfolio. The "discard" fashion plates may have meaning, and you may have to refer back to them as you go through this exercise. That is fine; answers to some of these questions may be hidden in the items you removed that won't be obvious until you go through these steps.

▶ Lay out your work on a flat table, or post it on a wall.

▶ Make copies of collections that are buried in your sketchbook pages, so you can review all of your work, both formal and informal.

▶ Display work in apparel categories.

▶ Question yourself: What do I have an affinity for? Make notes of your observations.

▶ Complete the statement, "In my illustrations/ layouts, I pay special attention to_____ _____."

Here are some examples of telltale signs of the specialized talents you may have in your work. These are only *possible* indicators and are by no means to be taken as the definitive way of determining which apparel category is best for you. If, in your work, you pay special attention to the indicators in the list under the category, you may find your specialization.

Accessories Hairstyles, nails, shoes, hats, legwear, handbags, jewelry.

Activewear Function, logos, hoods, zippers, rib knit closures, bright colors, color blocking, movement or action figures, illustration of muscular fashion figures, sneakers, technical performance fabrics, Lycra fabrics, props such as MP3 players, knit hats, baseball hats.

Bridal Lace, beading treatments, decorative motifs, ruffles, tulle fabrics, headpieces or elaborate decorative hats, plumage, evening wear.

Intimate apparel/lingerie Interest in drawing the body, lace, sensual poses, cuddly fabrics, detailed trims, interest in swimwear and dancewear.

Jeans Fabric or surface effects, topstitch details, layers, pant details, pant silhouettes, street attire.

Knitwear Tight-fitting or Lycra garments, yarns, color, brushed or plush fabric interest, fringe, handmade approach to garments from the inside out, sweaters.

Children's wear Playful elements, placed motifs, color simplicity, patterned fabric treatments, quilting.

Denim collections Sophisticated or complex design approach; surface effects; men's, women's, and unisex collections; silhouettes with hard edges; heavy or industrial fabrics.

Evening wear Elegance, beads, sequins, florals, satins, crepes, flowing or to-the-floor silhouettes, designing with a celebrity as a muse, tuxedos, suits, black and white evening attitude, drama in silhouette, poses, and background effects.

Footwear Function, technical fabrics, performance fabrics, detailed approach to patternmaking and the 3D form, attention to fit, shoes are an important part of the head-to-toe look, realistic approach to collection building.

Golfwear Casual sportswear, polo shirts, socks, love of sports and function of garments for performance, unisex interest.

Handbags Carrying handbags in a large portion of your collection, convertible clothing.

Leather Leather used in abundant detail, or as trim in many elements of your collections.

Outerwear Function, layering, fabric-driven designs, technical fabrics, tailoring and suits, fur, bulky fabrics, "away-from-the-body" silhouettes.

Sportswear Separate items, mix and match interrelated garments, unisex collections, prolific design vision.

Swimwear and beachwear Lycra fabrics, attention to function of garments on the body, attention to flattering the body, love of water sports.

T-shirts Graphic elements, hand-painted garments, placed motifs, logos, sportswear feel.

Urban streetwear Attitude poses, club attire, music-driven designs, sportswear feel, edgy apparel.

Chapter 2

THE IDEA STORAGE BANK

OBJECTIVES

+ Use a design process outline to create a collection concurrently with creating corresponding portfolio images.

+ Make a visual imprint of the Compile, Edit, and Finalize approach to working through the design process.

+ Use the Designer Filter to sift through the ideas taken into the ideas bank and the ideas that flow out in the form of a finalized portfolio collection.

+ Gather and process information from influential sources, including retail shopping, fashion shows, and trade shows.

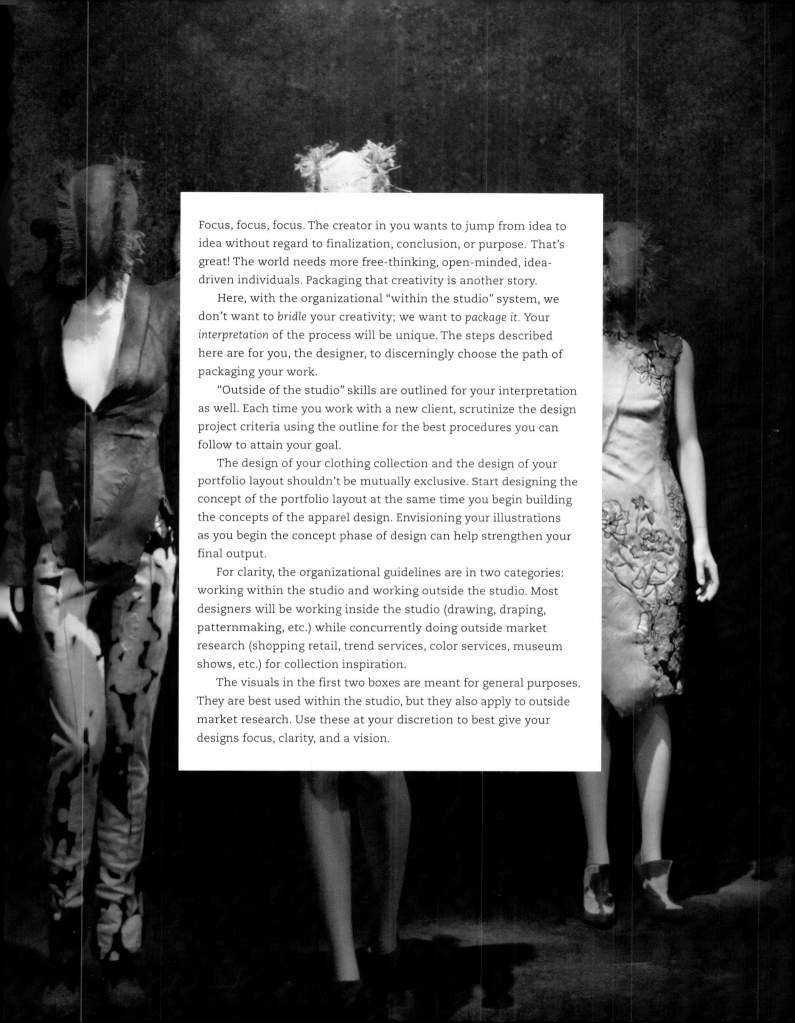

Focus, focus, focus. The creator in you wants to jump from idea to idea without regard to finalization, conclusion, or purpose. That's great! The world needs more free-thinking, open-minded, idea-driven individuals. Packaging that creativity is another story.

Here, with the organizational "within the studio" system, we don't want to *bridle* your creativity; we want to *package it.* Your *interpretation* of the process will be unique. The steps described here are for you, the designer, to discerningly choose the path of packaging your work.

"Outside of the studio" skills are outlined for your interpretation as well. Each time you work with a new client, scrutinize the design project criteria using the outline for the best procedures you can follow to attain your goal.

The design of your clothing collection and the design of your portfolio layout shouldn't be mutually exclusive. Start designing the concept of the portfolio layout at the same time you begin building the concepts of the apparel design. Envisioning your illustrations as you begin the concept phase of design can help strengthen your final output.

For clarity, the organizational guidelines are in two categories: working within the studio and working outside the studio. Most designers will be working inside the studio (drawing, draping, patternmaking, etc.) while concurrently doing outside market research (shopping retail, trend services, color services, museum shows, etc.) for collection inspiration.

The visuals in the first two boxes are meant for general purposes. They are best used within the studio, but they also apply to outside market research. Use these at your discretion to best give your designs focus, clarity, and a vision.

WORKING WITHIN THE STUDIO

As you work on your collections and on representing them in your portfolio, follow the steps of the design process, and use your "Designer Filter" (discussed later in this section) to channel your creativity in a productive direction. Being aware of your creative process will not inhibit your creativity, as you'll discover with practice.

AN ORGANIZED APPROACH TO A DESIGN PROJECT

Use the six basic steps of the design process to contain your thoughts, workings, and completion phases of portfolio development.

1. Set the goal.
2. Examine outside influences.
3. Establish criteria.
4. Make a plan.
5. Carry out a plan.
6. Evaluate.

When you are creating your collection, write or sketch each of the six phases of your project's work. Refer back to your annotated list to track your progress, and keep a copy taped into your sketchbook or on your bulletin board. Briefly outlined here is an example of a design project.

1. *Set a goal.* To create a portfolio collection for my interview with Calvin Klein Jeans. Get savvy about jeanswear surface finishes and fit requirements in the market. Create a contemporary look to my illustrations, with lifestyle interests of the Calvin customer included in my layouts and new looks in my design approaches to the company product line. Concentrate on male and female croquis used together on a page, and illustrate groups of four to eight croquis on a page. Finish project in 5 days, for my interview date. Prioritize Points 2–5 to be completed in this time frame.

2. *Examine outside influences.* Visit retails stores and Internet sites that carry the CK Jeans label, the competing brands, and edgier jeans labels. Visit and research denim fabric resources. Discuss wash finish trends with trend service reports, and talk to consumers about what finishes and silhouettes they like, and what they may be looking for. Research period pieces of manufacturers and designers that inspire me to influence this collection.

3. *Establish criteria.* Decide on the silhouette and direction I want for this line. Contemporary, with the need for supreme quality control. Use current fit standards and silhouettes of the CK label, and create my illustrations and designs in a stylized manner based on the influences. Stylization is a key factor in my illustrative narrative. Mood and color boards have to project a brand image while still being design driven.

4. *Make a plan.* Sketch silhouettes and model/croquis layouts immediately. Refine illustrations based on market research and outside influences as I do my research. Work using the art supplies I currently have to meet my deadline. Use my knowledge of the computer programs I have and not try any new techniques for this project because I am pressed for time.

5. *Carry out the plan.* Illustrate and render the croquis with the fabric, color, and mood choices I have made as background images. Render denim washes with realistic hand for appeal to the interviewer. Finish the layout on Day 4.

6. *Evaluate.* Look at my work; make minimal changes to the rendering and layout choices. Decide on the page order of the new collection and how it works with the rest of the images in my portfolio.

The three basic phases of portfolio refinement can be summarized with the Compile, Edit, and Finalize sequence, outlined in the box with that title. Keep this as a visual imprint of the work you are performing to perfect your portfolio.

OBJECTIVE: Follow the design process to set up the Portfolio Project.

Use the steps of the design process listed on page 50 to set up your portfolio project. Follow the example in the text for comparative reference. Check off the steps as you complete them as you develop the project. Follow the six steps in a linear sequence. However, the creative process does not always follow this sequence, so give yourself a lot of wiggle room to jump out of sequence from time to time to check your work. Play with the sequence of the steps as you tweak your line, but keep in mind that the final touches need to be carried through by following the steps in numerical order for a completed project.

COMPILE/EDIT/FINALIZE

During the design process, there are three basic phases you go through to get to your final goal of a completed design presentation in the form of illustrated fashion plates.

View the descriptions below with their logo attached to each. As you go through the book, the logo will be in the margin as a reminder of which phase you are working in, helping to keep you on task and on schedule.

1. Compile The Fantastic Creative Genius: Gather all information from outside sources for the concept, trend, mood, textile, color, retail, silhouette, and brand imaging from current and historical resources.

2. Edit The Compromiser: Sift through all of your gathered information, using the Designer Filter. Edit the materials for designing your final line. Only the strongest ideas survive.

3. Finalize Further edit: Render your collection, and assemble the portfolio.

THE DESIGNER FILTER

The second box shows the Designer Filter at work during portfolio building. The filter is your brain, processing the information that you take from the left column, "Formulating the Concepts." The output, which is the items listed in the right column, "Bringing It Forward," is the final decisions you make for putting your portfolio into its strongest presentation form. The filter acts a sieve for the input information. At the end of the chapter, Exercise 2.2 will challenge you to create a design project using the Compile, Edit, Finalize formula and your Designer Filter.

Some designers have an inherently trend-savvy filter and can appear to be effortlessly tuned in to the pulse of fashion. Others have to work harder to filter through trend information, and some may acquire an effortless filtering technique as time goes by. What counts is being able to take trend information and use it to illustrate a layout story for a portfolio. The more you design and build upon each successful line, the better your filter will become at interpreting trends and creating market-right merchandise *in portfolio format*.

Practice getting trend-savvy by looking at your work from past seasons. Go through the listings in the box "The Designer Filter" to determine what went right or wrong in your collection building. Keep notes of each initial idea, the filtered decision, and the final output. Refer back to each point, and see where you might need to improve. For instance:

1. *Fantastic concepts* OK, you have an idea. Go through Exercise 2.1, "The Basic Design Process," and set the idea in motion. Using *your* inner filter, edit and finalize your plan to come up with a final concept that has a grounded presence and answers all of your questions. Keep checking yourself during the design and layout of a portfolio collection to keep it true to your concept.

2. *Trendy is not a trend.* Reading *Us* or *People* magazine or seeing what a celebrity is wearing is not discovering a trend. Nor is today's fashion today's trend. The same holds true for fashion presentations. Take in what is out there in *all* visual resources, and *filter* the information through your designer brain. Your designer brain needs to have an inner eye on "what's next," not "what's now." There has to be the next version of what you see now that makes commercial sense. Try to predict the next wave of presenting merchandise, fiber, color, and silhouette. As you prepare your portfolio, you will also be researching presentation and layout trends. As you review your student portfolio, see how close your predictions were to what really happened in fashion trends. For your next project, remember to adjust your filter to get closer to the pulse of the next wave of fashion presentations. Depending on your targeted consumer, you may need to be way ahead of, right on top of, slightly ahead of, or just a tad in front of the next coming trend.

This will be checked by your referencing of all the different market research channels to determine where your collection needs to be for your particular end-consumer. The presentation format must be in sync with the sensibility of the apparel collection. Think, for example, of Vivienne Westwood. Her merchandise that you see on the runway, in magazines, and in stores have the same aesthetic. If you viewed her illustrations, you would get the same powerful feeling of her designs.

THE DESIGNER FILTER

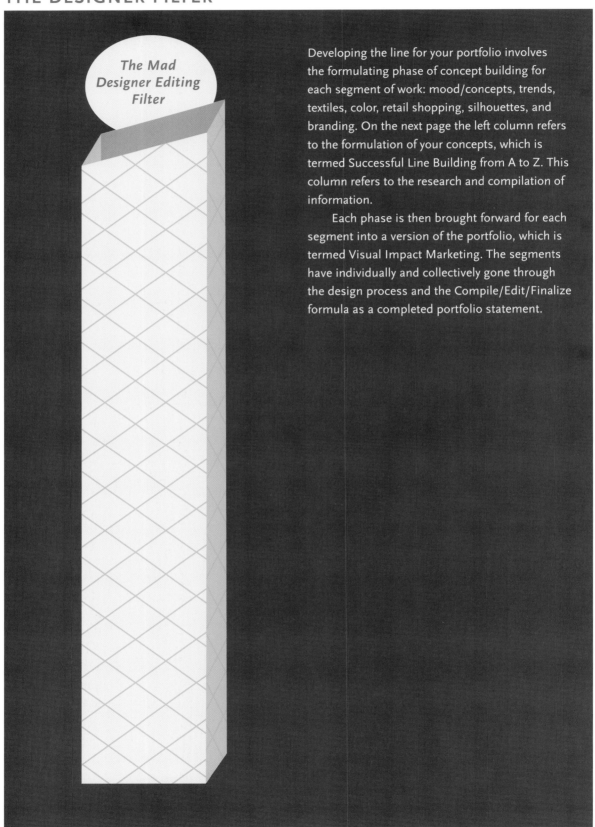

The Mad Designer Editing Filter

Developing the line for your portfolio involves the formulating phase of concept building for each segment of work: mood/concepts, trends, textiles, color, retail shopping, silhouettes, and branding. On the next page the left column refers to the formulation of your concepts, which is termed Successful Line Building from A to Z. This column refers to the research and compilation of information.

Each phase is then brought forward for each segment into a version of the portfolio, which is termed Visual Impact Marketing. The segments have individually and collectively gone through the design process and the Compile/Edit/Finalize formula as a completed portfolio statement.

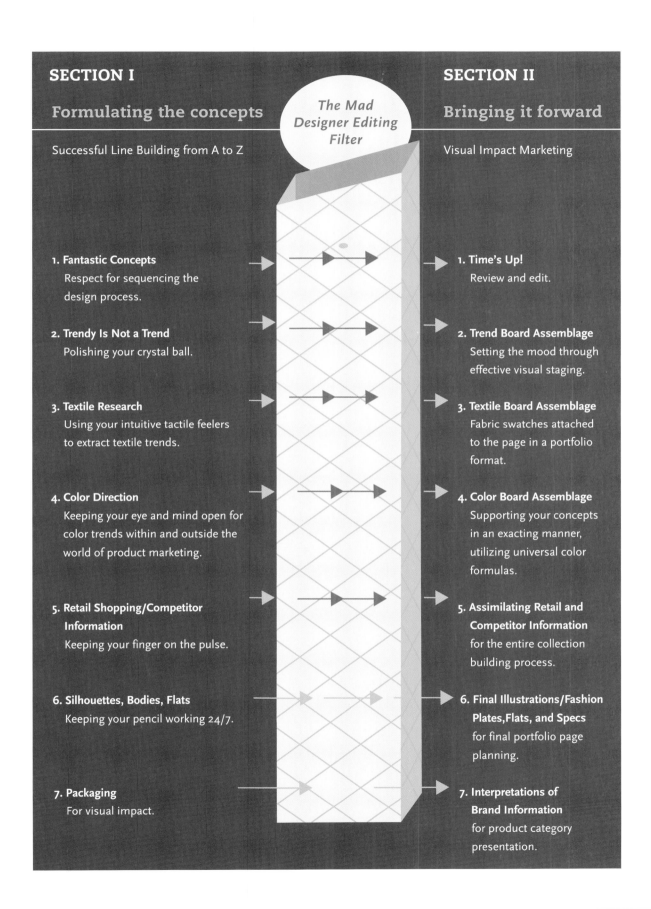

SECTION I

Formulating the concepts

Successful Line Building from A to Z

The Mad Designer Editing Filter

SECTION II

Bringing it forward

Visual Impact Marketing

1. **Fantastic Concepts**
   Respect for sequencing the design process.

2. **Trendy Is Not a Trend**
   Polishing your crystal ball.

3. **Textile Research**
   Using your intuitive tactile feelers to extract textile trends.

4. **Color Direction**
   Keeping your eye and mind open for color trends within and outside the world of product marketing.

5. **Retail Shopping/Competitor Information**
   Keeping your finger on the pulse.

6. **Silhouettes, Bodies, Flats**
   Keeping your pencil working 24/7.

7. **Packaging**
   For visual impact.

1. **Time's Up!**
   Review and edit.

2. **Trend Board Assemblage**
   Setting the mood through effective visual staging.

3. **Textile Board Assemblage**
   Fabric swatches attached to the page in a portfolio format.

4. **Color Board Assemblage**
   Supporting your concepts in an exacting manner, utilizing universal color formulas.

5. **Assimilating Retail and Competitor Information**
   for the entire collection building process.

6. **Final Illustrations/Fashion Plates, Flats, and Specs**
   for final portfolio page planning.

7. **Interpretations of Brand Information**
   for product category presentation.

3. *Textile research* Keep an open, tentacle-like research mind when examining textile mills and fashion runway collections. Put the available information into your filter, and determine what is right for your end product use. *Visualize* the fabrics in your silhouettes and on your illustrations as you shop the market. Begin to develop rendering skills to draw your fabrics in your portfolio.

4. *Color direction* Compile and play with color from all avenues. The filter needs to determine which colors are right for your market, for the collection/season you are working on, and for your portfolio presentation. *Imagine* your portfolio pages utilizing these colors as background colors, accent colors, or collection colors, and where your color trend information would be best utilized. As an example, grays are all the rage. Your filter tells you that the shopper who purchases for the 5-year-old would never expect the child to wear gray. Your filter helps guide you to think of gray as the outline color for your hangtags you are designing and for the logos applied to neon-colored T-shirts. Another designer knows that five shades of gray for his or her 55-year old customer will be used in the textiles and color statement, as well as the presentation boards in a matte silver background. All hair and makeup will be powder gray, as the filter reacts to the color direction information for the vision the designer has for the end consumer. Interpreted here for the presentation, the gray message is right for each market when used properly.

5. *Silhouettes, bodies, flats* When you are drawing in your sketchbook, on a table napkin, on scrap paper—wherever and whenever you get an idea—your filter can review each drawing and make decisions about the layout direction of the portfolio. Playing with different illustration styles as you research, design, and sketch will force the filter to work as you are developing the collection. An attitude toward the drawing page or presentation style begins to develop as the collection is drawn in thumbnail form.

6. *Branding/packaging* This is the trickiest task to finesse. You can't fool your consumer or interviewer with gimmicky, predictable logos or branding labels. The finest screen filter needs to be working overtime for the most effective end product.

As you get a feel for logo ideas from consumer branding effects you gather from magazines, the Internet, and all commercial venues, sketch different ways you can apply the thoughts to your garments and/or page layouts.

Maybe your filter tells you that the best way to brand your collection is in your page layouts. You can build a brand thematically on the page with formatting borders, color backgrounds, color blocking, poses that are unique to your design/illustration style, stylized texture details, logos, and typefaces. Similar to the staging of a play, the pages of the portfolio can act as the backdrop or stage for the brand.

Keep in mind that there is a difference between slapping a logo on your apparel, and forward-thinking, even subliminal nuances that make your brand, or your designer look, distinguishable from others. Fine-tune your filtering skills by practicing the filter technique as you build your portfolio collections. This experience will help your filter work in overtime mode to keep a cohesive, logical presentation format to building the face of your fashion presentation.

Use the design process exercise and the two boxes throughout your student design projects, in exercises in the text, and in your career. The inside studio work can overlap with the outside studio work. The research done outside the studio can also use the inside studio criteria.

WORKING OUTSIDE THE STUDIO

At the beginning of a project, when designers are actively seeking inspiration for a collection that will balance current trends with the wants and needs of the target market, they work outside of the studio to collect and research information.

The following is a list of places outside the studio where your work as a designer will take you:

+ Retail shopping
+ Attending forecast and color trend services' presentations
+ Shopping the textile and print market
+ Attending fashion shows and trade shows
+ Online research

RETAIL SHOPPING

When entering a retail store to research a particular collection, a designer looks for answers to the following questions:

+ Where is this designer line showcased on the retail selling floor? Near what other designers is this collection hanging? How much retail space does this designer have in this particular store? How does it compare with the other stores that I have shopped in terms of the size of the collection, the position within the store, the display items, and the collection color, silhouettes, and fabrics?
+ What fixtures are being shown with this collection to further reinforce this designer's brand image?
+ What silhouette, fabric, surface treatments, and accessories are being showcased?

- What is the mix being shown in relation to tops to bottoms, skirts to dresses, outerwear, accessories, and so on?
- What colors does the designer believe in this season? What do I think of the appeal of these colors to the consumer? What shade of black does this designer believe in?
- What silhouettes, colors, and fabrics stand out to me as key trendsetters?
- What garments do I think might be selling out now? (The designer can confirm this later by asking a retail associate.)
- What type of size/fit and silhouettes (length, width) are the garments and what shape would these garments take on the body?
- How do textiles and surface treatments feel, and how would they feel on the body? (Examine the label inside of the neck or on the side seam of the garment.)
- How does the consumer wear the garments, and how does it feel when I wear them? What do I see when I look in the mirror? Who is this person, and what does he or she want to purchase? (Depending on whether the designer is part of the target market, you might answer this question by trying on some of the garments or asking a cooperative friend who is in that market segment to try them on.)

This designer is researching retail garments in a department store, zeroing in on a designer collection to better understand its label in preparation for an interview with this design company. He has a pencil and sketchbook in his backpack. He is examining the silhouettes, shapes, labels, hangtags, trim details, finishing touches, and price points. His research is intended to answer the question: what makes this collection unique to the design firm? *(© Corbis Super RF/Alamy)*

- ▶ Speak to the trend services, fashion experts, and friends for the "hot" stores to visit a few days before your shopping trip.
- ▶ Shop for design ideas by viewing garment presentations and details.
- ▶ Gain product knowledge by examining price points, product presentations and placements, sell-throughs, and markdowns.
- ▶ "Hit the streets" with a plan. Have a list of store hours and street addresses. Map out your route via car, mass transportation, and/or walking. Project the number of hours it will take you to see each store, including travel time.
- ▶ Put your must-see stores on the top of the list.
- ▶ Examine the outside of the store windows. Look at all product categories, fashion and otherwise. Notice the unified story displayed as the store's brand merchandising. This is similar to how you will package your individual collections in one package: your portfolio case. Each collection will be different to show your design range, but the pages will be grounded with a sense of visual organization, similar to the 3D images of the exterior and the interior floor layout of the retail store.

- ▶ Make notes and sketches, and take pictures of store windows. View the items of interest inside the store.
- ▶ Enter the store and take in the broad picture. Notice which lines are showcased throughout the main floor. Take notes on color, materials, and textures used in the displays and display backdrops.
- ▶ Shop each collection and take notes or make sketches. This is best done in the dressing room with several key garments. Most stores will not allow you to take notes and sketch on the selling floor.
- ▶ Speak to the salespeople about market or trend information. What items are selling well? If you have an upcoming interview with one of the companies you are researching, tell the salespeople your purpose to gain better insight into the products and/or the company.
- ▶ Shop the specific designer lines and categories of design apparel in your area of specialization. Identify and compare competitive lines.
- ▶ Shop different price point categories, and make notes of the current trends/details/fabrics that are interpreted differently for each market.

OBJECTIVE: Conduct a design search for a category or specialization

1. Decide on one or a few categories for which you might be interested in designing. Refer to the choices in Exercise 1.8, "My Preferred Categories of Design: Figuring It All Out."
2. Shop retail in your categories of interest, examining the details as outlined in the Basic Designer's Guide to Retail Shopping.

3. Research the category(ies) on the Internet. Choose companies that are in the category, and check competitor differences, and price points.

4. Spend at least 3 hours in the library researching the categories of design and the companies you are interested in. Study period pieces from the past century and take notes; draw ideas in your sketchbook.
5. Thumbnail design 20–40 sketches for the categories you have chosen.
6. Upon completion, evaluate your work with an instructor to see whether you should pursue one of these collections for your portfolio and/or career path.

COLOR FORECAST AND TREND SERVICE PRESENTATIONS

Forecast services send out a flyer or an e-mail to their clients announcing the available show dates/times for the presentation of the upcoming season's trends. There are typically several days and times offered by the forecaster over a period of a few weeks to accommodate clients' schedules. The presentation can run in length from 45 minutes to 2 hours. There are typically 2 to 25 attendees per show, unless it is a presentation at a trade show, which might have hundreds of attendees in a larger venue. The designers (and other corporate executives) attending the shows take notes and sketch from the presentation's visual and oral presentation. There may be many inspirational details to capture on the written page, and designers can be sketching and writing these in their journals or on individual pieces of paper. They may gather mood and color inspiration, color references from universal color systems, and/or silhouettes/shapes to develop, inspirational sources of museum exhibits to visit, music sources to listen to, nightclubs or street scenes to research, and so on, which will lead to further research they will do after the presentation on their own.

A visit to a color forecast service. The designer attends a scheduled presentation by a color forecast service in its offices or showroom. *(Courtesy of WWD/Robert Mitra)*

THE DESIGNER'S BASIC GUIDE TO ATTENDING FORECAST AND COLOR TREND SERVICES' PRESENTATIONS

▶ Attend all forecast and color presentations that you can. They can be very useful, even if you don't agree with the information. Use each presenter as a benchmark for valid phrases, catchwords, and trends. Gather trends from different sources, then use your designer filter to sift through and edit information that you want to work with.

▶ Use the Compile/Edit/Finalize method while attending presentations.

▶ Don't apply the trends directly from the forecasts into your design collection.

▶ Interpret what is shown for all markets (not just your specialization).

▶ Use a mix of trend reports from different and varied sources. Runway presentations, runway slide shows, color services' presentations, retail reporting seminars, street scene reporting, and overall trends are just some of the subjects to choose from.

▶ Your company should subscribe to services in the industry for this information. As a student, look in your school library for archived trend resource materials.

▶ Seek out trade shows that feature seminars for designers.

▶ Gather useful information from the presenters by writing down all of the words and phrases that resonate with your creative side in short, stacked lines in a stiff-backed memo book. Review the words in your hotel room, if you are traveling, or in your studio, if you are not on the road, as soon after the presentation as possible.

▶ Rewrite or highlight the key words that you want to explore for your collection.

▶ Sketch any ideas you may have.

▶ Take notes on the museums, sites, music, books, and so on that you may want to visit for further inspiration.

▶ Make a point to introduce yourself to the trend reporting staff.

▶ Discuss key points with the reporters, and ask questions that you may have immediately following.

TEXTILE AND PRINT MARKETS

Designers schedule a time to visit a particular vendor to research the fabric assortment for the design of their upcoming collections. The fabric source is selected prior to setting up the appointment, as it is identified as a source to meet this particular designer's types of fabric for the season at a price point established by the company's production, marketing, and sales team. Designers know their customer, and assortment mix will require a fabric at a price their target consumer can afford. They choose a company as a source of textiles based upon the fabric blends, construction, and prices the company is known for. The vendor makes a presentation of the fabrics of interest to the designer and presents possible fabric trends for the designer to consider. Each designer will take notes on the fiber blend, width of the goods, the construction, weight, gauge (if the fabric is a knit construction), price per yard, production and sample availability dates, production and sample yardage minimums, and dye lot minimums.

In the textile designer's showroom, the apparel designer is shown the paintings or CAD designs of the textile design studio. The studio may represent hundreds of different designs by several design studios and/or many textile designers. Fashion designers know beforehand the manufacturing capabilities of their factories to produce the prints on fabrics in mass quantities—which might be limited to how many colors or what type of textures the designer can actually purchase from the textile print studio. The designer might chose ten prints for a season in which they wish to actually produce only three of the prints. Also, the designer might borrow the prints to look at with their design team and corporate decision-makers and then narrow the purchase of the artwork down to three or four prints.

A designer at an appointment in a textile vendor's showroom to research its fabric assortment for the design of his upcoming collection. The designer selected the fabric source prior to scheduling the appointment as it was identified as meeting his needs for the types of fabric for the season at a price point established by the company's production, marketing, and sales team. This designer knew his customer and assortment mix would require a stretch fabric at a price his consumer could afford. The vendor will make a presentation of the fabrics of interest to the designer and suggest fabric trends for the designer to consider. *(Courtesy of WWD/John Aquino)*

A designer on an appointment at a textile design studio's showroom, where she is shown paintings or CAD designs available from the studio. The studio may represent hundreds of different designs by several design studios and/or many textile designers. The designer knows beforehand the manufacturing capabilities of the vendor's factories to produce the prints on fabrics in mass quantities—which might limit the number of colors or types of textures available. The designer might chose ten prints for a season in which she wishes to produce only three of the prints. The designer might borrow the prints to share with her design team and corporate decision makers and then narrow the purchase of the artwork to the three or four prints. *(Courtesy of WWD/Robert Mitra)*

THE DESIGNER'S BASIC GUIDE TO ATTENDING FASHION SHOWS AND TRADE SHOWS

Use these two sets of basic guidelines to shopping trade shows and attending fashion shows throughout your design career.

Trade Shows

▶ Choose shows that are absolutely necessary for inspiration. Target shows that offer an overview of all categories, as well as highly specialized trade shows for your market specialization.

▶ Choose shows that make logistical sense. Many trade groups that once held shows only overseas now have shows in New York or California. Tie a retail shopping trip together with a trade show in one of the major market cities.

▶ Most trade shows will allow students in with a student ID; call or e-mail the management company in advance to confirm.

▶ 2 months in advance of the show: preregister for the show online, by fax, or by phone. You will receive an E-badge prior to show date for admittance.

▶ Register online for special trend or market seminars, and/or purchase a color card from the trend forecasts on-line.

▶ Book appointments with vendors prior to arrival.

▶ Familiarize yourself with the list of vendors by visiting the trade show website.

▶ View the map and venue layout at the website, and map your course.

▶ Upon arrival, check your coat and/or luggage at the registration desk. As you walk through the show, you will want your hands free to touch and feel fabrics and/or garments, to take notes at vendor's booths, to exchange business cards and shake hands with new business acquaintances. An outdoor coat and/or luggage or extra carry-all bag will get cumbersome

and will add extra weight to carry as you walk (sometimes miles!) through the show. You can also avoid losing your belongings as you move from one vendor to another.

▶ Go through the entire show floor plan and map to get an overview sense of what's happening.

▶ Be sure to visit trend, color, and textile forums and fashion shows. Keep informed by reading the daily bulletins at the entrance.

Designer Fashion Shows

▶ Admittance is by invitation only, and it's usually difficult to gain access. To get into a show, work or intern as an extra for a design house backstage.

▶ Consider an outfit befitting the performance. It is usually a place to see and be seen.

▶ Upon arrival, expect to wait. Most shows do not start on time. Anticipate some degree of difficult crowd control from the crush of editors and fashion followers.

▶ Expect that every seat in the house will be occupied, and your seat is coveted by many.

▶ Take notes on the music, staging, lighting, and performance aspects of the show.

▶ Take notes, and sketch details of garments.

▶ Observe the designer's color palette. How do these colors relate to your vision for the upcoming season?

▶ Observe the designer's color combinations that are being shown together in outfits and in surface details.

▶ Observe how the colors are being used. Are they main colors or accent colors?

▶ Which tones of colors are right for your market based on what you see?

▶ How do the fabrics move on the body?

▶ How do the fabrics relate to each body in a collection?

- Ask yourself, "Am I seeing an abundance of a certain fiber (for example, linen or silk)? How do I interpret these fabrics for the market I am designing for?"
- What reasonable fiber blends will help you get the look of the finer fabrics, maintain a high taste level, yet bring your price to your consumer's target price points?
- What textures are being shown?
- What is the balance or ratio of knits to wovens, sweaters to blouses?
- What silhouettes are being shown on the runways? Are dresses making a comeback? What are the hemlines? Are pants, shorts, or skirts dominant?
- Which bodies work for your customer or can be interpreted for your line?
- What shape is dominant? Is it tight to the body, away from the body? Are the garments structured or fluid?
- Enjoy the show!

FASHION AND TRADE SHOWS

It is rare that a designer would have the opportunity to attend a fashion show by a competitor. Designers can purchase tickets for some shows on an availability basis at the website www.couturefashionweek.com/tickets.htm. Tickets are sold for general seating through platinum VIP seating, by the day or by the show. The invitation-only seats in the audience are usually reserved for buyers, editors, retail executives, public relations executives, debutantes, patrons of the arts, socialites, and celebrities. The entrance to the show is carefully monitored by security guards, and a printed invitation must be presented at the door. The front-row seats are designated for the elite attendees, carefully chosen by the fashion show presenter's show team. Many shows start very late (up to three hours past the time on the invitation) and the wait can seem endless. The crowd scene outside and inside of the show can be a study in trends and inspiration for the designer. Taking notes and sketching in your seat (quietly and unobtrusively) is acceptable.

A designer typically preregisters online or through the mail for a trade show of particular interest to his or her line development. The designer checks in at the registration desk to get a visitor's badge, which must be worn to walk the show. The designer studies the layout map of the show; makes notes as to the vendor's and/or manufacturer's sections of the show that will be most productive to shop; and walks the aisles of these section, viewing the current garment presentations of the different manufacturers to keep a finger on the pulse of current trade show and fashion trends.

Designers may be among the attendees at a runway show during fashion week if they have been fortunate enough to obtain an invitation through, for example, an editor friend who works for a major publication. *(Courtesy of WWD/Giovanni Giannoni)*

Sportswear designers attending the MAGIC trade show. They preregistered online or through the mail. Typically held in Las Vegas twice a year, the show originally started as a men's trade show held in the Los Angeles Convention Center (MAGIC is an acronym for Men's Apparel Guild in California), and the show grew to a larger venue in Las Vegas to include women's and children's apparel and accessories.

THE DESIGNER'S BASIC GUIDE TO
SHOPPING THE TEXTILE AND PRINT MARKETS

▶ Contact the fiber companies. Fiber trade organizations and companies (e.g., Cotton, Inc., The Wool Bureau, DuPont Fibers) supply lists of the fabric companies and their contact information for specific fabrics.

▶ Search the Internet for fabric companies by category.

▶ Set up your appointments to visit fabric houses, or have the sales representative come to your studio. Time your appointments, taking into consideration the travel time in between appointments. Plan to spend roughly 45 minutes at each house.

Print studios are based in major cities and are also available for on-line perusing. Visit print studios based on your specific market and customer needs.

ONLINE RESEARCH

The modern designer can make use of the Internet to research websites that feature designers, runway presentations, companies, and retail stores. Individual designers' websites and portfolio websites also yield a wealth of information about current trends and resources.

OTHER RESOURCES

In addition, design research should encompass the categories listed below and any other informative bases you deem important to your line research. You can work with the methods described above or work in a spontaneous manner. Observe people's mannerisms, their dress, and the "big picture" of all scenes. "Packaging" surrounds you everywhere, occurring through natural causes, by cultural norms, or by marketing experts. Primarily, it is your goal as a designer to observe the influential sources that are not necessarily focused on fashion but reflect the zeitgeist.

Following are some ideas for research:

+ Street scenes.
+ Nightclubs.
+ Concert venues and live performances in the arts.
+ News reports, newspapers, and magazines.
+ Music television, YouTube, and similar media venues.
+ Museums, art galleries, and special exhibitions: Attend local exhibitions and read about international shows. Can you attend traveling exhibitions that are shown globally or nationwide?

Example of a source of online research for designers.

+ Libraries: Design reference books in all categories and old issues of magazines.
+ Celebrities: Oscar night, Emmy Awards, Grammys, etc.
+ Movies and theater performances.
+ Sporting events: Observe both national and international sports and sports marketing. Product placement should be observed. Is this an Olympic year? Rider's Cup and World Cup Soccer, to name a few events, highly influence fashion and function trends.
+ Read *Women's Wear Daily*, W magazine, *Vogue, Elle, GQ,* and international style magazines.
+ Alternative art and music: What are they producing, wearing, saying?

HATS OFF

John Galliano

Christian Dior

Giles Deacon

Marking the 30th anniversary of Stephen Jones Millinery, the MoMu fashion museum in Antwerp, Belgium, hosts "Stephen Jones & the Accent of Fashion," a retrospective of the designer's oeuvre, starting September 8 and running for six months.

"It's extraordinary to have done this for 30 years. It still feels like Day One," says Jones. "This is all my hats—it is like climbing into my mind."

Among the donors are private local collectors Geert Bruloot and Eddy Michiels, who loaned more than 120 pieces for the show, including the early hats Jones designed for John Galliano.

"It all started with Geert Bruloot, who invented the Antwerp Six," Jones says. "He has been a collector of my hats for years and he has over 200 that neither I nor John Galliano have seen [in years], and they will all be on show. The curators are creating the exhibition around me and it is fascinating to see someone else's point of view."

Jones points out that hats are becoming quite popular for museum fodder: Another anthology on the history of hats, which traveled from the Victoria and Albert Museum and recently closed in Brisbane, Australia, registered more than a quarter-million visitors.

"It is going to be a real adventure," Jones says. "There are very few fashion museums. It's quite amazing that the entire museum is dedicated to me. It's strange to have your life on view."

—Katya Foreman and Natasha Montrose

STEPHEN JONES PHOTOS BY ETIENNE TORDOIR/CATWALKPICTURES.COM AND YANNIS VLAMOS/CATWALKPICTURES.COM

THIS JUST IN HATS JEWELRY SHOES BAGS WATCHES SUNGLASSES HATS JEWELRY SHOES BAGS WATCHES SUNGLASSES HATS JEWELRY SHOES BAGS WATCHES SUNGLASSES HATS JEWELRY SHOES

DIY handbag lovers can customize their own totes with more than 50 pairings of colors and materials, including pony and suede, from Fratelli Rossetti ($1,900, Fratelli Rossetti, New York, 212.888.5107).

Giorgio Armani and Reebok are going retro with a collection of six sneakers under the Emporio Armani and EA7 labels ($150 to $450; emporioarmani.com and reebok.com).

8 **WWD**ACCESSORIES

Clippings from newspapers and magazines make a huge difference in the influences designers use to broaden their scope of information. Here are examples of pages from *Women's Wear Daily* and from *Vogue* magazine—showing trend information. Designers may paste these into their sketchbook, pin the influence to their bulletin board, or place the information in a file for line development information. They may read through these sources and sketch 20 or more ideas based on the written information they culled. (© *Avital Aronowitz and Courtesy WWD*)

An example of a special exhibit featured at the Metropolitan Museum of Art's Costume Institute. The number of garments shown and curated by world-renowned experts make this museum a must-see when you are traveling to New York. Go online to the museum's special exhibit website (http://www.metmuseum.org/special/index.asp) to see the list of current, past, and future special exhibits to plan your trip and research. Top: *(Courtesy of WWD/ Kyle Ericksen)* Bottom: *(Courtesy of WWD/ Kyle Ericksen)*

Check reference sections in your local public libraries and your college library for reference periodicals (old magazines catalogued from the turn of the twentieth century in bound books) that cannot be taken out of the building but can be viewed and sketched from. Here, a student is carefully tracing fashion influences from the 1930s *Vogue* magazine she found with an inspiring silhouette. Careful to preserve the archival quality of the old magazine, she uses her pencil lightly to get a tracing of the photograph. She will collect many tracings, sketches, and notes from the racks of magazines and look through them later in her studio for inspiration for her line. (© *Avital Aronowitz*)

Celebrities hold a place of high esteem in today's fashion market. Until about 20 years ago, fashion trends were dictated by the designers and artists of the era. Celebrities in today's fashion arena can dictate trends and have lines with their names stamped on them. Some celebrities play a large role in designing the lines bearing their label, and others put their stamp of approval on the garments at the very end of the process. Gwen Stefani is shown at left on the runway at the end of her fashion show featuring her signature collection. Shown in the middle and at right, Lady Gaga is another example of an influential celebrity to follow. Observing the habits of celebrity designers and other trendsetting celebrities through fashion magazines and celebrity tabloids can help a designer keep up-to-date about what is hot now. Designers then needs to use their Designer Filter to sift through how the garments are being worn to translate these influences to a collection they are designing for their own portfolios, which should be innovative and take the trend to the next level for the upcoming season. Left: (Courtesy of WWD/Thomas Iannaccone) Middle: (Courtesy of WWD/Steve Eichner) Right: (Courtesy of WWD/Steve Eichner)

Staying on top of sporting events, which can influence fashion from couture design to budget lines, is essential. Here is an example from the FIFA World Cup opening ceremonies featuring the performing artist Shikira, which the designer can study for color, silhouette, and crowd behavior. All of this information influences the way consumers buy and wear garments; psychologically or literally. (Corbis/Andres Kudacki)

Learn to enjoy your research work, and it will become part of your daily routine.

As you work with the four Basic Designer Guides, it is important to understand that you can garner inspiration from the top down, the bottom up, or any combination in between. Mixing up this formula will keep your merchandise looking fresh and modern.

Inspiration can come from the streets and be taken *up* to the couture market. Conversely, one can find inspiration from the couture market and take it *down* to a mass-merchant collection. It's best to remember to mix it up by drawing from all avenues but keep in mind, first and foremost, that interpreting better design details for the mass market is a sure winner—if done correctly.

Visualize interpretations of the trends you observe at all levels, so that your garments will have the best interpretations of all the markets for the market that you serve. If you are designing for the mass/budget market, for example, and you adapt the look of a "better" collection by using inexpensive fabrics and take-down versions of elaborate design details shown in the other markets, you should have a collection that reads consumer-right. Practice to become skilled at this technique of observation and adaptation.

OBJECTIVE: "Hit This Mark" with an informal sketch collection

Sketch 20 designs in thumbnail form as a collection in the category of your choice and "hit the mark" of the market you are designing for. Follow the schematic drawing and the outline below.

1. Research the avant-garde and better collections for inspiration, even if you selected a different market segment. Formulate your plan on your dream concepts. Make your initial sketches "out there" with the freedom to design a collection with pure inspiration. Make this your dream collection.

2. Research the mass market/volume retail stores for inspiration. Research the street and moderate retail stores for inspiration. Again, this research may provide inspiration even if you are designing for a different market segment.

3. Modify your initial collection with 20 sketches of your collection that hits the mark by pulling in your ideas for the market you are designing for.

4. Evaluate your work for market correctness. It should have the flavor of innovative newness, combined with market-right clothing.

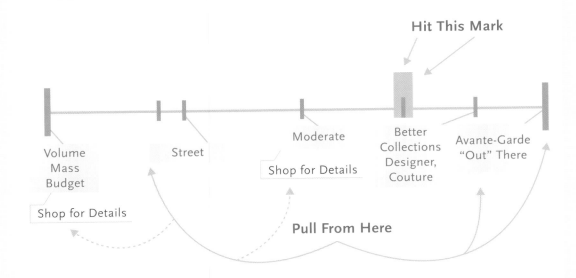

Hit This Mark

Volume
Mass
Budget

Shop for Details

Street

Moderate

Shop for Details

Better
Collections
Designer,
Couture

Avante-Garde
"Out" There

Pull From Here

OBJECTIVE: To prepare for the completed portfolio project in Chapter 6 in a shortened condensed form.

Using the visual imprint of the Compile/Edit/Finalize logos, work on this exercise with the mental reminder that there is a start (compile), middle (edit), and end (finalize) to all design projects. This will help you develop a pace to achieve a final goal to reach an identified customer.

    This is a practice exercise for the Portfolio Project, which will be to develop your final portfolio collection.

1. Compile

Design a line of 10 sportswear outfits for the male or female customer, ages 25–35, for in-store placement 6 months from now. First, compile information. Information should be entered into the sketchbook journal by sketching/pasting/rendering/writing.

- ▸ Examine the age group of consumers ages 25–35. For example, included in this wide age range are recent college graduates to young, upcoming executives with their careers on the rise, young adults planning to or in the beginning phases of starting a family, adventure-seeking national or world travelers, recreational athletes, students in graduate school, a cutting-edge avante-guard personality, a wanna-be rock star/gangster/pop idol, an artist, volunteer worker, social service or government worker, etc. Look through the Internet and library sources for profiles on this age range to get an idea of the consumer, their spending power, and their lifestyles. You can interview relatives or friends in this age group to get an idea as to their lifestyle and consumer likes and dislikes. Focus on one group of consumers in this age

group that has one type of lifestyle. Take the answers and apply them toward the ideas you will put together for your collection. The consumer's needs/wants will help focus your direction. Keep their needs in front of you as you develop the collection. You can do this by researching this age group, or through the interview. Here are some sample questions to answer through your research or in an informal interview of a consumer:

- ▸ What type of clothing do you wear to work (weekends, leisure time, etc.)?
- ▸ What do you look for when you buy clothing that you need?
- ▸ What was the last "impulse buy" you made (clothing or otherwise) which you had to absolutely have? (An impulse buy is an item that catches your eye either through reading about it, seeing an advertisement about it, or seeing it at retail/on the internet/on a TV shopping network that makes you just *have* to buy it on the spot or go out and get it immediately.)
- ▸ What colors, fabrics, and silhouettes do you like to wear and why?
- ▸ Mood concepts: Collect images from magazines, websites, drawings, etc. that inspire you to create a new collection with a vision for what sportswear will be worn on the body in this age group 6 months from now.
- ▸ Trend information: Answer the question in your sketchbook through writing, drawing, or cutting/pasting information from publications: What are the trends that affect this customer and what will he or she be looking for in 6 months in my collection? Women's Wear Daily's buying and retail trends are an excellent source for incoming trends.

- Textile research: Indicate through swatches and/or renderings textile ideas you think suit the collection. Search the Internet and fashion publications for what types of surface effects are forecasted to be popular for the next seasons. Women's Wear Daily Textile issues, which report on trade show buying and shopping trends, are an excellent source.
- Color direction: Visit stores, view magazines, and visit Pantone websites for color direction for the upcoming seasons. Paste color swatches/renderings into your sketchbook.
- Retail shopping/competitor information: Select three sportswear companies that fit this demographic. Shop their lines at retail. Log (through sketching and writing) the silhouette, color, price and fabric information into your sketchbook that you deem important to line development. Your first notes can be in a portable notepad. Transfer the most important or pertinent information to your sketchbook.
- Sketch silhouettes of the designs in your sketchbook using the influences of the research materials you gathered.
- Sketch ideas of branding or packaging in your sketchbook. Think about how you would like the hangtags, logos, inside or outside garment labels to be designed to make the garments appealing to the consumer.

2. Edit

Sift through all of your information by using the Designer Filter. Decide which of the ideas need to be reworked, which need to be discarded, and which need to be refined. Use your information of the consumer to help you evaluate the concepts to make these changes. The direction should be as focused as possible so that your final fashion illustrations "speak" to this consumer. Cull down your ideas to eight outfits, five fabrics, and six colors.

3. Finalize

Closely edit and refine your collection to 6–8 final outfits. Complete illustrated fashion plates for each outfit, showing individual or multiple figures on the page. Render fabrics, colors, and silhouettes to the best of your ability to showcase a refined collection aimed at the target consumer.

4. Add these illustrations to your temporary student portfolio case.

REFERENCE

Davis, Marian L., *Visual Design in Dress*, 3rd edition, Prentice Hall, Inc., Upper Saddle River, NJ, 1996.

Chapter 3

ENTERING THE MARKET WITH PROFESSIONAL FLAIR

OBJECTIVES

+ Focus your portfolio collection for a specific distribution within retail venue(s).

+ Decide on a specialized market for your portfolio presentation or a generalized sportswear or eveningwear portfolio presentation.

+ Develop an ideal vision of your best portfolio images.

+ Complete the designer grid for working on the final illustrations.

Now you have a traveling artist's tool box set up with the following:

+ Materials needed for portfolio presentation.
+ A purchased portfolio case.
+ A trusty sketchbook chock-full of sketches, themes, and doodles.
+ An idea of an interview.
+ Completed self-evaluation forms.
+ An overview of the basic design categories.
+ An imprint of the design process, design editing, and
  the designer filter.
+ Designer's guides to market research.

The next steps in linking all of these elements are presented in this chapter. They will sharpen your ability to market yourself and your designs in a portfolio package.

FOCUS ON A RETAIL VENUE

A focused retail venue for selling your collection is a necessary first step in planning your portfolio collection. A retail venue is defined and broken down as follows:

Retail Venue: Where the fashion designs in your portfolio will be sold: retail store, Internet, mail-order catalogue, or television purchasing; or a combination of these venues.

Here is a list of retail venues to consider:

+ Individual mom-and-pop stores or boutiques, which can be the one and only store that exists and has an assortment of just a few pieces of each item offered.
+ Small retail stores with 2–10 locations throughout the country or world.
+ Nationwide or worldwide specialty stores, such as Ann Taylor, Banana Republic, Gap, Gap Kids, Old Navy, Express, American Eagle, Ron Jon, Henri Bendel, Lane Bryant, Forever 21, Hollister, Abercrombie & Fitch, Victoria's Secret, and H&M.

+ Department stores, such as Neiman Marcus, Bergdorf Goodman, Nordstrom, Saks Fifth Avenue, Bloomingdale's, Lord & Taylor, Macy's, Burdines, Dillard's, Belk Stores, Sears, and JCPenney.
+ Large apparel specialty chains that sell to a specialized market, such as active apparel stores (Sports Authority, Dick's Sporting Goods, Models).
+ Designers' own stores, such as Ralph Lauren, Armani, Chanel, Missoni, Sonia Rykiel, Prada, Donna Karan, and Calvin Klein.
+ Direct Internet sites for the manufacturer or designer.
+ Internet sites that carry many different assortments of merchandise.
+ Collections made exclusively for eBay Internet sales.
+ Mail-order catalogues from department or specialty stores that sell an assortment of goods, or designers' own catalogues featuring only their own merchandise.
+ Cable shopping networks such as QVC or HSN.
+ Smartphone apps.

Within each of these channels of distribution are different price categories of clothing. The consumers who shop in some retail stores or boutiques are willing to pay higher prices for the exclusivity of their clothing, since they might be one of only a handful or hundred people who will buy a particular garment. Some freestanding retail stores distribute merchandised collections:

+ Only in select major cities throughout the United States or the world.
+ Only in select regions of the country.
+ Only in select malls or demographic areas that have the population that would shop at the right price points for their merchandise.
+ In major shopping malls scattered throughout the country.

Within these retail categories, the manufacturing company you will be working for might choose to put select collections in certain key areas of the country or the world, as the consumer's needs are sharply identified by market research. As a designer, you will be acquiring or honing this basic "read" of the consumer markets that you are designing for.

A collection aimed at the consumer who shops at Walmart and Target stores will require different planning from that of the internship position you might be interviewing for within an haute couture or designer house. Some designers can choose and work only with fine fabrics and can produce only made-to-order garments. This is a very limited market, as is haute couture. Get a reality check by going through Exercises 3.1, 3.2, 3.3, and 3.4. This should help you establish the consumer and retail venue that you could be designing for.

In addition to the market tiers of distribution that are listed on page 80, some successful designers and manufacturers are able to straddle multiple distribution channels without tarnishing their brand's image.[1] These designers create a different name or label to their line for a select venue. See, for instance, how Vera Wang reaches customers with a range of spending power, from her high-priced lines to moderate or budget categories.

The categories of retail distribution for you to consider for your portfolio are couture, designer, young designer, bridge/better, contemporary, upper moderate/lower bridge, moderate, and budget. Here is an overview of these categories:

Haute Couture Collections by designers such as Karl Lagerfeld for Chanel, Givenchy, Christian Dior, Jean Paul Gaultier, Giorgio Armani, and Yohji Yamamoto. The fashion runway shows may highlight a made-to-order design collection combined with a ready-to-wear version of their high-end couture pieces, which are produced in the designer price points. Haute couture garments can range from $2,500 to upward of $50,000 for a garment.

Portfolios with this category of consumer in mind show complete fantasy and extreme use of luxury imagery.

There are designers who cater to celebrities or a small following of customers for whom they custom-design and machine-sew all of the garments exclusively. This is not haute couture, but it is small-business design, which is a limited market.

Designer Top-tier department stores and freestanding stores in high-end retail malls distribute these collections. Bergdorf Goodman, Neiman Marcus, Barneys, Saks Fifth Avenue, Bloomingdale's, and Nordstrom carry designer collections, and they are usually showcased on a separate floor from all other collections. Target locations in large metropolitan areas are the department and specialty stores on Fifth Avenue and Madison Avenue and some parts of Tribeca and Soho in New York; Rodeo Drive, Robertson Avenue, and Melrose Avenue in Los Angeles; Palm Beach, Bal Harbour, and Miami, Florida; Michigan Avenue in Chicago; Newbury Street and Back Bay in Boston; and the top malls and avenues of Las Vegas, Dallas, Houston, Seattle, Phoenix, Short Hills, New Jersey, and Washington, DC and its Virginia and Maryland suburbs. Smaller cities with high-spending demographics carry these collections on a smaller scale. Price points can range from $500 through $3,000 for a garment. Portfolios for collections for this market show minimized fantasy, but use of luxury settings and accessories.

Young Designer These designers are found in most department stores listed in the designer category, and in some department stores in major cities, such as Macy's, Dillard's, and Lord & Taylor. Garment prices average $300 to $800. The garment collections and portfolios are trendy and status conscious, showing an in-the-moment lifestyle. Marc Jacobs and Anna Sui are two examples of the designers.

Bridge/Better This is the category of clothing that falls in between the designer level and the more moderately priced lines. It covers the secondary lines created by designers such as Donna Karan and Ralph Lauren. DKNY, RL, Lauren, AK by Anne Klein, Dana Buchman, Tahari, and Ellen Tracy are

some examples. Jackets in this category are in the $250 to $450 price ranges. The collections are carried in all of the major department stores listed previously. Portfolios for these collections show the target consumer doing ordinary things at work or at a recreational event

Contemporary These collections appeal to a broad group of consumers, and portfolios depicting the garments show a sense of fun or glitz applied to ordinary consumers doing extraordinary things, or playing in a fantasy-like environment. The prices for jackets average between $150 and $225. Jones New York and Evan Picone are some examples. They are carried in most major department stores.

Upper moderate/lower bridge Labels include Chaus, Karen Kane, and Evan Picone, sold in most department stores. Price for jackets range from $100 to $120. A practical approach to advertising or packaging to appeal to the price-conscious consumer is reflected in portfolios featuring these collections.

Moderate A price-conscious consumer shops this category. Prices range from $70 to $100 for jackets. Distribution channels include JCPenney, Sears, and Kohl's. In portfolios for collections for this category, prices may be listed. You may recognize "take down" versions of the better design houses' collections, and in advertisements there is a sense of practicality and function to the model and backdrop, and a message of "style at the right price."

Budget This is the lowest level of the price structure. Stores include Target, WalMart, Kmart, Costco, BJ's, and Payless. Portfolios featuring collections for this category look similar to portfolios for the moderate category.

CONSUMER BUYING HABITS, RETAIL VENUES, AND YOUR PORTFOLIO

A portfolio can be focused for a general consumer in various categories of lifestyle, income, and buying power characteristics. This attention to detail interpreted in your collection designs will help you keep your portfolio fresh and ready for multiple interviews aimed at a range of consumers. Your portfolio can be edited and updated and/or revised based upon specific research for an interview with a company.

Basic characteristics of consumer spending are outlined below.

Consumers shop brick-and-mortar stores, the Internet, mail-order catalogues, and television venues based upon their income, lifestyle, age, and occupation. Getting to know your consumers and their buying habits is essential to creating designs for them to wear. The reflection of this research in your portfolio design illustrations is readily visible to an interviewer.

A designer or potential employer who reviews your portfolio has a trained, professional eye and is looking for your keen understanding of what a targeted consumer will wear, and where that consumer will shop for it.

Consider these breakdowns of consumer buying habits as they relate to retail venues and to the categories of price levels described above. Keep in mind, however, that there is no magic formula for understanding how individual consumers' lifestyles affect their buying habits. As you grow in your design career, you will become better able to gauge the buying habits of your targeted consumer based upon how your designs sell at retail. These retail observations can meld directly with your trend forecasting for the company or designer you will be worsking for.

Following is a general introduction to consumer buying habits and retail venues. There is not a straight line between income level with select stores or buying habits. For instance, a wealthy person may spend more money at a lower-end retail store per year than a person with a lower income, based upon the size of their respective discretionary incomes.

Breaking the population into three levels of upper, middle, and lower income helps you see in your mind's eye just whom you are targeting your products for.

+ *Upper class: 3 percent of the population*
  - Upper-upper class understated elegance:, inherited wealth, socially elite, unconcerned about cost
  - Lower-upper class conspicuous consumer, the nouveau riche (new rich), status/label conscious, unconcerned about cost

Categories of retail aimed toward this population: haute couture, designer, young designer.

+ *Middle class: 42 percent of the population*
  - Upper-middle class cautious spender, prefers designer status labels, but usually will purchase the lower-priced lines of designer labels
  - Lower-middle class purchases lesser-quality designer knockoffs, searches for buys at discount stores, and purchases take-down or knockoff versions of trendy merchandise

Categories of retail aimed toward this population: designer (at discount stores), young designer, bridge/better, contemporary, upper moderate/lower bridge, and moderate.

+ *Lower Class: 55 percent of the population*
  - Upper-lower class/value-conscious consumer: shops at discount retailers and off-price stores
  - Lower-lower class/survivors, only makes fashion purchases as a necessity at the discount and off-price retailers

Category of retail aimed toward this population: budget.

VERA WANG: THE DESIGNER AND THE BRAND

Born June 27, 1949, American fashion designer Vera Ellen Wang is based in New York City. She is known for her couture bridesmaids' gowns and wedding gown collections. Wang was a senior fashion editor for *Vogue* for 16 years. In 1985, she left *Vogue* and joined Ralph Lauren as a design director for 2 years. In 1990, she opened a design salon featuring her trademark bridal gowns.

Well-known clients for Vera Wang wedding gowns include Chelsea Clinton, Ivanka Trump, Alicia Keys, Mariah Carey, Victoria Beckham, Jennifer Lopez, and Uma Thurman. Her gowns have often been referenced in popular culture. In the *Sex and the City* TV series, Charlotte York found a Wang wedding dress to be perfect for her wedding to Trey MacDougal. In the film *Sex and the City*, Vera Wang was featured among the bridal gowns Carrie Bradshaw wore in her *Vogue* photo

Diana, an ivory strapless organza sweetheart gown with tulle draped bodice, swirling tissue organza flange skirt, and ivory double-knotted tie at waist, from Vera Wang's 2011 wedding collection. *(Courtesy of WWD/Robert Mitra)*

shoot. In the film *Bride Wars*, Anne Hathaway and Kate Hudson both wore custom-made Vera Wang gowns. Vera Wang's design was referenced in the NBC television show *The West Wing* in the episode "The Black Vera Wang."

As a former figure skater, Wang designed costumes for figure skaters, including Nancy Kerrigan, Michelle Kwan, and Evan Lysacek. And she designed the two-piece uniforms for the Philadelphia Eagles cheerleaders.

Her awards include CFDA's women's wear designer of the year in 2005 and the Andre Leon Talley Lifetime Achievement Award.

The designer Vera Wang *(Courtesy of WWD/Robert Mitra)*

Following is Vera Wang's product range, to date, is:

▶ Vera Wang ready-to-wear (Saks Fifth Avenue, Bergdorf Goodman, Neiman Marcus)

▶ Bridal (Vera Wang Chicago; Vera Wang Boston; Vera Wang Manhasset, NY; Saks Jandel, Washington, DC; Bergdorf Goodman; Saks Fifth Avenue; Neiman Marcus)

▶ Vera Wang Tabletop (Bloomingdale's, Macy's, Dillard's, Bed Bath & Beyond)

▶ Vera Wang Fragrance (Macy's, Sephora, Dillard's)

▶ Simply Vera Vera Wang (exclusive to Kohl's)

▶ Vera Wang by Serta Mattresses (Neiman Marcus, US Mattress, Horchow Collection, Mattress Joint, CSN Mattresses)

While this list is impressive, it is a difficult task for a designer or label to manage successfully. There are many tiers of executive management, business, marketing, sales, design, and development teams that make this happen for Vera Wang, herself, as the designer and overseer of her brand's image.

A sample of Vera Wang's better women's Pre-Fall 2012 collection [a–c], Vera Wang Resort 2012 Jewelry [d], and her Princess fragrance from her better-priced retail offerings [e]. Compare these styles and prices from the Vera Wang's Simply Vera collection she designed for Kohl's Department store [f–h], which range in price from $24 to $64, to her designer lines. Vera Wang's ability to maintain luxury brand status as a better designer label and also design successfully for the lower-priced market is unusual and well worth studying for career planning. [a–c] *Courtesy of WWD/Thomas Ianoccone*, [d] *Courtesy of WWD/Kyle Erikson*, [e–f] *Courtesy of WWD*.

CONSIDER A MARKET SPECIALIZATION

Choosing a market specialization is not mandatory. As a student designer, you can represent basic sportswear in your portfolio, for example. You will assemble both the specialized portfolio and the basic sportswear portfolio after completing market research. Market research is composed of the retail, forecast and color, textiles/prints, and online research of designer houses and designer portfolios. It is described as "understanding the consumer." Your finished portfolio should demonstrate this understanding of the consumer from conception to finalization. The exercises in this chapter will develop your sense of understanding.

THE BASIC SPORTSWEAR PORTFOLIO

The basic sportswear portfolio is anything but generalized; it is a highly focused portfolio for a specific segment of the sportswear market. The basic sportswear portfolio can be targeted at the women's or men's sportswear market, or it can be unisex. The focus you demonstrate in this area is critical; you must identify an end consumer before designing the collection by following the exercises for this consumer. The consumer must be easily envisioned by an interviewer when he or she looks through your book. The basic sportswear portfolio can be very helpful in landing a job in specialized markets. The gamut of sportswear items and accessories you show in your portfolio can exhibit great strength of your range and breadth of your talents to design-related separates. As the interviewer sees your ability to design trousers, skirts, or blouses, you may land a job as a specialized designer within one of these categories.

After you complete your basic sportswear portfolio, you can choose to identify a specialty market and design a collection of 16 ensemble pages as a part of your portfolio. You can also design a specialty collection specific to a company you are going to interview with.

The **specialized portfolio** showcases your complete desire to work in a given category of design. Some specialized categories cover many segments of the market, so "specialized" does not necessarily mean "narrow." For instance, a portfolio specialized in active sportswear is limitless in its end uses and how it can be interpreted by the interviewer. Because active sportswear encompasses such a broad market composed of men's, women's, children's, pro sports, team sports, exercise, recreational sports, and specific sports categories of swimming, basketball, football, soccer, tennis, dance, track, running, cycling, camping, outdoor sports, skiing, rollerblading, skateboarding, snowboarding, motor sports, ice hockey and ice skating, baseball, softball, fencing, and many more, the portfolio can show one or two of these categories, show a general view of athletic attire for many categories, or show a feeling of athletic influences. Any of these combinations can appeal to the interviewer in an active sportswear company.

Most importantly, the designer depicts the target consumer on the page in the way of a fashion figure. The fashion figure can be inspired by an imagined consumer with an imagined lifestyle; or the designer may model the fashion figures on a celebrity who represents a particular consumer demographic. For specific categories within active sportswear, a highly focused collection for a particular company would be required for an interview. Alternately, an active sportswear portfolio might appeal to a company that is seeking an activewear designer's look to influence another category of design, such as urban streetwear or men's outerwear.

THE SPECIALIZED EVENING WEAR PORTFOLIO

There are many examples of specialized portfolios that can showcase your talents in multiple categories. Another example of diversity is the category of eveningwear. If your portfolio shows women's evening gowns, and you go on an interview for a day-dress designer, your evening gowns can be interpreted into day dresses. You can also add a collection of dresses for a particular interview and explain to your potential employer that you want to gain experience in the day-dress area as part of the development of your design career. The evening gowns you show are related in nature to the day-dress area. To broaden your visual presentation in evening gowns, you might choose to put your portfolio collection together with menswear partner outfits; and/or cocktail dresses as part of a separate collection. The elements of the design collection can be connected through fabrics, details, and presentation layout from the eveningwear to the cocktail dresses, thereby helping the portfolio flow better. The evening wear portfolio might also appeal to an interviewer for bridal, certain areas of costume/theater design, made-to-order, celebrity, one-of-a-kind, and/or couture design houses.

DEVELOP AN IDEAL VISION OF YOUR BEST PORTFOLIO IMAGES

Preview the specialized portfolios shown in the illustrations in Chapters 4 and 5 as an overview. You can look for inspiration for the development of your ideal portfolio by referring to the illustrations in Chapters 4 and 5 and the list of categories in Chapter 2.

Look over the chapters with an open mind, and take notes on which lines you might want to explore. Complete Exercises 3.1 and 3.2 to help you determine your career portfolio path.

Complete Assignments 1–5. Upon completion of the assignments, fill out the questionnaire that follows, "What Area of Apparel Most Motivates Me to Produce a Portfolio?" At the end of the questionnaire, decide on a consumer and category direction for your portfolio. Here is an overview of the assignments, followed by details for completing each:

Assignment 1. Preview the portfolios in Chapters 4 and 5.
Assignment 2. Identify your consumer.
Assignment 3. Identify your taste.
Assignment 4. Identify your price points.
Assignment 5. Identify your retail venues.

Assignment 1. Preview the Portfolios in Chapters 4 and 5

Chapters 4 and 5 have examples of many different types of portfolio collections with the emphasis on focusing the portfolio for an end consumer. Chapter 4 features portfolio representations in women's, men's, and children's wear. It also discusses key categories, retail size considerations, and fashion figure attitudes. Chapter 5 depicts the specialized portfolio and how these categories can overlap into a general sportswear portfolio presentation.

1. Briefly skim through Chapters 4 and 5, and observe the following:
   ▸ Your likes and dislikes of a product category you want to pursue
   ▸ The design approaches to focused collection building
   ▸ The stylization techniques, layouts, and attitudes of the fashion figures and how these features of the portfolios relate to the garments being shown
   ▸ The difference in a general sportswear portfolio and the tightness of a specialized portfolio

Assignment 2. Identify Your Consumer

Materials needed: Tracing paper, file folders, pencils, current magazines you can cut from.

1. Collect information from designers and design houses. Spend 3 hours in the library looking through periodicals both current and from the last decade. Make photocopies of select merchandise from select designers you are interested in. Also, trace the garments you are interested in, noting the designer or manufacturer.

2. Collect information from current periodicals, catalogues, and Internet sites. The periodicals can be from the most recent editions and from the past 4 years. Label each with the name of the designer. Print the information from the Internet collection sites with the designer reference on each.

3. Make piles of each picture or tracing from each designer or design house. Make file folders for each label. Place the pictures in the file folders.

4. Seek out the particular designers or labels you might be interested in designing for from the top markets all the way through to the budget houses. Seek out competitive lines from within a category.

5. Choose from these detailed folders a consumer you would like to design for by examining the marketing techniques and materials used in the ads or fashion layouts. Make a list for each folder, identifying each according to what you perceive to be its consumer base.
   ▸ The list for each folder should include (a) fabrics used and a rough estimated wholesale price per yard of each fabric; (b) trims used and their respective estimated wholesale price per yard; (c) shapes and silhouettes used;

(d) colors, including how they are used in a current season and how they evolve over several seasons; (e) approximate price points and fabrics/materials used for the accessories shown: hair styles, eyeglasses, jewelry, shoes, handbags, and belts; and (f) what attitude or style is shown.

6. Answer these questions:
   ▸ Do the fabrics, trims, shapes/silhouettes, and colors appeal in price point and sense of style to a consumer in one of the categories listed from haute couture to budget?
   ▸ Do the ads and/or fashion spreads' backdrops appeal to the same category by depicting a certain lifestyle? Examine the photographs or layouts. Examples of the categories' looks are listed on page 80. Some of the category images can blur the lines of price and consumer base. Some garment companies attempt to appeal to a perceived consumer need for product purchase by showing ads or catalogue layouts that have an upscale look for a moderate consumer base. Examine the visuals carefully.
   ▸ Do the ads show a certain type of style— attempting to appeal to the luxury consumer? Is the ad aimed at the budget consumer? Identify the consumer category that the ad is attempting to lure.

7. Keep the notes that you have accumulated in their respective folders. You will use them to help you set an image for your portfolio collection.

Assignment 3. Identify Your Taste

1. Look through the temporary portfolio. What taste does your work portray? Use the categories of the market listed on page 80 to make an assessment. Assignment 2 should have given you critical experience in finding this answer. Does it portray the taste level you wanted to portray,

or can you do a better job to reach the mark that you had wished to achieve? Ask yourself:
   ▸ Do my illustrations work for the taste I want to portray:
     ▹ Are the fabrics in the taste of the consumer I designed for?
     ▹ Do the trims cheapen or enrich the image, based on my consumer's taste?
     ▹ Are my silhouettes appropriate for the taste of my consumer?
     ▹ Are my colors correct for this category of taste—are the colors too brash, too dull, too complex, too simple, too cheap, or too rich looking for this consumer?
     ▹ Are my accessories realistic for this price point and taste preferences of my target consumer?
     ▹ Is the attitude/style/gesturing appropriate for this consumer's taste?

2. Look at your work and try to gauge generally how it could appeal to your customer's expectations, based upon the following criteria. Have you illustrated a collection that matches the style to the price categories that will appeal to your target consumer?
   ▸ Luxury, celebrity, upper-upper class consumers (haute couture and designer)
   ▸ Upper-class consumers who enjoy a rich lifestyle and shop at department stores (designer)
   ▸ Youthful consumers who want the latest fashions without regard to price point (young designer)
   ▸ Consumers from many age ranges who need functional garments for the workday and weekend activities within a mid-range price point (bridge/better, contemporary)
   ▸ Practical purchasers who have a high regard for price points and value but who want today's looks and fashions (upper moderate, moderate)
   ▸ Practical fashions with a wide range of styles and basic garments for the lowest price points (budget)

3. Evaluate your perception from the time you created this collection to your perception today.

4. Decide whether or not you can make the appropriate changes to appeal to a different level of consumer. If you believe you can, then decide on this consumer for your portfolio collection. If not, you are best suited for this particular price point customer. If you do it well, then your collection will be successful. This is the level at which you design best.

Assignment 4.
Identify Your Price Points

1. Shop the retail stores according to the Designer's Basic Guide to Retail Shopping Box in Chapter 2. Before going out to the market, decide on the segment you want to design for, based on the price point/taste level.

2. Shop the stores that carry merchandise you most identify with, and take notes on the price points for the items you will be designing: tops, bottoms, skirts, jackets, coats, etc.

3. Shop the Internet sites that carry these lines, and make notes on the price points.

4. Add the notes to the respective designer folders, or create new folders for additional labels.

5. Keep these price points and basic taste levels in mind when you design your collection.

Assignment 5.
Identify Your Retail Venues

1. Begin to evaluate which category of design you are choosing to design your portfolio collection for.

2. According to your ability identified in the evaluation assignments, choose the retail venues (brick-and-mortar stores, mail-order catalogue, Internet, shopping networks) that would carry your line.

3. Keep in mind the visual of the consumer who shops in these outlets as you begin the design process of your portfolio collection.

Questionnaire:
What Area of Apparel Most Motivates Me to Produce a Portfolio?

Answer the following questions to help you decide the direction of your design category for your portfolio collection. Completing this questionnaire might leave you with many open-ended answers to the questions. There are no final or correct answers. Think about what works best for you and your abilities and current career goals. These factors could change, and you will evolve within the industry as you develop further design skills.

▶ When you reviewed the portfolio in Chapters 4 and 5, per Assignment 1 determine the following:

▷ Which categories make you most instinctively excited about designing?

▷ Which categories translate best to your chosen style or illustration ideals?

▷ Did you sketch ideas for the categories that interest you? Which ideas flowed most freely for you?

▷ Which categories have you designed collections for in your student work? Which of these categories do you feel you have strength in?

▷ Have you specialized in a category of design and construction at your college? Does it make the most sense to pursue this category for your portfolio collection, or are you more interested in another category? Deciding now can better channel your energies in the correct direction for your career path.

- Do you feel you want to pursue a technical designer portfolio? Is this your area of interest? If so, it's best to focus on this for your portfolio collection.

- Are your interests and designs in accessories design strong enough to specialize in accessories? Does your college support any courses to study these areas? If not, have you explored summer/winter/graduate programs in these areas so you can compete with the trained designers who will be interviewing for the same jobs as you? A strong portfolio in accessory design combined with some (even a small portion) of technical training in these areas will give you credibility upon your entry-level job search.

▶ Taking the information folders from Assignments 2–5, review and evaluate your abilities to bring forward a collection in a chosen category. With this research, you should have a better knowledge base to go forward with a decision. Closely look at the following quesions:

- Which of the designers/manufacturers you researched do you have a feel for as a working designer?

- Can you create prolific designs for this category, or is it a real struggle? If it is a real struggle, and you are highly motivated to make this work, it will take extra time and work to complete your portfolio. Allow extra time for yourself to explore, experiment, learn, and apply your new category to your portfolio story. If the struggle is just not working for you, evaluate your timing for getting your career launched in a timely manner. Perhaps staying in a more general category or a category you have more experience in is the best entry-level path for you to pursue.

- Do the magazine/catalogue/Internet visuals give you ideas for your portfolio layout? You might be attracted by the layout, but not by the product content. Determine this by sketching the poses or gestures you want to capture from the layout. Decide on a category to sketch your designs on these poses. Is your sketching naturally going into a category that is different from the products shown in the ads? If so, keep the ads for your portfolio/illustration layouts. Perhaps you are not interested in the types of products shown, just the presentation.

- Do feel better suited for a certain consumer price point?

- Have you concluded that your temporary portfolio exudes the taste level you *thought* you were designing?

- Are you comfortable with the taste level you are showing in your current portfolio as it applies to a category you would like to design? Have you determined that your category of design has the range of taste levels that would support that which you will have the ability to illustrate?

- Do you need to revisit your fabric resources, use of art supplies, color choices, or collection styling to achieve the ideal results/category choice? If so, do you have enough time in your schedule to complete this transformation?

- Be aware of the price points your designs will support for your portfolio collection.

- Be aware of the retail venues you will design for—and visualize these venues as you design going forward. Think about the selling floor space (or catalogue/Internet/cable site) your garments will be selling in. Visualize your garments hanging in these venues when you design your collection.

- Be aware of the age group and body type of your upcoming collection. In your illustrations, show the idealized body type best suited to your target consumer.

OBJECTIVE: Plan an idealized portfolio
Materials:

Paper for notes (size and style of your choice)
Transparent sheet of acetate (size and style of
your choice)
Permanent Sharpie marker to write on the acetate
sheet (color and nib size of your choice)

Complete this exercise by drawing on the
work, exercises, completed temporary portfolio
project, research, and compilation of information
you have gathered in Chapters 1 and 2. Answer
the questions as best you can on a sheet of paper.
(See Item 1 below.)

Use the notes and answers to these
questions to create the transparent overlay of
the Idealized Final Portfolio Plan. Some of the
answers will be left open-ended, for you to finish
as you begin the design process of the final
collection. (See instructions in Item 2 below).

Answer the questions that follow. Visualize and set
your mind to the task of completing your portfolio
to the best of your ability. These answers lay the
ground work for your final goal. As you create the
collection through the next chapters, change your
mind or direction as you wish to better your work.
Some of the answers you will *not* have completed.
The object is to keep this overlay of direction as
a working structure to guide your designs into a
showcased body of work. Similar to the working
process of designing a line in Adobe Illustrator or
Photoshop, think of the "layers" of the process.
Think of keeping this transparent layer or open
window that you continually reference and update
as you work through your collection. The answers
could come to you as you work through the design
process of creating your collection.

Think about the four effective areas of
refining your portfolio as

► Materials
► Motivational thoughts, goals, inspiring details,
   trendsetting responses
► Layout
► Extras

Materials:

Have I focused on materials for my final portfolio?
Have I purchased and tested my materials?
Have I purchased my final portfolio case that will
house or stage my work? (You can't stage a play
without a set.) Have I purchased my portfolio
sleeves in the polypropylene/archival quality only?
Make a list of the medium choices for hand-
rendering you think you will use to achieve the
mood of the collection.

Motivational thoughts, goals, inspiring details, trendsetting responses:

What are my realistic refinement goals to meet my
portfolio completion deadline?
What sets my design line apart from the current
market trends?
How will I apply fashion-forward styling and
forecasting to the initial offering?
How do I step out of my comfort zone and reach
to the next level?
What illustrators' or layout artists' work do I most
admire?
Have I examined, collected, and organized
my visual references from the illustrators and
designers that I strive to emulate?
Have I identified the ideal or dream illustration or
presentation style I may go after?
Am I willing to go the extra mile and create work
that is one notch above my last work? How will I
do this?

Can I use better paper, better quality medium?
Can I improve my textile, color, mood, or silhouette work?
How can I better my technical flat drawings?
How can I better integrate computer driven images into my mixed media presentation?

Layout:

What is my orientation on the page (vertical or horizontal, but not both)?
How will I plan my layout to demonstrate interaction of figures and gestures to tell a collection story?
How will the pages of my portfolio unfold?
Will my figures be one on a page—or two, three, multiple figures?
Will I showcase my flats on individual pages, or will I combine them with the pages with the fashion figures?
Will I include fabric swatches on the figure page?

Extras:

1. Visualize a front page, an introduction page, and/or a logo/business card design. Will you create a leave-behind piece, CD-ROM, or Web page? Think about how these materials will enhance your image.

2. Use a sheet of acetate as an overlay for your project of creating your best portfolio. In the next chapters, you will set up a bulletin board, poster board, or journal of your design plan. This see-through acetate page will be the guiding overlay for you to push your collection into the best light.

3. Transfer your answers to the acetate sheet as best you have answered them. Change or add direction as you go through the chapters of creating your collection.

COMPLETE THE DESIGNER GRID FOR WORKING ON THE FINAL ILLUSTRATIONS

In Chapter 6, you will build your final portfolio. In Chapters 4 and 5, you view specific portfolio images. Prepare for the job in front of you now with Exercises 3.3 and 3.4. Both of these exercises can be updated as you learn more about your designer direction in Chapters 4 and 5.

OBJECTIVE: To prepare for the Portfolio Project in Chapter 6, create a Designer Grid.

There are four material options: A, B, C, and D. Read through the options to see which one works best for you.

Option A is a foam core layout board, or a bulletin board.

Option B uses four boxes as the layout vehicle.

Option C uses four file folders or four Bristol boards.

Option D uses the designer sketchbook.

For each option, the materials needed are listed with the directions.

The designer grid will be used as a backdrop to build your collection's mood, color, textile, and silhouette ideas through the conceptual evaluating, editing, and finalization processes. Experiment with a layout option that will let your thoughts flow freely.

Option A:

Materials: Large foam core board (40" x 60"), or a bulletin board
Sharpie pen for creating line grid and labels
Push pins to put ideas onto board

▶ Section the large board into four equal parts with a ruler and pen.
▶ Label the four sections: Mood, color, textiles. silhouette.

MOOD	COLOR
TEXTILES	SILHOUETTE

The large foam core board divided into a grid and labeled.

Option B:

Materials:
Four boxes (cardboard, plastic, used shoeboxes, wicker, canvas, etc.) of uniform size, approximately 9" x 12" x 3" (or large enough for you to store your collected ideas)
Sharpie pen for labeling
Optional materials: Push pins, 1½" Velcro adhesive strips, cork bulletin board

▶ Label the four boxes: Mood, color, textiles, silhouette.
▶ You can keep the boxes stacked on a shelf, or use push pins or Velcro strips to attach the boxes to a bulletin board.

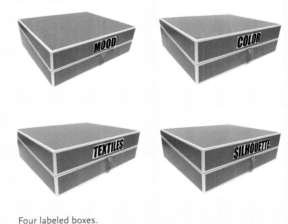

Four labeled boxes.

Option C:

Materials: 4 manila file folder or envelopes (sized 8.5" x 11" or larger) or 4 pieces of Bristol board (sized 9" x 12" or larger) to use as dividers
Sharpie pen for labeling
Optional materials: Scotch Tape for adding ideas to the Bristol boards

▶ Label the four folders, envelops or boards: Mood, color, textiles, silhouette.

Four manila folders labeled for the Portfolio Project.

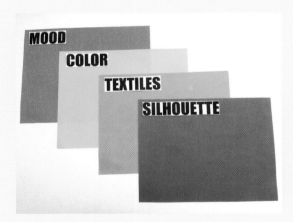

Four Bristol boards labeled for the Portfolio Project.

Option D:

Materials: Sketchbook.
Any choice of medium to enter your ideas: Pencils, markers, pens, colored pencils, paint, etc. Color swatches and textile swatches that you collect for each concept.

▶ Use your designer sketchbook as your work pad. Divide your workbook into sections for mood, color, textiles, and silhouette. You can also create your system of tracking these four phases of mood, color, textiles, and silhouette in a scattered or haphazard fashion and then gather your thoughts into the final phases of illustration and presentation.

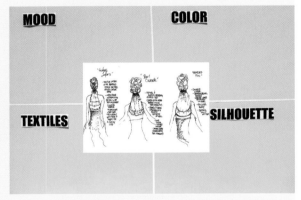

Here the designer develops concepts for her bridal veil designs by sketching and writing notes. She will later develop her mood, color, textiles, and silhouette pages based upon her original inspiration shown here. Inspiration and product development need not follow the grid pattern. This exercise, which uses the grid, is for organization, demonstration, and teaching purposes, The designer can follow or break apart and customize the grid, experimenting for each design project.

REFERENCES

WWD, Wednesday, December 30, 2009, The Multichannel Road Map to Fashion.

Diamond, Jay and Ellen, *The World of Fashion*, 4th edition, Fairchild Publications, Inc., New York, 2008., pp. 72–75.

Chapter 4

FOCUSED
PORTFOLIOS

OBJECTIVES

+ Define a market-focused portfolio through viewing, planning, and technique.

+ Explain the options of a gender-based collection.

+ Understand the sizing of women's, men's, and children's wear and how sizing affects the approach to assembling the pages of the portfolio.

+ Identify key categories and influences and overlaps of collection merchandise.

+ Identify specialized portfolios and influences and overlaps of collection merchandise.

+ Attitudinize the fashion figure for a specific market.

What makes a portfolio specific to a market? The end consumer, competitive retail market, and trend research completed in Chapters 2 and 3 are the foundation of a market focus. You were challenged to discover an age group and a lifestyle of your consumer. These findings contribute to the decision-making process of line development.

Designers create portfolios that focus on a particular gender or age group, and/or they create portfolios that combine genders and/or age groups.

MARKET PORTFOLIOS DEFINED

As discussed throughout this book, a focused portfolio is crucial to career success. The focus of the portfolio can be gender- or size-specific; based on a functional category, such as sportswear or formal wear; based on a key category; or based on a narrowly defined specific category.

GENDER- AND AGE-FOCUSED PORTFOLIOS

Portfolios that focus on gender, on age, or both have many possible variations.

+ Gender-specific portfolios feature
  ■ Women's wear
  ■ Menswear
  ■ Girls' children's wear
  ■ Boys' children's wear
+ Mixed-gender portfolios combine
  ■ Men's and women's wear
  ■ Children's wear for girls and boys

Portfolios focused on an age or size specification include the following:

+ Women's wear
  ■ Misses sizes (usually ages 25 and older)
  ■ Junior sizes (usually ages 12–25)
  ■ Full-figure, or Plus sizes
  ■ Maternity
  ■ Petite sizing (not a usual focus of a portfolio, except for the experienced designer)

+ Menswear
  ■ Men's sizes
  ■ Young men's sizes
  ■ Big and tall sizes (not usually a focus of a portfolio)
+ Children's wear by specific size breakdowns
+ Newborn/Layette through 24 months
+ Toddlers (ages 2–4 years) sizes 2T, 3T, 4T, and 5T
+ Preschool girls and boys (ages 3–6 years) sizes 4–6X, and boys 4–7
+ Girls (ages 6–12) sizes 7–14
+ Boys (ages 6–12) sizes 8–20
+ Preteen or Tweens (ages 12–14) Girls Junior sizes 0–16, Boys 8–20 or conversions to young men's sizes.
+ Teens (ages 13–17); depending on the size of the child, most children fit into women's junior sizes and young men's sizes.

FOCUS ON FUNCTIONAL CATEGORIES

The portfolio can focus on a functional category, such as generalized sportswear. In this category:

+ The portfolio presents basic mix and match separates that relate to one another in color, mood, fabrics, and silhouette.
+ The garments are planned to work well with one another, or they can be worn on their own as separate items.
+ The basic items are cut-and-sew tops, knit tops, lightweight jackets, pants, shorts, and skirts.

For designer sportswear collections:

+ Portfolios showcase a broad range of sportswear and related merchandise.
+ The basic items are knit tops, woven tops, sweaters, dresses, skirts, pants, shorts, suits, lightweight jackets, outerwear jackets, and coats.
+ Most of the better designer collections feature misses or men's sizing. A junior women's, young men's, or children's wear portfolio is also a viable alternative.
+ The merchandise mix features clearly related items that reinforce the designer's brand. They are generally shown as mini-boutiques within retail stores with their own section that may carry signage for the brand name, or as free-standing designer retail stores.

Layouts of two fashion plates of a general women's misses sportswear portfolio. *(Courtesy of Jane Henry)*

- Because designer collections can be shown as related pieces so effectively in one selling area of a department store, or exclusively in their own store, the consumer can get a sound image of their
  - Fit.
  - Proportions.
  - Trendiness: Criteria such as location of the collection on the selling floor (for instance, collections that are shown right where you enter the store, in the outside display windows, or right where you get off an escalator), number of customers you can observe are shopping in this section, type of fixtures, type of music playing in the section, sell-out items that aren't available, and trunk shows are all indicators of how "hot" or "in" a certain designer label is with different levels of trend-driven consumers.
  - Sophistication level.
  - Attitude.
  - Style.
  - Texture and color direction.
  - Reinforcement of the brand as an image.
- The designer collection portfolio showcases the illustrations in the same way as the store model and should entice the reader to want or need this well-put-together designer look or the stand-alone separates.

KEY CATEGORY PORTFOLIOS

The portfolio can be designed exclusively as a key category portfolio, which is characterized as follows:

- Focus exclusively on a specific area of merchandise, *not* on generalized mix-and-match items. The collection is designed only for a category listed below.

- The items presented may include *only* the garments within that category. For instance, a sweater designer might present a sweater portfolio by showing the sweaters on a cropped figure only from the waist up with graphic layouts of sweater patterns.

- The items presented might be supported by surrounding garments to link the key category designs into a head-to-toe look. For instance, a sweater designer may feature sweaters in a head-to-toe look with jeans and trouser separates that complement the sweater designs. The company for which the designer is designing this collection most likely does not design or manufacture jeans or trousers, but the lifestyle of the consumer is captured on the page. This helps the viewer comprehend the lifestyle that the designer is promoting along with his or her sweater designs.

- Key category apparel is presented on the selling floor of a retail department store or smaller retail store as separate merchandise. The consumer purchases these items for a specific end use, which may or may not involve a mix-and-match collection purchase. For instance, a consumer might decide to purchase a coat that works with all of the clothing in his or her wardrobe without shopping through a designer's collection of sportswear. The retail selling floor meets this need for the key category shopper by segregating coats into a separate area, so the consumer can run into the store and purchase a coat for a cold day or a dress for a special occasion in the dress department, and so on.

- Key category items are highly specific to the consumer's desire to shop for apparel with a multitude of choices. A consumer who is shopping for a coat wants to see all coats together. It is possible to comparison shop for price, fit, and style all in one section of the store. The key category portfolio showcases these items similarly to the way they are shown in the store, as a separate, well-thought out grouping.

Key categories are as follows:

- Coats and suits
- Denim collections (which include jeans as a portion of the separates collection, but also include tops, jackets, skirts, etc.)
- Dresses
- Evening wear/special occasion/black tie
- Jeans (which are jeanswear bottoms only)
- Knitwear
- Outerwear and coats (usually represented by all-weather gear such as parkas, snow jackets, raincoats, ponchos, furs, etc.)
- Sweaters

Two key categories in this list that generally are not combined with sportswear garments are dresses and evening wear/special occasion/black tie.

SPECIALIZED PORTFOLIOS

Specialized portfolios, described in detail in Chapter 5, are directed to a specific segment of the market. The difference between the key category and the specialized portfolio collections is the highly focused attention in the specialized portfolio categories over the last century. They are segregated here to help you make decisions about your levels of concentration within a given market and how specialized you want to become. Choices of how and when to make the decision to specialize in these categories are outlined in Chapter 6.

Many design colleges offer a general apparel design and art design program that overviews most of the key categories. Many design colleges offer programs specifically concentrated on the specialized fashion categories, as well as a specialty in men's fashions.

Specialized portfolios include the following:

- Accessories: Most entry-level accessory portfolios will feature a combination of subcategories of accessory design, such as footwear, handbags, small leather goods, gloves, and hosiery)
- Activewear
- Bridal
- Costume/theater design
- Eco/green apparel
- Golfwear
- Intimate apparel, lingerie, and underwear
- Millinery (which can be an accessory subcategory or a more exclusive category limited to headwear)
- Swimwear and beachwear
- T-shirts
- Technical design
- Uniforms
- Urban streetwear

A generalized portfolio may "steal" some influences from these markets and may also include garments from some of these segments. An example is a generalized sportswear portfolio collection that has separates that mix and match with lingerie pieces under a jacket, T-shirts worn with jeans, and urban streetwear sneakers worn with an activewear top and cargo pants. All of these are considered sportswear in a sportswear portfolio. However, in a specialized portfolio, the garments are all merchandised and planned *only* for a specific market. Depending upon the specialization (such as intimate apparel) the merchandise mix fits a specific need that, may be segmented by age, retail selling/buying category, size, or gender. Portfolios in these categories are represented in Chapter 5.

A portfolio can also be a combination of generalized sportswear, key category items, and/or specialized portfolio items. This technique can help build a brand and expand the merchandise mix.

GENDER-SPECIFIC PORTFOLIOS

A portfolio presentation can be exclusive to women's, men's, boys' or girls' collections. The collection is assembled with the knowledge of the end-consumers' age and appropriate apparel size ranges.

WOMEN'S WEAR

Categories of sizing in women's wear take into account variations in body type based on age and other factors.

Misses Sizes

Misses sizes are intended for ages 25 and older. Most colleges stock the misses size range dress forms for draping, patternmaking, and construction. Most garment companies and designers work their samples and prototypes in size 8 or 10, which is the fashion industry's norm of the average size misses woman. Some luxury designers work with a smaller size, such as size 4 or 6.

Misses sizing is for a woman with a mature and fuller torso dimension. If she has borne children, her hips are wider and proportioned differently from when she was younger. With age, the anatomy of the female figure widens or relaxes slightly. Designers strive to make clothing that flatters this female form, and conversely to cover or disguise any flaws or less slim areas of the body.

Most companies hire **fit models** to try their garments on for fit on a perfect size 8 or 10. Fit models are typically not hired for their looks but for their perfect measurements to the company's established size 8 or 10. Bust, waist, hips, arm length, torso length, inseam length, and height need to exactly match the measurements of the company's standards. Height is usually established at 5 feet, 6 inches or 5 feet, 8 inches. Runway models typically have smaller measurements and are taller than fit models.

Junior Sizes

Junior sizes are intended for girls and young women ages 12–25, and are odd-numbered sizes 1–11. Most colleges have a limited number of junior size range dress forms for draping, patternmaking, and construction. Many sportswear/pant-leg, full-size dress forms in college classrooms are in junior sizes. Most junior designers and companies make their prototypes and showroom samples and hire fit models in a size 7 or 9. Again, the fit models' measurements need to exactly match the company standards.

Junior sizing is for a youthful figure, probably one that has not had children. The shape of proportions is much less full. The body type is slim in the waist, hips, and thighs. Designers strive to make clothing that works well with this body type, which is not that concerned with covering anatomical flaws. Essentially, a junior customer who wears a size 5 might be a size 2 if she shopped a misses line. See the box for comparison sizing information.

The main differences between misses and junior styling are as follows:

+ Misses is more traditional, with the exception of avant-garde designers and contemporary ready-to-wear brands. Garments might be less form-fitting. Even form-fitting styles have more ease built into the garments than a junior fit.

+ Juniors are trendier, less interested in investing in a "look" that might last a few seasons. Their purchase is for now and is more of an impulse buy. Many styles are form-fitting without a lot of ease. The body can be more restricted by the garments, as the body can move better in youthful years; therefore, a tight pair of jeans on a junior body feels like it "fits like a glove." The same garment on a misses customer would be too tight, restrictive, and uncomfortable.

A group figure layout of a junior sportswear portfolio and a page showcasing one figure for a junior sportswear collection. Both layouts are suitable for the same portfolio. The designer will make the pages flow by working the sequence of the pages in the portfolio. These two pages are two contrasting collections and would be shown in a portfolio in two separate sequences surrounded by pages that supported each collection's story. Marker rendered figures and garments. Multi-fashion figure layout assembled in Photoshop/Illustrator. *(Courtesy of Cat Craig)*

MISSES AND JUNIOR SIZE COMPARISONS

Junior sizes are cut slimmer than a misses sized garment. To convert a junior-size into a misses size, see the table that follows as a guideline for fit.

Because every manufacturer has a different fit standard for all size ranges, a junior size 5 from The Limited is different in size and structure from a junior size 5 from dELiA's. A misses size 8 from Calvin Klein will fit differently from a Tory Burch size 8.

The fit of the garments can give you an idea of the shape and fashion demands of the target customer of a particular designer.

The range of sizes in the conversions reflects these differences. As you can see from the following table, a junior size 7 may fit into a 4, 6, 8, or 10 based on the established standard fit measurements of each individual designer or company. A size 7 might fit into a 2, if the customer is very slim and the designer's fit standard is a full fit.

In general terms, the following table describes what the industry would perceive the evolution of a woman's sizing might be as she matures, and if she stays the same relative weight and height. The body would shift to slightly wider proportions with age, and develop into the size in the right hand column.

A Junior Size Woman Might Mature into a Misses Size

1	2
3	4
5	6
7	8
9	10
11	12

A Current Size Junior Would Fit into a Misses Size

1	0
3	0 or 2
5	2 or 4
7	4, 6, 8, or 10
9	8, 10, or 12
11	12, 14, or 16

OBJECTIVE: To understand the sizing of design brands that you are interested in possibly working for and designing your portfolio for.

1. Choose one category for research: Misses, junior, large sizes, maternity, or petite sizing.
2. Identify two stores that carry the brands in these categories that you most want to pursue for your portfolio.
3. Shop the stores with a pen and paper or a device on which to take notes.
4. For the category you have chosen, research five different brands. Take their garments, including tops and bottoms, into the dressing room. (Male designers: Bring a female friend to try on the garments for you. The friend would have to come out of the dressing room to show you the fit you are researching.)
5. Try on the garments or have your friend try them on, and make notes of the way that the same sizes fit from brand to brand.
6. Visualize this customer, and how the customer would like the clothing to fit her body.
7. Take notes on your findings.
8. Apply your findings to your portfolio designs.

Women's fashion figures directed at the misses, junior, large size, or maternity market can be attitudinized in different forms. Your particular drawing style may be limited to one type of stylization, you may simply be comfortable with one style of drawing, or one style of drawing works very well for you. Whichever size category best meets your drawing style, it is important to research, develop, experiment, and be influenced by new drawing styles based on market trends. In addition, these influences will keep your portfolio looking fresh. You may also discover new techniques and artistic/design talents you otherwise would not have explored.

You can adopt an entirely new style of drawing figures for different collections within the same portfolio. Each style/collection should be connected by a common graphic or layout element. These include line quality, background, scenery, choice of mediums, and general aesthetics.

In Exercise 4.2, research illustrations from past to present to develop an illustration style that showcases your garment details and designs with a powerful message for your chosen market.

You illustration style will be enhanced by a given attitude of the figure on the page. Posing the fashion figure a certain gestural way develops a personality for the figure best suited to show off your designs. The attitude can be obvious, exaggerated, simply sublime, or naïve in nature. You can be strongly obvious with the attitude of the fashion figure or use the influences of these markets to imply an attitude in your fashion figures.

Most current portfolios show a range of cultural diversity within each fashion plate. By showing diversity within the figures on the page, you demonstrate your knowledge of the consumer base for your designs.

Some women's attitude ranges for the fashion figure are listed below. See the examples of attitudinized figures as inspiration to research and develop these looks:

+ Haughty, formidable woman
+ High-fashion woman
+ Relaxed or casual woman
+ Sporty woman
+ Dressy woman
+ Princess
+ Ladies-who-lunch looks
+ Wholesome woman
+ Naughty woman
+ Athletic woman
+ Graphically drawn or animated woman
+ Party-celebrity woman
+ Naïve woman
+ *Sex-and-the-City* urban woman
+ Executive woman
+ Shopping woman
+ Student or studious woman
+ Beach or surf woman
+ Night club woman
+ Dominant or dominatrix-referenced woman
+ Diva
+ Retro-referenced woman from different time periods or decades
+ Cropped-figure layouts
+ Catalogue figure layouts
+ Manga-inspired woman

OBJECTIVE: To absorb illustration style details from historic and modern culture to influence your drawing style.

1. Find a library that stocks:
   ▶ Periodicals from the past that have illustrations and reference books of illustrators and illustration styles (see the references listed in Appendix I).
   ▶ Trend and forecast sketchbooks.

2. Go to the library with a pad of tracing paper, pencil, and pencil sharpener.
3. Gather illustrations from many different periods of time.
4. Trace the illustration styles that are inspiring.
5. Trace the design style details that are inspiring.
6. Absorb and stylize your illustrations based on your findings.

Haughty, formidable woman. Here, Lela Rose and Adam Lippes showcase their muse, which can be interpreted as haughty and formidable. The designers use gestures, postures, and attitudes to best portray this. Left *(Courtesy of Lela Rose)* Middle *(Courtesy of Lela Rose)* Right *(Courtesy of Adam Lippes and Fairchild)*

Drawing by Antonio Lopez

High-fashion woman. There are so many different ways to draw high-fashion woman. Here is Antonio Lopez's interpretation. High-fashion illustration stylization can be researched at length (see Appendix I). *(Courtesy of Antonio Lopez)*

Relaxed, casual woman. The designer captures fashion and style with a relaxed, casual approach to real-life dressing. *(Courtesy of Jerry Dellova)*

Examples of a sporty woman fashion figure for better designer sportswear, by Christian Siriano. This type of fashion figure can be a benchmark for presentation of sportswear collection fashion figures for any segment of the market. *(Courtesy of Christian Siriano 2011)*

Princess woman. An example of a princess-inspired fashion figure. *(Courtesy of Kelly Moore)*

Naughty woman. A more risqué pose for an appropriately researched and executed vamp collection. *(Courtesy of Alexandra Palmisano)*

For the lingerie or intimate apparel market, these figures suggest the act of primping. Their gestures and poses (arms extended) are good for showing details of lingerie collections. *(Author's collection)*

Athletic woman. To develop poses for general athletic collections, it is important to show figures in motion. Athletic figures can be proportioned to have more athletic bulk than the figures shown here, depending on the market segment the designer is appealing to. Athletic figures can also be shown performing in specific sports. Although active-sportswear collections are designed for function, the presentation of the garments is usually illustrated on a figure with movement that can show the clothing, not the specific sport. The current trend of blending athletic looks with fashion and celebrity attitudes gives the designer a wide range of poses and fashion figures to experiment with. *(Author's collection)*

Graphically drawn or animation-influenced illustrations by Peter Som and Adam Lippes. Left *(Courtesy of Peter Som)* Right *(Courtesy of Adam Lippes and Fairchild)*

Party or celebrity woman. Michael Angel's fashion illustration gives inspiration for a portfolio collection designed for a specific celebrity or for a designer collection that is aimed at the celebrity-wannabe. The attitude and layout are exaggerated for dramatic effect. *(Courtesy of Michael Angel)*

This fashion illustration shows the influence of glam and *Sex-and-the-City* urban style. *(Courtesy of Hintergrund and Fairchild)*

These illustrations have the feel of a female student. *(Courtesy of Alexandra Palmisano)*

Bibhu Mohapatra evoking night-club style. *(Courtesy of Bibhu Mohapatra)*

Diva-type woman. *(Courtesy of Kelly Moore)*

Retro-referenced woman from different time periods, influenced, respectively, by a 1920s Erté illustration and by the 1970s roller-disco era. (Author's collection)

Catalogue-influenced figure layout. This fashion presentation board is easy to read and very clearly sells the garments, much like a fashion catalogue directed to the consumer. *(Courtesy of Jerry Dellova)*

Three different ways to show cropped figures on the page. The first figure (left to right) is developed to take up the entire page. The advantage to this close-up view is to magnify the details of the garments or accessories designed for the upper portion of the body. This can be especially helpful for portfolio illustrations of swimwear; intimate apparel; and such accessories as jewelry, millinery, glasses, scarves, belts, wrist-watches, or sweaters/knitwear. The next figure, by Michael Angel, is cropped in a way that might be shown on a page of a portfolio with a full-length figure wearing another ensemble in a collection. The last figure shows a smaller-scaled full-length figure in the background with a cropped figure in the foreground as a layout plan for a 1980s key category dresses collection. *(Left and right, author's collection; Center, courtesy of WWD)*

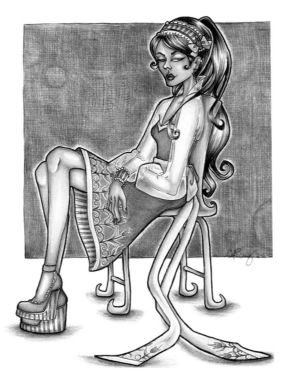

Animation-influenced woman: The designer's style is naturally animated. Many designers are influenced by different animation artists' work, and still others study manga-style drawing and use all or aspects of that style in their illustrations. *(Courtesy of Cat Craig)*

WOMEN'S FULL-FIGURE OR PLUS SIZES

Designed for any age range that fits appropriately into a plus-size 14, 16, 18, 20, 22, 24, 26, 28, 30, 32, 1x, 2x, and 3x, women's plus sizes are styled to flatter the body type of this end consumer. See page 125 for a measurement size chart of from www.lanebryant.com.

Color, texture, print pattern, fit, and style lines are carefully thought out to please the way the plus-size woman wants her clothes to flatter her. Comfortable knit fabrics are often used by designers so the clothing is fashionable, functions well, and is comfortable to move and sit in. Proportions of print patterns are carefully scrutinized for the way it will flatter or distort the body. Textures are chosen that aren't weighty, heavy, or plush, as these fabrics are not usually desired by this end consumer. Colors are often dark neutrals, black, navy, and bright color accents or base colors. Style lines and silhouettes are carefully planned by the designer to cut the body to flatter the figure.

Plus-size fit models and dress forms vary from company to company. Most times there is a standard that the company prefers to work with, based on availability of models and the experience of the pattern makers, technical designers, and the designer. Most showroom sample sizes and prototypes are in size 1x.

Designers who specialize in plus-sizes may have started their careers designing misses-sized women's wear collections, and they use that experience to translate looks for the plus-sized market. These multitasking designers may size up the misses silhouette designs with minor or major changes for the plus-size collection and may also design silhouettes that are exclusively designed for the plus-size range. If the plus-size market is an area of interest for you, it would be smart to include a collection in your portfolio. See Exercise 4.1 to research this field.

Like individual designers, some companies produce a version of their misses collections designed for large sizes. The styling may be different from that of the misses styles. Some companies take advantage of the fabrics, dye lots, and patterns created for a misses collection to produce a collection of large sizes. For other companies, the large-size collection is the sole focus. For example, Lane Bryant stores cater to women who wear the large sizes; a company design team creates clothing exclusively for its stores, and this merchandise carries the store label.

Large-size fashion figures should be shown on the page similarly to a fashion print advertisement layout. The same layout and research guidelines for women's portfolios apply to the large size portfolio development.

The fashion figure body type has a fuller width. Using the same 9½–12 head fashion figure you have developed as an initial template, increase the body features as listed here:

+ Wider, fuller face.
+ Broader chest, thicker waist, wider hips.
+ Wider and broader legs, hands, and feet.

See the women's large size fashion figure template. Use this as a basic visual guideline for your fashion figure, or trace over the template. Change the template by drawing over it with your own illustration style. Use your vision of proportion and attitude to have the figure "come alive" as your fashion muse. Develop different poses and views (side view, three-quarter view, back view, etc.), the same as you develop figures for women's fashion portfolios.

Reference the attitudinal illustration specifications for layout and design as outlined in the women's wear section for taking your large size fashion plates to the next level of presentation.

PLUS-SIZE MEASUREMENTS

Size	Bust	Waist	Low Hip
14	40	34	42
16	42	36	44
18	44	38	46
20	46	40	48
22	48	42	50
24	50	44	52
26	52	46	54
28	54	48	56
30	56	50	58
32	58	52	60

Use this plus-size croquis for designing a plus-size collection. If you choose to create a collection for this market, add your own gestural poses and attitudinized style to more plus-size figures. *(Author's collection)*

MATERNITY COLLECTIONS

Maternity collections are sized for all women of child-bearing age. The sizing is based on a pre-pregnancy misses size. The garments have fabric and fit accommodations for a woman's pregnancy shape. For example, if a woman wore a size misses size 4–6 or extra small (also designated as "XS") before pregnancy, when she shops a maternity line, she should fit in an extra small garment, or a size 4–6. See the maternity charts for sizing.

There are three trimesters of growth for pregnancy: The first trimester is 0–3 months, which brings a relatively small amount of size change for the average woman. She may remain in her pre-maternity clothing, or she may purchase maternity clothes as sized above. The second trimester is 3–6 months, with moderate growth or size change to the woman's body, when she is more likely to purchase maternity clothing. During the third trimester, she can expect the most change in her body size, most likely leading her to purchase maternity clothing.

Maternity designers concentrate on the function of the clothing for the growing stages of the baby and the mother's body. Many maternity garments have stretch panels in the torso area to accommodate the three trimesters' body growth. Many garments have stretch support layers built into the torso area to add comfort for the expecting mother.

Today's modern maternity clothing lines stay on top of current trends. The maternity clothing trends are on par with the current fashion trends, built with comfort and function first and foremost in the fashion styling.

Develop the maternity figure by using the template of your 9½– to 12–head fashion figure from your women's collections. Increase the width of the hips to accommodate the width of the lower abdomen for the pregnant silhouette. Reference the template for proportion guidelines, or trace over the template to develop your own figure. Remember to move the figure into different poses on the page for interest and vitality. Today's maternity consumer is most likely active in the same lifestyle as that before pregnancy.

The illustrated maternity figure should have allure equal to that of the women's and large size fashion figure. Follow the attitude suggestions from the women's fashion figure for layout and design.

MATERNITY SIZE CHARTS

These size charts from A Pea in the Pod Maternity Clothing line suggest the guidelines that customers should use to determine their maternity size. If the customer's pre-pregnancy size is XS (for example), and her pregnancy bust measurement is 33"–34", then she would purchase Pea in the Pod size XS. Pea in the Pod cuts garments in size XS to fit the bust measurements listed below, and it includes the extra room in the shirt (or pant) for the increased size of the waistline in the garment. If a customer was a pre-pregnancy size XS, and her pregnancy bust measurement is 35", A Pea in the Pod specialist recommends she purchase the Size S garment so it isn't too tight of a fit in the bust.

Table 1

SHIRTS AND TOPS

Pre-Pregnancy Size	Bust	Maternity Size
XS (2)	33"– 34"	XS
S (4–6)	35"– 36"	S
M (8–10)	37"– 38"	M
L (12–14)	39"– 40"	L
XL (16–18)	40"– 41"	XL

Table 2

PANTS AND BOTTOMS

Pre-Pregnancy Size	Hips	Maternity Size
XS (2)	36"– 37"	XS
S (4–6)	37"– 38"	S
M (8–10)	39"– 40"	M
L (12–14)	41"– 42"	L
XL (16–18)	44"– 45"	XL

Use these maternity-sized croquis for designing a maternity collection. The templates can be changed to match the size of the women's fashion figures you have planned in your portfolio by enlarging them on a copier. If you decide to include a maternity collection in your portfolio, the maternity figures should be in the same size, scale, and proportion as your fashion figures (except for the maternity-shaped torso). If you design a maternity collection for your portfolio, it is essential to develop various gestural poses that consider the consumer's lifestyle and incorporate an attitudinized illustration style. *(Author's collection)*

MENSWEAR

Clothing for males who have outgrown the boys' sizes are categorized as men's and young men's sizes. As with women's portfolios, menswear portfolios show a range of cultural diversity within each fashion plate.

Men's Sizes

Sizing for men's casual clothing is S, M, L, XL, XXL, and sometimes XXXL. Sizing is very specific for sport coats, coats and suits, dress shirts, and trousers. See the box, Men's Sizing Specifications.

Men's showroom sample size, fit model size, and forms are generally size medium.

The style of a menswear portfolio can be driven by the look of the body type of the male figure. The figure types can be used for any kind of menswear portfolio:

+ The general men's sportswear portfolio
+ The men's key category of apparel portfolio
+ The men's combination sportswear and key category portfolio
+ The mixed gender portfolio

There are two distinct stylized men's body types that depict two different styles:

+ The more rugged male body, which has more muscle mass and fuller proportions
+ The metrosexual male body, which is thinner and has more elongated proportions and an androgynous appeal

An example of a rugged male fashion figure. You can use this croquis to design a men's wear collection. If you develop final images in men's wear for your portfolio, be sure to enhance the presentation layouts with your own figures that you've developed using the attitudinized method. *(Author's collection)*

Portfolio illustrations and layout for the current market can have an affected attitude for any given market, which takes careful planning and research. In the past century, most men's portfolios had a Hart Schaffner Marx attitude of the well-dressed male. In the last 20 years, the male figure and fashion image have given way to different approaches to the illustrated page and the fashion attitude of marketing clothing.

The affected attitude (of either the rugged or androgynous male figure) is based on the designer's approach to fashion combined with extensive market, trend, and retail research in the exercises in Chapters 2 and 3. Here is a list of some attitudes for male figures:

+ Traditional guy
+ Casual weekend guy
+ Executive guy
+ Metrosexual male
+ Retro-style man
+ Very formal, bespoke guy
+ Preppie guy
+ Rugged outdoors man
+ Trucker guy
+ Sporty guy
+ Surfer dude
+ Athletic performance guy
+ Team-sports guy

+ The logo man
+ Urban street guy
+ Gang-culture guy
+ Rapper/hip-hop man
+ Rock-and-roll guy
+ Alternative music guy
+ World music man
+ Reggae dude
+ Indie music man
+ Man from the UK
+ Night club man
+ Student or studious guy
+ Cropped figure layouts
+ Catalogue figure layouts
+ Manga-influenced man: Many designers are influenced by animation and/or manga-style illustration. There are volumes of instruction books on this subject that can be researched.

The affected attitude of the figure can be further enhanced by background, scenery, or props that the chosen type of man relates to. Researching print periodicals and tearing out marketing and fashion spreads can give you insight and ideas into how to show the particular type of male you choose to depict. You can exaggerate by taking on all of the affectations of a given look, or scale back and just use minor inferences.

MEN'S SIZING SPECIFICATIONS

Men's fit standard measurements also run differently from designer to designer; therefore, a men's size medium from Brooks Brothers is different from a men's size medium from Gap.

Men's dress shirts are sized by neck x sleeve length, and men's suits are sized by the chest size. Men's suits become specific to short, regular, long, and large or portly sizes.

Here are a few size charts for men's standards for an overview of different men's sizes.

Table 1 | Men's Fox Racing Sizes

	XS	S	M	L	XL	XXL	XXXL
Chest	32–33	34–35	36–38	40–42	44–46	48–50	52–54
Sleeve	31	31½–32½	32½–33½	33½–34½	34½–35½	35½–36½	35½–36½
Waist	26–28	28–30	31–33	34–36	38–40	42–44	46–48
Inseam	30	30–30½	30½–31	31–31½	31½–32	32–32½	32–32½

Brooks Brothers Men's Sizes

Brooks Brothers presents its dress shirt sizes in four different fit styles: traditional fit, slim fit, regular fit, and extra slim fit to suit a range of customer's sizing needs. Table 2 is a traditional fit dress shirt size chart.

Table 2 | Brooks Brothers Traditional Fit Shirt Size Chart

Neck Size	14½"	15	15½"	16	16½"	17	17½"	18	18½"	19	20
Center Back Length	32	32⅜"	32¾"	33⅛"	33½"	33⅞"	34¼"	34⅝"	36	36⅜"	37⅛"
Center Front Length	28¾"	29⅛"	29½"	29⅞"	30¼"	30⅝"	31	31⅜"	32¾"	33⅛"	33⅞"
Center Measurement at Armhole	47½"	49½"	51½"	53½"	55½"	57½"	59½"	61½"	63½"	65½"	69½"
Waist Measurement 8" Below AH	43¾"	45¾"	47¾"	49¾"	51¾"	53¾"	55¾"	57¾"	59¾"	61¾"	65¾"

Table 3 | Brooks Brothers Men's Trousers Size Chart

Inseam	Waist Size											
	30"	31"	32"	33"	34"	35"	36"	37"*	38"	40"	42"	44"
30"	•	•	•	•	•	•	•	•	•	•	•	•
32"	•	•	•	•	•	•	•	•	•	•	•	•
34"			•	•	•	•	•	•	•	•	•	•

Table 4 | Brooks Brothers Men's Regent Suit Size Chart

Suit Size	36	38	39	40	41	42	43	44	45	46	48	50	52	54	56
	Waist Size														
Short	29	31		33		35		37		39					
Regular		31	32	33	34	35	36	37	38	39	41	43	45	47	49
Long			32	33	34	35	36	37	38	39	41	43	45	47	49

Table 5 | Brooks Brothers Size Translation Chart for Shirts

	S		M		L		XL		XXL	
Neck	14"	14½"	15"	15½"	16"	16½"	17"	17½"	18"	18½"
Sleeve	32½"		34"		35"		35½"		36"	
Chest	34"	36"	38"	40"	42"	44"	46"	48"	50"	52"
Waist	30"	32"	34"	36"	38"	40"	42"	44"	46"	48"

Casual weekend guy. These garments and attitude work well for a casual, weekend collection for the better designer market. (Author's collection)

Executive guy: Traditional in stature and gesture, he can be a blend of "rugged guy" and "androgynous guy," and for a multi-figure presentation in a portfolio, it can be best to show diversity in these body types and attitudes (as well as cultural diversity)—just like the executive work force. There is nothing frivolous or flamboyant about these presentations; they are all work, no play. (Author's collection)

Metrosexual male presentation page. The figure is more stylized and the collection is more intensely fashion conscious. (Courtesy of David Bermingham)

Preppie guy presentation. More traditional in nature; and with a relaxed or sporty attitude. *(Author's collection)*

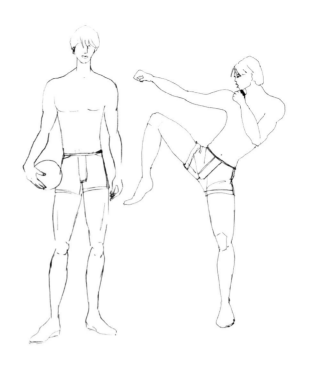

Athletic performance guy presentation. *(Author's collection)*

Urban street guy. A relaxed, "chill" attitude figure. He is generally very planted on the ground with a strong presence. He should be surrounded on the page with fashion figures that are a multicultural mix with different gestural stances. *(Author's collection)*

Hipster/street/music/art-influenced guy: A figure that is seemingly "in the moment" of the current scene. *(Author's collection)*

Young Men's Sizes

In the menswear trade, both at the wholesale and retail end of the business, clothing is broken into menswear and young men's wear. Young men's apparel is sized the same as men's apparel, but similar to women's and juniors, there are differences in the fit. The men's fit is fuller and has more ease built into the standard measurements established by a company. Young men's fit is closer to the body. Good examples of young men's merchandising and design are Abercrombie and Fitch and Aeropostale clothing lines. Young men's wear, intended for ages 16–25, is sized S, M, L, XL, and XXL.

Young men's apparel lines are more contemporary and trendy in design and merchandising than men's lines. The retail turn of merchandise is quicker. The young men's companies trend toward the distinctly more stylized, youthful customer. For example, the customer accepts and wears less traditional colors, printed patterns, tattooed or logoed garments, embellished garments, and newer or trendier garment washes. He is inclined to be style driven by:

+ Peer pressure
+ Music videos
+ Sports celebrities
+ Current movie influences
+ Video gaming images
+ Skateboarding, street basketball
+ Gang influences
+ Night club influences
+ Pop culture

The fit models and body forms used in colleges and in the industry are either a men's size medium or size small.

The young men's figure type is slightly smaller than the 9½- to 12-head figure for men's figure. Work with an approximate 8-head figure. Change the angular features of the fully developed male to be a bit softer or rounder, as in the figure shown at right.

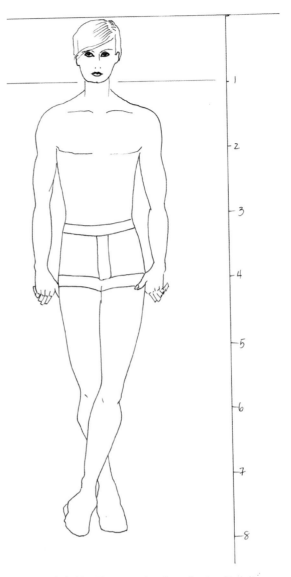

Young men's fashion figure template for stylization (*Author's collection*)

OBJECTIVE: To understand the sizing of design brands that you are interested in possibly working for and designing your portfolio for.

1. Choose one category for research: men's, young men's, or big and tall.

2. Follow instructions 2–8 from Exercise 4.1, substituting men's wear categories. Women will have to have a male friend try on the garments.

CHILDREN'S WEAR

Children's wear is grouped by age. Children's wear design portfolios focus on a specific age group by collection. If the designer shows all ages of children's wear, it is broken up into age groups. The ages can be combined with careful planning. Mostly, the following combinations are suitable on the portfolio page. In general terms:

+ Newborns: Mostly show as a separate category, not to be combined with any other size range. The clothing is specific to the needs of the child and the mother. Snap crotches on garments are a necessity while the child is still in diapers. Designers may show boys and girls as segregated categories, or they show them combined.
+ Toddlers, preschool, girls/boys, preteens and teens: The younger categories can be combined with the older categories of children's wear, but a clearer, more distinct statement is made by keeping this age group together. Many designers choose to show only boys or girls categories. The genders can be kept separate or combined.

Style and attitude for children's figures are mostly created by taking a playful edge and utilizing the particular stages of development, body gestures, and/or lifestyles of the age group. Because children grow quickly, remember to examine the age group you are designing for to show their gestural habits, facial expressions, and body stances by reading through catalogues, watching children's television shows, and observing children at play.

Generally speaking, younger children are drawn with rounder dimensions and a chubby appearance and without the angles or sharpness of the adult fashion figure. The figures are not elongated and follow the guideline head sizes listed below. Their head sizes are larger proportionately to the body sizes.

+ Newborns through 24 months: Draw as a four-head figure. Depending on the age, the newborns through 1 year are shown lying down, sitting up, or crawling. Toddling poses of the child who is just beginning to walk with an unsteadiness are fine for the 12–24 month old.
+ Toddlers: Draw as a four-head figure. Show in moving poses, standing with abdomens sticking out, barely established balance to their stance, awkward walking or movements.
+ Girls and Boys: Draw a five-to-six-head figure. Show with a thinner torso and limbs, in walking or sporty movements and casual stances.
+ Preteens, Tweens: Use a seven-to-eight-head figure. Show with more angular features, and as extremely influenced by media and current trends.
+ Teens: nine-head figure. Show more elongated in proportions, and as extremely influenced by media and current trends.

Following are some stylized suggestions for children's fashion figures. See the figures at right for reference:

+ Sweet child
+ Demure child
+ Bespoke child
+ Retro-influenced child
+ Turn-of-the century (1900s) child
+ Silly child
+ Mischievous child
+ Devious child
+ Sporty child
+ Athletic child
+ Rapper-influenced child
+ Urban street child
+ School-days child
+ Beach child
+ Cartoon character-wearing child
+ Animated child
+ Dancer child
+ Fashion-forward child
+ Manga child (See Appendix I for a list of reference sources)
+ Harajuku child

Children's wear portfolio page layout. This can be described as a "school days" children's fashion figure. Marker and pencil. *(Courtesy of Ithwa Huq-Jones)*

Children's "sweet child" pose. *(Courtesy of Miri Rooney)*

OBJECTIVE: To understand the sizing of design brands of children's wear that you are interested in possibly working for and designing your portfolio for.

1. Choose one category for research from the categories of children's wear

2. Follow instructions 2 to 8 from Exercise 4.1, substituting your children's wear category. Have a child of the appropriate age and gender model the clothes for you.

Children's wear portfolio page layout, "animated child figure." *(Courtesy of Lindsey Russell)*

MIXED-GENDER PORTFOLIOS: MEN'S AND WOMEN'S

Starting out in the fashion industry can be daunting for the about-to-be graduate. Many student designers like to design both men's and women's fashion. This works especially well in a portfolio aimed at a specific brand, label, or design house that has this breadth of merchandise.

Many designers aren't sure how to show the groups within a portfolio. The portfolio can be separated, showing either gender first. The men's and women's collections can be directly related, using the exact same fabrics and/or colors and silhouette influences, or as completely separate entities.

The collection can be combined into one presentation wherein the men and women are shown together in the fashion plates.

Portfolio page of separate men's collection. The designer's focus is on the bridge/better men's suits and coats market. She shows an interesting layout with one cropped figure, combined with two figures in the background on one page, and segues into the next page with two fashion figures. The segue figure is in an argyle sweater, which adds a visual change to the "read" of the two pages. The figures and layout make it easy for the viewer to understand exactly *where* these garments would be sold within a retail venue, and exactly *who* would wear them. It is easy to visualize this end consumer. Marker rendering. *(Courtesy of Ithwa Huq-Jones)*

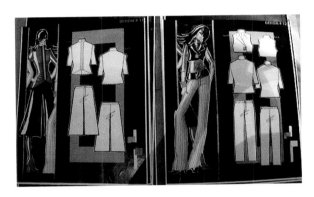

Portfolio page of separate women's collection that is shown in the same portfolio with a men's collection. A two-page spread from a special portfolio collection designed for the CFDA's Educational Initiatives Competition, for which the designer won an internship with Target Stores. The women's presentation became part of her portfolio as a women's segment, and she followed it with the men's collection in the menswear pages shown above to show her diversity in gender styling. Each collection stood separately on its own, and the transition within the same portfolio from women's to men's statements was made easily. Marker rendering. *(Courtesy of Ithwa Huq-Jones)*

KEY CATEGORY PORTFOLIOS

Key category portfolios are specialized and focus on one group of merchandise. Designers working within a key category typically know that they want to work in a specific area of design.

A key category portfolio can be shown on an interview for a different category, but if you want to design for a specific to the company that is not represented in any way in your book, you should create a collection that is geared to the category produced by that company.

View the designer portfolio pages of the key category portfolio. Create your portfolio pages within your chosen category to be as focused as this portfolio if this is your career direction.

Men's and women's combined collection portfolio page. The designer's avant-garde designer style is presented logically and one can easily view the retailer and customer. An easy retail venue for David's collection would be Patricia Field's House of Field boutique in lower Manhattan. Go to http://www.patriciafield.com/house-of-field-collection.aspx familiarize yourself with The House of Field Collection. To read about Patricia Field's start in the industry to her rise as the designer/stylist for *Sex in the City*, go to http://en.wikipedia.org/wiki/Patricia_Field. Marker and pencil. *(Courtesy of David Bermingham)*

COMBINING KEY CATEGORIES WITH SPORTSWEAR AND SPECIALIZED FASHION CATEGORIES

A designer can combine different key categories with one another, as well as with sportswear and specialized categories. This combination portfolio needs to be focused toward a design house that manufactures these multiple categories or one that might have possibility of understanding such breadth of merchandise. The design elements need to be interrelated, utilizing mood, color, textures, and silhouettes as one story.

For instance, a designer can show jeans with knitwear and sweaters, outerwear and coats, as the customer will be combining these items together, either from one company or from multiple companies. The interviewer can cull the items from the portfolio that will be best suited to the employer's merchandise mix. This could also be loosely considered a sportswear portfolio of mix-and-match separates. See the portfolio image at right.

Denim collection key category portfolio page. *(Courtesy of WWD/ George Chinsee)*

THE SEASONED DESIGNER'S LOOK BOOK

Designer's working for many years in the industry slowly begin to develop more of a "look book" than an illustrated story portfolio.

Some designers combine the illustrated portfolio with press release and press coverage printouts. As the press portion of their career blossoms, and they attain greater visibility with their accomplishments, they create a separate look book of their designs that becomes their portfolio.

The look book can contain the following:

+ Press releases
+ Press coverage (ads, quotes, statistical printed success stories)
+ Fashion photographs
+ Runway photographs
+ Celebrity endorsements with or without the designer
+ Magazine and periodicals featuring their styles in photo shoots

THE LEAVE-BEHIND PIECE

The leave-behind piece is optional. Some designers like to assemble a composite visual example of their designs in the form of a leave-behind piece for the end of an interview. The purpose of this is to leave the interviewer an impression or reminder of their design talents. It is a general overview of all of their collections and/or press release information. The leave-behind piece can be the following:

+ An 8½" x 11" computer printout or color copy montage of the designer's work. Included on the page is the designer's name and contact information.
+ A CD or DVD of JPEG files that showcase the designer's designs. The outside of the CD/DVD and the case or envelope in which the CD/DVD is encased are clearly labeled with the designer's name and contact information. One of the visual portions of the CD or DVD also has the designer's name and contact information included in it.
+ A memory stick of JPEG files of the same material as outlined for a CD or DVD, in a case that is clearly marked with the designer's name and contact information. The visual files also have the contact information included inside.

REVIEW OF DESIGNER PORTFOLIOS

Review the following figures of portfolio collection stories. Reference these photographs throughout your career.

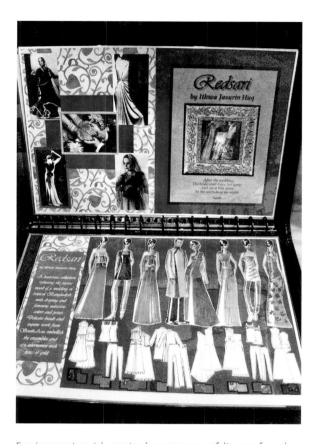

Evening wear/special occasion key category portfolio page from the designer's runway collection, which she designed and produced for Massachusetts College of Art's Senior Thesis Collection. The collection portfolio pages were her first pages in her exit portfolio. She skillfully showed additional pages of the fabrics and fashion plates of each ensemble (not shown here). She combined a title page with an inspiration/mood page and used Photoshop/Illustrator CAD programs to present her figures in a group page layout with a story about the inspiration. Her flats were hand-drawn and she included fabric swatches. *(Courtesy of Ithwa Huq-Jones)*

Importance of BASE LAYERS

asymmetric strapping

File Under: SPORT FUSION

x-static placed in key areas of interior lining, from neckline to waistline

X-static, a fiber created from 99.9% pure silver yarns, is antimicrobial, anti-odor, all-natural, thermodynamic, anti-static and therapeutic.

Silk and chiffon pieced, draped overlapped; fullness released at waist to fall into very wide sweep of hem

The ULTIMATE fusion of sport and fashion

Off the shoulder straps tucked beneath straps for halter neckline

sew-free seams- all seams tape bonded

body fabrication bonded to power- mesh backing

laser cut graphic elements

LASER CUT DETAIL

Importance of BASE LAYERS:

Laser cut detail

Interior compression corset with wicking (moisture management) properties, nylon spandex

Gruau's design for Miss Dior 1949

Dresses key category portfolio page. Jane's designer dresses are engineer-influenced. The fashion plate pages explain her process details, which she combines on the page with better-designer posed figures. She illustrates the fashion figure more like a retail store mannequin to add further focus to the "science" of her design process. Marker rendering. *(Courtesy of Jane Henry)*

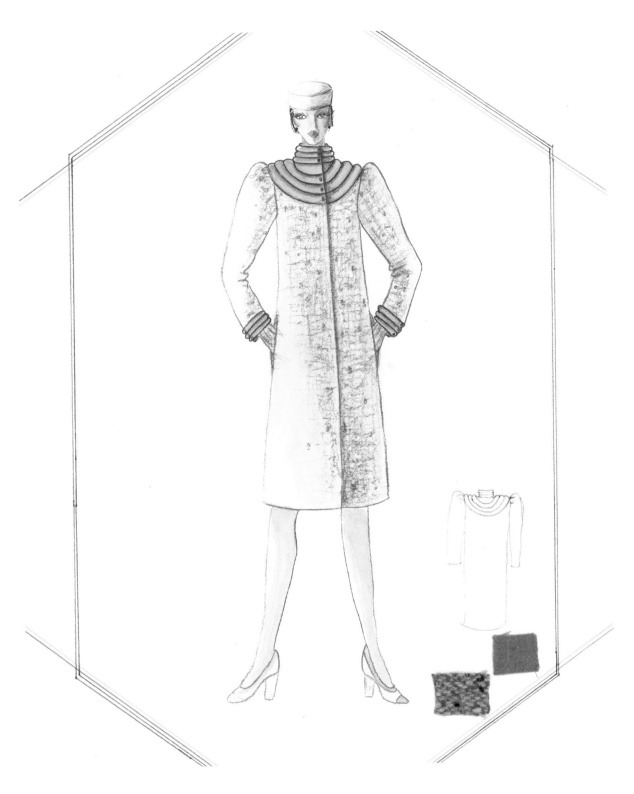

Coats key category portfolio page. In this fashion layout, it is all about one thing: the coat. This is a one approach to presenting coat designs for a highly focused market. *(Author's collection)*

Combination portfolio of Jeans, outerwear, sweaters, and coats. This collection is aimed at a moderate-to-better contemporary market. It could easily be shown on an interview for lines such as XOXO, Macy's private label design, JCPenney, or Target. Depending upon the interview, the designer could present different qualities of fabrics to suit the client's price points. During an interview, if the garments on the page appear to be over-designed or complicated in comparison to the garments of the interviewer's design studio, the designer can tell the interviewer that some of the details can be taken off the garments to lower the manufacturing costs and fit more into the firm's current design aesthetics. The designer could also customize a collection prior to the interview to complement this portfolio page with supplemental separates. Watercolor, acrylic, and pencil. *(Author's collection)*

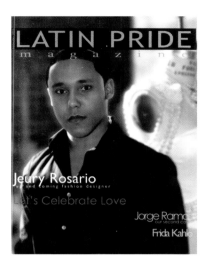

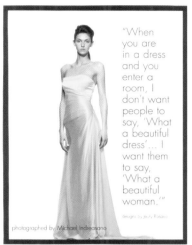

"When you are in a dress and you enter a room, I don't want people to say, 'What a beautiful dress'... I want them to say, 'What a beautiful woman.'"

photographed by Michael Indreasano

Layout of six pages from a designer's look book. Jeury designs exclusively made-to-order garments for select clients. He is a graduate of the Fashion Design program at Massachusetts College of Art and Design in Boston. He has a traditional illustrated fashion design portfolio as well as a look book of his press releases and public relations photography. You can visit his website for further inspiration at http://www.jeuryrosario.com. *(Courtesy of Jeury Rosario)*

Women's Sportswear Portfolio, Student CFDA Design Initiative Competition, Winner, 2010. Shawn designed this collection specifically for a student portfolio competition. He presents a relaxed yet fashion-conscious muse layout with figures standing, sitting and in a reclined position. The collection shown in the figure above and to the right helps to support his cohesive statement of color, line, and fabric quality. This is a young, better designer collection with a strong eye for the end-consumer. *(Courtesy of Shawn Reddy)*

Women's Sportswear Portfolio. A young designer collection, which can be used in a range of first exit interviews for the designer, young designer, bridge/better, contemporary, moderate, or budget market. The designer could present color and fabric schemes that could suit a specific interview. This is a multi-figure layout with supporting fashion plates; flats; and mood, color, and textile pages in the portfolio. *(Courtesy of Miri Rooney)*

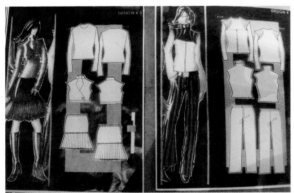

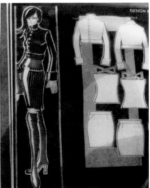

Women's Sportswear Portfolio, Student CFDA winner, 2006, Ithwa's collection for the CFDA Educational Initiative's student portfolio competition for a Target internship. The designer presents a multi-figure layout supported by individual fashion plates of each ensemble. She chose background colors and layout to complement the detailed flats drawings, which work well with the fashion figure illustrations. *(Courtesy of Ithwa Huq-Jones)*

Comparison of portfolio presentation styles. The figure at top left is a page from Pavlina's portfolio where she chose to put inspirational elements onto the same page that included a multi-figure layout. Her illustrations are hand-rendered, and the portfolio page is cut-and-paste; yet it has the "clean" look of a CAD-constructed page. The figure at top right is a very traditional format of presenting two fashion figures on a page. The figure at the bottom left is a seasoned designer's presentation board for a merchandising meeting, which could easily be part of his portfolio presentation. He used garment hangers instead of figures to show how classically ready-to-wear his collection is. *([Top left] Courtesy of Pavlina Gilson [Bottom left] Author's collection [Right] Courtesy of Jerry Dellova)*

Men's and women's combined portfolio. Although this presentation may seem outdated, the pages are part of a student exit portfolio for the bridge/better market. They clearly show garment detail and fabric-driven thoughts. The garments can be merchandised together or stand on their own as a gender-specific collection. There is an androgynous look to both the male and female figures, which is an approach to consider for forward-thinking designer layouts. *(Author's collection)*

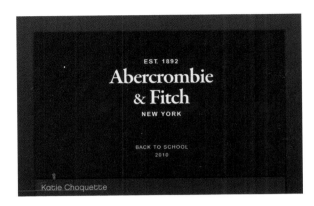

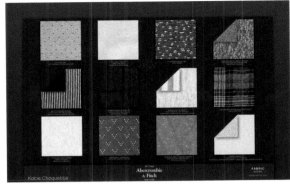

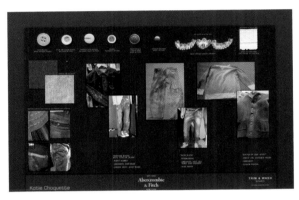

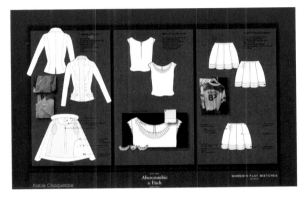

Men's and women's combined portfolio. The designer had a specific interview with Abercrombie & Fitch with this portfolio presentation. She presents a title/intro page, a fabrics page (note the neatness and uniformity of the fabric swatches—some corners of the swatches are turned over to show the double-side of the goods), a details page, figures page, and many pages of detailed flats showing construction information for the garments. *(Courtesy of Katie Choquette)*

Men's and women's combined portfolio. An exit portfolio page showing a men's and women's collection. The flats are colored for effect, and the figures are shrunk down to fit six poses on the page in a catalogue-inspired layout. These pages are shown in the designer's portfolio with the other student work featured on these pages, with the thought to flow and page-turning sequence. *(Courtesy of Ithwa Huq-Jones)*

Children's wear portfolio. The designer composed a fantasy background to create interest in the first two figures. For the next two figures, the designer was awarded honorable mention by the CFDA Educational Initiatives Portfolio competition for a Target internship. She used her book-binding skills to create a book with peep-hole cellophane covers, where she displayed tiny doll-sized garments that she had made. She surrounded the little garments with flats drawings. In the last figure in this group, Miri photographed her tiny garments on a clothing line for whimsy. *(Courtesy of Miri Rooney)*

Chapter 5

SPECIALIZED PORTFOLIOS: DIVERSE MARKET SEGMENTS

OBJECTIVES

+ Define specialized portfolio collections and explain the options.

+ Study examples of specialized portfolios for inspiration and guidance.

+ Combine generalized sportswear, key categories, and specialized fashion categories.

+ Review designer portfolios.

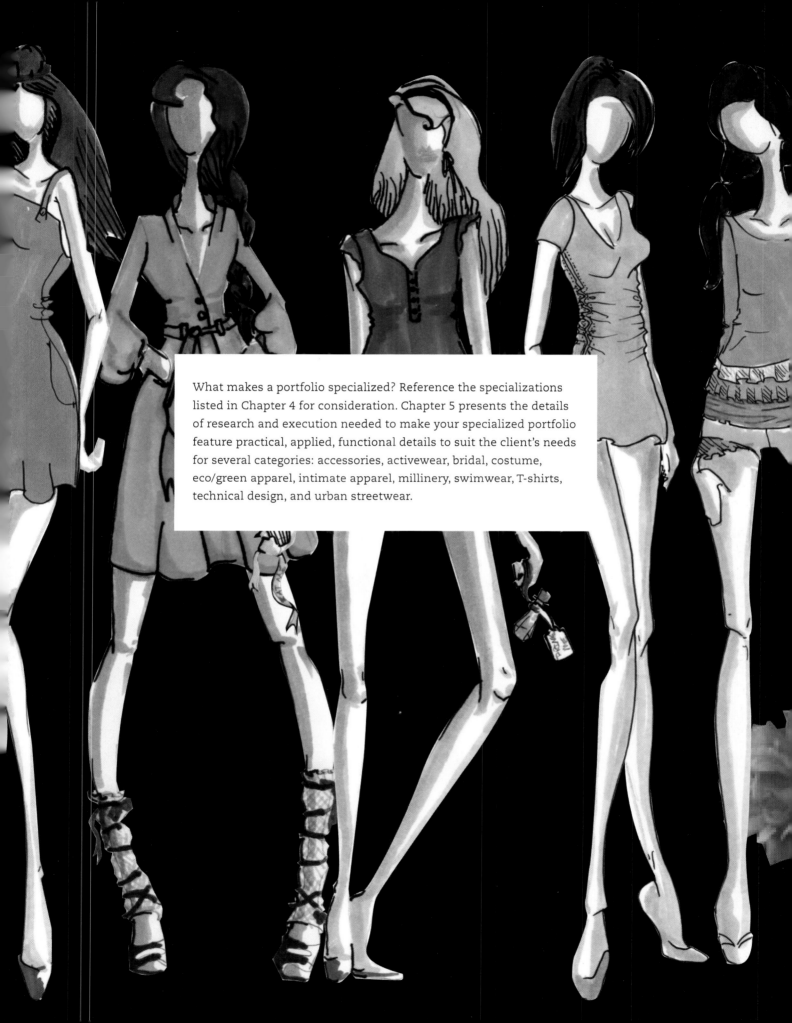

What makes a portfolio specialized? Reference the specializations listed in Chapter 4 for consideration. Chapter 5 presents the details of research and execution needed to make your specialized portfolio feature practical, applied, functional details to suit the client's needs for several categories: accessories, activewear, bridal, costume, eco/green apparel, intimate apparel, millinery, swimwear, T-shirts, technical design, and urban streetwear.

SPECIALIZED PORTFOLIOS DEFINED

As with all portfolio planning, the end consumer, competitive retail market, and trend research completed in Chapters 3 and 4 are the foundation of a specialized portfolio. The lifestyle and age group help define the functional demands of the specialization.

This description of a market-specialized portfolio can initially seem as if it would limit employment possibilities for a designer. The idea of specializing can scare many student designers from completing a tightly designed portfolio for a specific market. It may seem to keep them from being qualified for any number of jobs upon graduating from college.

As described in earlier chapters, if a designer *feels* a calling through design experience (in school or after graduation) to design for a certain niche market, that is an appropriate market for which to design a portfolio.

Many designers naturally develop styles during their school years in a broad range of categories with a resounding theme of a niche category. For example, a designer will create a denim collection and a sportswear collection for a student or professional portfolio with a clear message of urban apparel in every detail of the work. This designer could consider designing a portfolio exclusively for the urban streetwear market, featuring a complete package of competitive urban streetwear collections. Finely tuned garments designed exclusively for the urban market would need to stand head-to-head with established brands within the industry in order to be competitive.

Another example is a designer who features clearly defined millinery pieces in every collection of his or her student and professional work. This designer could consider pursuing an education and career in millinery arts. A millinery portfolio helps market the designer for the proper retail distribution channels or education program. The focus of the portfolio demonstrates a singular passion for hats and the people who wear them.

Your college may offer senior-level portfolio or design classes with options to explore a specialized fashion category. You can work within the structure of one of these classes to create a portfolio collection either featuring specialized categories or subcategories combined with a more generalized portfolio or complete a portfolio based solely upon a specialized category. In addition, you may choose to create these collections on your own by following the textbook as an outside-of-the-classroom project.

If you pick a specialization at a college such as knitwear, for example, and later decide not to pursue this category, the education or work completed for this niche market can help lead you to another specialization. This design route could also lead you to be a better generalist, with focused capabilities to design for many different markets.

Specializing tends to tighten a designer's talent base. This can be a launch pad for developing methods and skills that make designing other categories seem simpler or easier to tackle. By specializing a portfolio or studies during college or taking advantage of mentoring within the industry, you can become better able to zero in on the client's needs. Adopting this strategy helps you to work better in any general market, key category, or specialization.

Specialized education programs teach designers how to fine-tune their specific craft and focus on a specific category, which can lead into any facet of design. For example, you could use a specialized portfolio for a generalized sportswear position, with an added sportswear collection designed for the interview.

Focused specialized portfolios consider the function of the garment for a specific environment, task, duty, or activity to be performed. Therefore, you need to pay careful attention to the *functional* criteria of the specific client. Details from concept through completion need to be spelled out in the portfolio images. The function needs to be examined, researched, and problem-solved for practical use of:

+ The garment or accessory on the body
+ The color palette for a specific task
+ The durability and wearability of the fabrics for the task at hand
+ Hardware that enhances the garment's or accessory's use

During interviews or discussions with potential or established *informed* clients about what functional qualities they are looking for in your designs, it can seem that they are overwhelming you with unnecessary minutiae, but in fact, these performance details make or break the sale of the products and the immediate appeal to the consumer. Specialized portfolios need to have a single-minded vision, devotion, and "blinders-on" passion for the minutiae of the clients' needs and lifestyle. See the box, "Informed Needs of the Client." The graphic presentation in the portfolio must be compatible with the specialized content.

The Fashion Design Portfolio method suggests you design the specialized portfolio images to compete with the established brand for which you want to design. An interviewer may be reviewing the designs in your portfolio to see whether they would function better for the consumer than the company's current designs do. The designs should suggest change and an evolution of product.

The generalized fashion designer assembles a collection with fashion trends in mind that the target consumer "just has to have" and with a consideration of how the garments function on the body. The specialized designer designs first and foremost with critical objectivity for "what works for the client." This approach is successful at retail when a client touches the garment or views it on a screen and knows that it will deliver the desired performance features. The trends of color, textiles, brand image, and silhouette are integrated into the function of the garment to have an almost instant appeal to this informed buyer.

In the job application process, an interviewer knows how to spot this keen objectivity in the designer's portfolio images. The knowledge is built into the illustrations, which graphically depict the lifestyle of the client (for example, a swimwear collection shown in a beach scene, or a bride walking down an aisle), and in all the mood, textile, color, and flats presentations. Whether the applicant communicates this knowledge with effective interpretations of the target consumer's needs and demonstrates sharp follow-through skills on every portfolio page can make or break the interview.

INFORMED NEEDS OF THE CLIENT

When working in a specific category of fashion, you must get to know the client almost intimately. Here are some questions to ask your clients. Stay on top of your clients' needs by interviewing them with interest and taking notes.

▶ Where do you wear these garments?

▶ How often to do you wear these garments?

▶ What is your expected life span of the garments?

▶ What temperatures and environments do these garments have to function in?

▶ Do these garments perform one function, or do you demand multiple functions of them?

▶ What garments or designer apparel do you currently wear to perform these functions, and why do they work?

▶ What new features or changes would you like to see in these garments to suit your lifestyle?

▶ What is your favorite line of apparel in this category? Your least favorite apparel? Why?

▶ Where do you shop for these garments?

▶ How do you move your body when you are in these garments? How does the garment need to work with you when you perform in them?

▶ What restrictions on the body can you absolutely not have on these garments?

▶ Are there restrictions about color types and dye stuffs for your garment to function properly?

▶ Are there restrictions about fabrics or fibers for your garment to function properly?

▶ How durable do your fabrics need to be for the functions of your category?

▶ What performance properties of the fibers, if any, do you need to have built into your garment?

▶ What performance properties of the fit or construction, if any, need to be built into your garment?

▶ What type of hardware and closures work for the function of the garment? What type of hardware and closures don't work for the function of the garment?

▶ What is your basic day like when you wear these garments?

▶ How do you describe your lifestyle?

▶ What are your favorite things to do outside of this specialized category?

REVIEW OF SPECIALIZED PORTFOLIOS

A review of the specialized portfolios follows. This review will help you examine these choices for your current portfolio or for future portfolio presentations.

ACCESSORY DESIGN PORTFOLIOS

Your college's curriculum or degree program may offer courses in different segments of accessory design. Accessory design includes belts, gloves, millinery (see the section on millinery design later in the chapter), handbags, umbrellas, luggage, eyewear, legwear, and footwear. If designing for any of these markets appeals to you, you should target that product type in your portfolio.

Jewelry, as an accessory, can be explored for presentation in the portfolio. Jewelry design careers can be jump started in a fashion design program, but because the materials, construction, merchandising, and distribution are different from those aspects of fashion design, a fashion designer interested in pursuing a career in this field would have to focus on a jewelry design or merchandising program.

Four to eight illustration plates of jewelry as part of an accessory or generalized portfolio can show an example of your talent and passion for jewelry design and help in an interview. For example, an eveningwear portfolio presenting jewelry at the end of your book might spark the interest of the interviewer as a potential hire as an assistant to design evening bags with metalized closures to complement the design house's existing evening collections.

A student portfolio might represent different aspects of the design categories in which the student designer had as class instruction

An experienced designer might have a focused portfolio on the area of design he or she is specifically interested in working for or has had experience in, such as luxury handbags. A portfolio featuring luxury handbags might also include luxury wallets and luggage. Another designer may design sporting goods bags (duffels, backpacks, sport-specific tennis bags, etc.), and this portfolio could also show caps, headbands, wristbands, and socks. Within the accessory category, there are related items that work with the main product line.

Accessory designers have to consider first the category they are designing for. The focused research is carried out the same way as the line building process for apparel described in Chapters 1 to 3. The designer then needs to evaluate the category for how it functions for the consumer. Accessory designers also need to be aware of trends in apparel design because their accessories accessorize the apparel.

A designer's exit portfolio featuring a special collection designed for an in-class project, formulated in Photoshop and Illustrator. *(Courtesy of Alexandra Palmisano)*

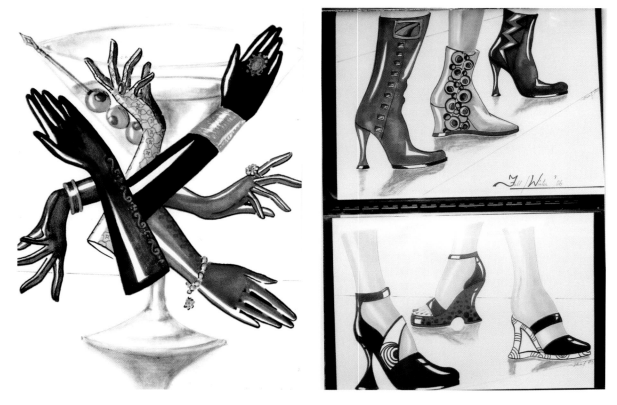

A designer's exit portfolio featuring marker rendering of gloves and dress shoes from in-class assignments for a specialized fashion class. *(Courtesy of Ithwa Huq-Jones)*

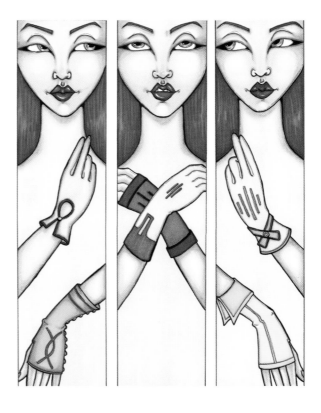

A designer's exit portfolio in which she designed dress shoes and gloves for an in-class project. On her own, outside of class, she added a combined junior sportswear collection in a lifestyle fashion plate showcasing headbands, a choker necklace, wristbands, cell phone bag, multiple handbags, hosiery, and luggage. Marker rendering. *(Courtesy of Cat Craig)*

Within each category of accessory design, there are three different aspects of design: 1) dressy, special occasion accessories, 2) everyday, recreational accessories, and 3) athletic, sporty, or sport-specific accessories. For instance, shoe design would have an area of dressy shoes for evening wear or party attire, everyday shoes for work or pleasure with more relaxed silhouettes, and sporty sneakers or sport-specific shoes for such activities as jogging, tennis, or golf. The same is true for instance, for gloves. Gloves are designed for weddings or ball gowns, for everyday driving and warmth, and as sporting goods.

Portfolios in this category can be gender- and age-specific or mixed gender and age.

The designer's study of the functional needs of the consumer includes the following:

✦ A close examination of how the product is used by the target consumer. Each category is broken down into different end uses. The luxury and better-priced items demand high-quality workmanship in the construction and details. Mid-tier to moderate-priced goods require careful craftsmanship, but are manufactured with less strict standards and less expensive materials. Budget items are manufactured with still less expensive materials and a different standard of quality workmanship. It is the designer's task to design quality silhouettes for the price point of the intended market.

For example, a luxury design house such as Coach manufactures a handbag design following its standards of craftsmanship using materials, machinery, and worksites that have been part of a legacy for generations. The brand has an established elite status and commands a certain price point based upon these manufacturing criteria as well as design and marketing aesthetics. If Coach wanted to enter the mass-market of moderate or budget accessories, the current criteria for such a "take-down" line would need to match or exceed the design, materials, manufacturing, marketing, and retail distribution criteria established by competing brands in Coach's moderate to budget product placement strategy. The price points, however, could match or undercut the competition, again depending upon the strategy of Coach. If the product offered more to the consumer than the competition, the retail venue and Coach's management could decide that the product warranted a higher price point than the competition. The chosen materials, factories, worksites, machinery, and craftsmanship would be scrutinized by Coach to be sure to maintain its luxury image and symbol of quality, but the final product expectations would be different. Coach would not lower its standards for quality product; it would just be appropriately matching or exceeding the standards of the moderate and budget competing product lines.

✦ The color palette for the portfolio is driven by the same trends as the fashion market. The colors need to work with the given trends of apparel, so they can complement the outfits they will be worn with. Consumer may shop for their accessory items after they've purchased an outfit or a garment and want the belt or the shoes to work with the clothes. Some consumers purchase the accessory, and shop for the garments to work with their specialty product. This is a less common way for a consumer to shop, but it gains popularity in periods of economic downturns, when shoppers concentrate their spending on fashion items that may be less expensive than a new wardrobe, thus creating accessory-driven trends.

✦ The durability and quality of the materials as well as the hardware used is driven by the area of design the product is for. Luxury and better-designer goods can support higher-priced leathers, animal skins, fabrics, and metals. Mid-tier, moderate, and budget design houses use lower-priced pelts and fabrics, and lower-priced hardware.

- The graphic layout and the illustrations should show the accessories being used or worn in the lifestyle of the consumer. Close-cropped, detailed illustrations are the preferred method of showcasing the products, as opposed to a full-page fashion figure. There can be fashion figures on the pages with the cropped versions of the accessory. Each accessory also should be shown with detailed flats, either on the same page or on a separate page.

ACTIVEWEAR PORTFOLIOS

Activewear portfolios can be general across many categories, or the portfolio can concentrate on a specific area of design. See the box "Activities Serving as Markets for Activewear Specializations" for choices.

Portfolios in this category can be gender- and age-specific or mixed gender and age.

The designer must consider the following to meet the functional needs of the consumer:

- Sporting goods apparel needs to function for a specific sport. For each sport, the athlete performs specific full-range-of-motion movements. Incorrect fit or seaming details can abrade the body and can lead to potential injury. Sport-specific silhouettes cannot create drag or wind resistance, as this could slow down the athlete's performance time. Gussets, princess line seaming, hidden pockets, padding, and lines that accentuate the body's form are important for certain sports. Style lines that support muscles and oxygen intake are critical to the athlete's performance.
- Sports apparel has certain colors and color blocking formulas that work for a "head-to-toe" look. The color relationship of the cap, top, bottom, socks, and shoes is part of brand imaging and is a look that many athletes prefer to wear. Some sports customers believe that the look of the apparel they choose helps them perform better. Certain outdoor sports

need bright colors for visibility, and other outdoor sports require neutral or colors that act to camouflage the athlete in the chosen environment. Social and performance indoor sports vary by regions of the country. Color selection may be predicated upon the climate of the region, and the local popular major league sporting teams. Other athletes need to have high-visibility colored clothing with florescent or reflective qualities for transition into night-time sports.

- Fabrics are developed to have appropriate **tensile strength** (breaking strength) for the given sport. Fabrics with perspiration management properties, such as **wicking** ability (the fabric/fiber's ability to disperse moisture through its surface so that evaporation can take place) are considered essential to the athlete's performance. Thermal warming fabrics are necessary for key sports categories.
- Hardware cannot hinder the athlete's movement. Elastics and drawstrings can't get caught on sporting goods equipment, nor can they cut off blood circulation or oxygen intake. Zipper pulls and buttons can't flap in the breeze or slap against the body, which distract the athlete or limit the body's movements.
- The layout and illustrations usually show the lifestyle and/or sport of the consumer. The footwear, hats, socks, and accessories are accurate for the sport or for the image of the weekend or professional athlete.

Activewear portfolio page, combining swimwear, gym wear, and outdoor apparel. Marker rendering. *(Author's collection)*

Activewear portfolio page, snowboard apparel. Color Matters CAD program. *(Author's collection)*

ACTIVITIES SERVING AS MARKETS
FOR ACTIVEWEAR SPECIALIZATIONS

Dance   recreational and competitive dance

Licensed athletic apparel   for *team sports and branded licensed apparel for streetwear:* Major League Baseball, National Football League, National Hockey League, National and International Soccer Federations

Performance sports   camping, cycling, golf, gymnastics, hiking, ice skating, rock climbing, running, skiing and snowboarding, surfing, swimming, tennis, triathlon, and weight lifting

Recreational weekend wear   windsuits, jogging

Team sports   baseball, basketball, football, hockey, soccer, and softball

Workout activities   aerobics, Pilates, studio and exercise classes, and yoga

BRIDAL DESIGN

Bridal design portfolios can be exclusive to bridal gowns, or they can include mother-of-the-bride gowns and bridesmaids' gowns. The bridal designs are usually shown as gender-specific, and usually include bridal headpieces and bridal shoes shown on the illustrations. Attire for the groom and other male participants in a wedding would be shown in a portfolio dedicated to formal wear.

Growing in numbers are same-sex weddings, for which a designer may choose to create a collection. Since this area is currently evolving, there are no social norms for the attire of same sex couples. One or both may want to wear a traditional bridal gown or a tuxedo. As more same-sex weddings take place, there may be an outfit that is exclusive to a bride and groom of the same gender. If you are designing for this group, it would be a niche market to research fully by visiting bridal shops and interviewing sales and management staff as to what garments are being purchased. You can also search the Internet to view weddings for trends in same-sex wedding attire.

The functional needs of the traditional bride of any sexual orientation include the following:

+ Being able to walk and/or dance in the gown. If there is a train on the garment, it should transition to a to-the-floor length for after the ceremony with the proper buttons or hardware hidden within the back of the gown. The silhouettes are created for different body types and diverse religious/civil ceremonies. The silhouettes are planned to be voluminous or to fit the body tightly. See the box "Bridal Gown Silhouettes" for details.

+ The new trend, still for a very small minority of bridal customers but gaining popularity is for the bride to purchase two gowns. The first is the formal gown for the ceremony. The second gown is less elaborate and is worn for comfort and movement for the reception or after-party.

Bridal design portfolio page. Gouche and pencil on watercolor paper. *(Author's collection)*

BRIDAL GOWN SILHOUETTES

Bridal gown design details can be combined to create a distinctive silhouette.

Necklines

Asymmetric
Bateau
Halter
High neck
Illusion
Jewel
Scoop
Square
Strapless
Sweetheart
Tip of the shoulder
V-neck

Silhouettes

A-line
Cocktail length
Mermaid
Princess/ball gown
Sheath
Tea length

Straps and Sleeves

¾ length sleeves
Cap sleeves
Long sleeves
Spaghetti straps
Tank

Train

Cathedral
Chapel
No train
Sweep

Waistline

Asymmetric
Basque waist
Dropped waist
Empire waist
Natural waist
No waist/princess seam

Source: http://www.kleinfeldbridal.com/images/dresssearch (accessed July 14, 2010).

- Mother-of-the-bride gowns are created to flatter the body, and to complement the bride's and bridesmaids' gowns. The bridesmaids' gowns are created to work well with the bride's dream wedding plans.
- The colors of bridal gowns are usually ivory or white, but the range of these hues can be bright white, off-white, natural white, antique white, ecru, champagne, tea-stained, pink-white, or blue-white. The accessories all need to have the same tone of color as the dress, if the look is meant to have an exact match. Lace, stitching, fabric, or beading detail may be intentionally dyed to match the dress, or planned to be contrasting in color.
- The colors of the mother-of-the-bride and bridesmaid's gowns can be chosen by the bridal party as a group, but it is generally a choice of the bride. Colors of mother-of-the-bride dresses follow trends for what is in for the look of weddings of the particular period in time. The colors are planned to flatter the more mature figure and personality of the mom. Colors of bridesmaids' dresses also follow trends of social norms of the period but can be any color or group of colors that the bride chooses.
- Fibers for the bride and the bridal party fabrics include silk, polyester, nylon, rayon, cotton, and wool. Trimmings in tulle, lace, and beading are carefully researched and help set the wedding mood. Fabric constructions come in a broad range of goods, such as satin, brocade, pongee, double-faced fabrics, homespun, and voile.
- The garment details and hardware must function for the bride to be comfortable on her day. The train holdings must hold the fabric in place for the bride to leave the ceremony and enjoy the reception or after party. The boning and fabric stays must complement and hold the dress silhouette in proper shape throughout an approximate 8-to-10 hour period. The headpiece may transition from a long veil to a small headpiece.
- The layout style of bridal pages may take inspiration from formal or informal wedding settings. The layout can show an indoor or outdoor setting or can feature a runway bridal show. Another popular layout for illustrations can show the bride's dressing room, or the salon in which the bride purchases the dress. Romantic backdrops and garden settings are also choices for illustration backdrops. The focus of the illustrated page is primarily on the details and embellishments of the dress.

COSTUME/THEATRE/FILM DESIGN

Costume/theater/film design portfolios can be mixed gender and age. It's best to show two to three collections of different artistic productions, either real or imaginary stories.

Costume designers draw with a realistic hand. The figures are drawn with the realistic eight-heads proportions instead of the exaggerated nine-and-a-half-head fashion figure used in a traditional fashion portfolio. In a fashion portfolio, the apparel is the focus of attention. The figure or muse that wears the garments is an idealized mannequin on which to drape the garments. In costume portfolios, the character of the figure on the page is as important as the apparel. The figure is portraying a part in the play or production, and the clothing designed for the role is a part of the character. The costume designer brings the character to life with the clothes.

The costume designer's job is that of collaboration with the set and lighting designers, makeup and hair designers, producer, director, actors, and support staff. These collaborators depend on the costume designer to enable the play or film to be aired without interference by "wardrobe malfunctions."

Costume designers may be one of the main venues in which to bring a character to life in a dramatic form for the stage or film. This can make the costume/theatre designer's occupation very exciting and rewarding.

Considerations of the functional needs of the actors and production team include the following:

✚ How will the actor's body move in the production? How many costume changes are required? How much time does the actor have to get changed? Is this an action production involving extreme movements of dance, flight, water sports, winter mountain climbing, and so on? The costume you design will work with the body to make these actions happen and look seamless on the production set.

✚ The designer brings the silhouettes forward as an interpretation of the production's story-line. The effect may be highly stylized, hauntingly realistic, or any dramatic interpretation in between. Historic period productions depend on the designer to use the right silhouettes to make the viewer believe the character is in the correct time period.

In costumes for film, the color palette must work with the cinematography and the collaborative efforts of the entire team. The color of the clothing helps set a mood for a stage production and must complement the staging. Color is carefully selected to work cohesively with the production team's visions.

✚ The fabrics and hardware must be true to the character's spirit to make the actor believable to the audience. The fabrics may be true to a time period, and may have to endure different environments and costume changes without interfering with the acting.

✚ Graphic layout and illustrations depicting the lifestyle of the characters within the story line help market the designer's ability to work with a production team. The figures are drawn to reflect the proportions and body types of the actors, such as short or tall, or stocky, slightly overweight, or slender. Actors' features are drawn realistically in the illustrations.

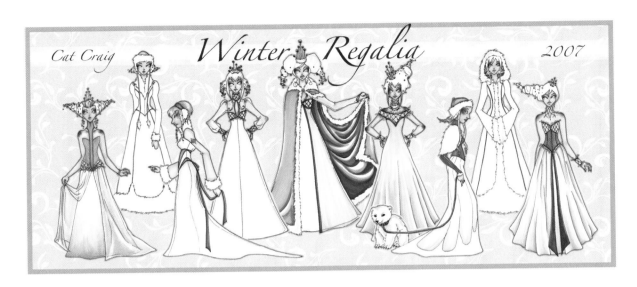

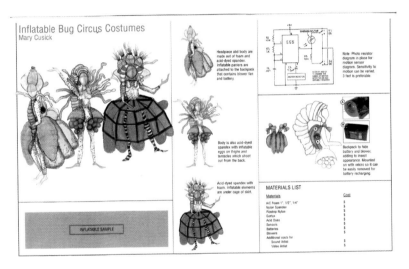

Theater design portfolio images from three different designers. In the first image, the designer presented this collection as her final thesis in portfolio form as well as creating the garments. Her technical details are added to the portfolio page in marker and Photoshop rendering. The second designer's fantasy is spelled out as a storyboard of collective designs in marker rendering. The last image is a more classic presentation of costume designs in a watercolor rendering for an in-class project. *(Courtesy of Cat Craig [top], Courtesy of Mary-Francis Cusick [left], Courtesy of Katherine Waddell)*

ECO/GREEN APPAREL

Eco apparel portfolios can depict garments that are planned to be manufactured only under green or eco guidelines. They can also show garments that feature fabrics made from sustainable resources, from organically grown fibers, or from organically raised animal fibers. The hangtags and packaging can be planned to be made from completely recycled or sustainable materials. The clothing can be made from recycled clothing or materials. The presentation in the portfolio should clearly explain these features in a stylized manner.

Meeting the functional needs of the consumer includes the following considerations:

+ The category of design for eco apparel will determine how the garments should work on the body. Eco apparel areas are growing for every category listed in this book. While eco merchandise is currently reaching a relatively small portion of the population, the anticipated growth of eco-minded products is substantial. The designer should plan to research this market to become versed in the inner workings of the manufacturers and retailers that support green merchandise.
+ The colors and dyestuffs used in eco or green apparel have varying degrees of tolerance, and the designer needs to research this information.
+ The fabrics and hardware are a specialized category, and the designer has to plan time to be educated as to their availability, cost structure, manufacturing, and consumer handling guidelines.
+ The graphic layout and illustrations can show earth-conscious fashionistas wearing the garments as the designer sees the consumer wearing them.

INTIMATE APPAREL, LINGERIE, AND INNERWEAR

Most portfolios in the category of intimate apparel, lingerie, and innerwear are gender- and age-specific. Although it is atypical, they can be shown as mixed-gender collections.

These categories are primarily segmented within large retail department stores to be worn specifically for innerwear and sleepwear. Consumers sometimes layer garments in the innerwear category rather than wearing them as undergarments. Current trends forecast this area of innerwear as outerwear to be growing in popularity. Therefore, if you design a collection for this category, take this trend into consideration in developing the designs for multiple use.

Some lingerie items are impulse sales and/ or gifts purchased by significant others for their mates. There is a strong level of hanger appeal to certain apparel lines in this category. In some lingerie specialty stores and department store venues, the garments are fully displayed on front-view racks, as opposed to crowded rounder racks. The hangers can be boudoir-esque, adding to the point-of-sale appeal. Visualize the display of the garments as part of the conceptual development of the product, as well as the portfolio presentation. There is a fine line within the industry between maintaining a level of allure and vulgarity, which is an always changing cultural norm, and it varies among distribution channels. It is also expressed differently in different regions of the United States and the world. The designer has to focus on the furthest point at which to use this appeal to sell adult garments, maintain a fashion edge, and keep in what is considered to be good taste.

Addressing the functional needs of the consumer includes the following considerations:

+ How do the garments work on the body as possible innerwear and layering pieces? The garments are designed for different end uses within the category: to flatter the body, to be comfortable for sleeping, to hide certain figure flaws, for support, for hygienic purposes, for a honeymoon penoir set, to be worn as a flattering top, for the waistband to show beneath a pair of pants, as a layering top, as flirtatious items, and so on. The garments can't restrict movement by being designed too tight, or conversely so loose that they hang on the body and create folds and bunches to the garments being worn over them. Foundation garment designers need to fully understand the needs of a range of body types and their specific fit requirements.

+ Color palettes are driven by the same fashion-forward trends as the industry. There are specific color groupings that are forecast for the intimate apparel industry. Colors that can be layered under transparent clothing are considered, as well as colors that will peek out from layers of outergarments.

+ Fabrics and hardware need to be soft and comfortable as the under pieces. Stretch goods in different weights are produced specifically for this market. Hardware, elastics, and trims are finely tuned to be wearable close to the body.

+ Some choices for graphic layouts and illustrations in this category can be playful, serious, alluring, or mainstream wholesome. Understanding your consumer and distribution channels will be the key to your success in depicting your fashion muses in the right poses, gestures, and postures. Props are used more often in this category to fill up negative space on the page, and to add to the idea of sensual pleasure on all levels. Figures can be shown cropped, focusing only on the torso, which shows the intricate details up close.

Intimate apparel/better designer portfolio page. Watercolor, gouche, pencil, and marker on watercolor paper.

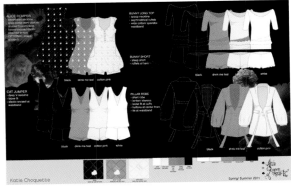

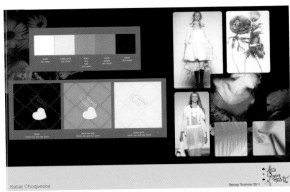

The designer assembled a lingerie collection for her portfolio. For the mood board, [Top left] she gathered images to support her theme and used Photoshop to create her final mood page. The garments are shown as flats [Top right] in the colors of the palette, are very easy to read, and include detailed information about color, findings, and construction. The next page in her portfolio collection [Bottom left] showcases her textiles and logo, supported by garment influences and mood images. A fourth page [Bottom right] shows the garments as a collection on fashion figures. *(Courtesy of Katie Choquette)*

MILLINERY

Millinery portfolios are for the very focused designer who is working toward fine-tuning his or her craft. Some colleges offer millinery classes and/or minor or specializations in this area. Some colleges have true millinery equipment for forming and shaping hats. This can be a very rewarding niche market for the talented designer who is passionate about hats.

The portfolio can be mixed gender and age.

The considerations for meeting the functional needs of the consumer include the following:

+ What is the hat being worn for: warmth, cooling, protection, sun blockage, fashion, special occasion, attitude, a head-to-toe look, athletic performance, health reasons, chemotherapy recovery, etc.?
+ What size is the head? How is the hat going to stay on the head? Does it need pins or a hair comb to stay on? Is it one-size-fits all?
+ Are you designing brimmed or unbrimmed hats?
+ Knowing your customer's head is the essential key to success of the millinery designer. Some designers have carved a niche for themselves in this industry for their stylized kitsch, drama, fashion runway, street appeal, and special events. talents. See the box "A Window into Millinery Design" for a short biography of milliner Philip Treacy, and a brief history of Kangol hats.

+ The colors for your target customer can range from radical show-stopping colors to subdued effects, depending on the end use of the hat. Dyed-to-match headpieces are carefully planned with their apparel and/or footwear counterparts.
+ Durability and wearability of the fabrics are driven by comfort or high style. Balance and weight of the hat follow a careful plan. Fabrics include beaver furs (for steamed and fitted hats), felted wool, buckram starched forms, polyester canvas, leather, suede, and other materials. The trims and hardware are sometimes exclusive to the millinery industry. Feathers, furs, ribbons, metal hardware, inside sweatbands, and millinery wire are all essential materials to consider.
+ The graphic layout of the illustrations supports the lifestyle of the consumer. The illustrations can be shown with matching outfits, or they can be drawn as cropped figures from the waist up, or the shoulders/neck up. The technical flats are details of how the hat is made from the inside out.

Two designers' portfolio pages in marker renderings created for a millinery design class. If the designers wanted to specialize in millinery, they would need to add renderings of flats to their portfolios. *(Courtesy of Ithwa Huq-Jones (top) and Cat Craig (bottom))*

A WINDOW INTO MILLINERY DESIGN
FOCUS ON PHILIP TREACY/MILLINERY DESIGNER
AND KANGOL HATS

Philip Treacy

Most recently gaining notoriety as the milliner for 36 guests of the 2011 royal wedding of Prince William to Kate Middleton, Philip Treacy first showed an interest in fashion design by sewing dresses for his sister's dolls at the age of five. He graduated with his degree in fashion design from the National College of Art and Design in Dublin, Ireland, in 1989. While studying there, he discovered he'd rather design hats than clothing. After doing his graduate work in millinery at the Royal College of Art in London, he took one of his hats to the fashion director of *Tatler* magazine and met very briefly with Isabella Blow, the style editor, while he was there. She recognized his talents and commissioned him to design her hat for her wedding, and he moved into her house, where he set up a millinery workshop. Isabella Blow was photographed many times in his hats, and many of her friends also wore them.

In 1991, Karl Lagerfeld invited him to design millinery for Chanel, which he did for 10 years. In addition to designing for Lagerfeld/Chanel, he has designed couture hats for Valentino, Versace, Alexander McQueen, Ralph Lauren, Donna Karan, and Rifat Ozbek.

In 1994 he opened his first store on Elizabeth Street in London, where his clients ranged from young girls ordering their first trilby to a 70-year-old man that came in every summer to order 20 haute couture hats for his travels on his yacht.

Treacy's name and millinery styles have become synonymous with one-of-a-kind showpieces for royalty and celebrities alike. He was appointed the honorary officer by The Most Excellent Order of the British Empire by HRH Prince Charles and HRH The Duchess of Cornwall in 2007.

Photo Princesses Eugenie and Beatrice in Philip Treacy fascinators (elaborate crosses between hats and headbands) at the wedding of Princes William to Kate Middleton, 2011, and the milliner with the model Iman wearing one of his creations. [top] *(Courtesy of WWD/John Calabrese)* [bottom] *(© IAN LANGSDON/epa/Corbis)*

Treacy is quoted at his website (http://www.philiptreacy.co.uk/bio.swf) as saying about hats:

"It's an enigmatic object that serves the human purpose only of beautification and embellishment and making one feel good whether you're the observer of the spectacle or the wearer".

"I started designing hats ... while a student at the Royal College of Art. It was a time when hats were perceived publicly as something worn by ladies of a certain age, and something from a bygone era. I thought this was totally ridiculous, and simply believed we all have a head, so everybody has the possibility to wear a hat."

Kangol

Kangol is a millinery company founded in 1918 in Cumbria, England, by Jacues Spreiregen, as an importer of Basque berets from France. This beret became a post war fashion item for 20 years. In 1938, Spreiregen decided the company needed a distinct name, so, according to the most believed theory, he created the name from *K* for knitting, *ang* for angora, and *ol* for wool.

The brand became a main supplier for the British Army in World War II, most notably for General Bernard Montgomery. In 1964, with the rise of the Beatles from the UK music scene, Kangol hired Eileen Greig to design a line of Beatle caps and berets and became the sole manufacturer world wide of headgear featuring the image, endorsement, or name of the Beatles.

In 1981, Graham Smith, milliner, teamed up with Kangol to design hats for British Airways. In 1983, Princess Diana wore one of Kangol's hats. In the same year, Americans became interested in the hats, and kept asking retailers for the "kangaroo hat" (mispronouncing *Kangol*) and Kangol officially added the kangaroo logo to

The artist LL Cool J wearing a Kangol hat. *(Janette Beckman/ Getty Images)*

its products. At that time, LL Cool J, a famous rapper, was always photographed in his videos and press appearances wearing his Kangol hat with the highly visible logo. Over the years, hip-hop artists such as Slick Rick, Erik B and Rakim, and Grand Master Flash wore their Kangol hats, making them popular with a generation of music-followers. The actor Samuel L. Jackson is regularly photographed in his Kangol hat. This has lead to a sub culture of non-designer hats that are in high demand.

In the past decade, Kangol has worked with Comme des Garçons, Katherine Hamnet, and Catherine Malandrino developing headwear for their collections.

Sources: http://www.philiptreacy.co.uk/bio.swf
http://www.kangol.com/html/retrospective.asp

SWIMWEAR AND BEACHWEAR

Swimwear and beachwear portfolios can be shown as gender-specific or mixed gender. It is best to focus on an age group within this category, as the fit, style, and distribution of the apparel has established itself as a highly specialized, segmented group of industry professionals.

There are designer or brand collections that feature an entire lifestyle collection that includes swimwear and beachwear. If you are pursuing a career in this area, create a portfolio collection showing the full range of merchandise that the brand or designer carries in the stores.

The functional needs of the consumer that the designer must consider include the following:

+ Swimwear is designed for fit, comfort, and style. The shape and age of the body is the basis of the silhouette development. Consumers have certain ideas of what they can or cannot wear predicated on their body type, body image, modesty factors, and social norms; these considerations are especially of concern to the female consumer. Regions of the world have different criteria as to what the same consumer might wear. For example, in certain European cultures, women's swimsuits can be topless, and men's suits are sized smaller and are tight fitting, like competitive swimsuits sold in the United States. In Latin America, thong bathing suit silhouettes are a dominant fashion garment for women. The selling season of Holiday/Cruise in November through January is an important time to sell the garments, as well as the spring/summer months. In some climates, the swimsuit season is year-round.

+ Color palettes follow trends specific to the swimwear industry as well as the general fashion trends. Many styles are color- and pattern-driven. The colors can be in various ranges from sophisticated to seductive, youthful, playful, nautical, trendy, fashion-forward, eclectic, or athletic/performance-related. The color direction can depend on the brand's history, the particular market niche of the designer's label, and fashion and buying trends. Men's colors may tend to be more traditional, depending upon the consumer. Many young men's swimwear colors can be radically off-the-charts bright and powerful.

+ Woven fabrics, stretch fabrics, and stretch linings for women's and men's swimwear must meet guidelines for chlorine and salt resistance for the swimwear industry. The cotton/Lycra and nylon/Lycra blends used for swimsuits have different properties from these same blends used for streetwear. The designer considers one-way or two-way stretch fabric for the swimsuit's silhouette on the body. Woven fabrics are used for men's and women's suits and cover-ups. Women's cover-ups can include transparent voiles and homespun fabrics.

+ Graphic layout and illustrations can be cropped to show just the torso or full-length fashion figures. Beach or pool scenes can be included in the backgrounds.

Swimwear portfolio page in pencil and marker showing misses better designs. *(Courtesy of Shanna Jones)*

Swimwear design portfolio pages in marker and pencil showing junior designs. *(Author's collection)*

Swimwear portfolio page in marker and pencil showing misses/better designs. *(Author's collection)*

T-SHIRTS

T-shirt portfolios can be gender- or age-specific, or they can be mixed gender and/or mixed age. Mixed-gender and -age portfolios should have technical flat drawings that clearly delineate the ages, genders, and size ranges. The fashion illustrations can show the different age groups together. Portfolio presentations generally keep the genders and ages separated by category in the portfolio, so that each gender and age takes on an identity and has more impact on the viewer.

T-shirts can be purchased in bulk amounts from T-shirt manufacturers without the artwork on them, and they are called **blanks**. Blanks come in a full range of sizes, colors, and tie-dye. T-shirts can have graphic prints silk screened, heat transferred, or felt flocked onto the front, back, and/or sleeves.

The T-shirts should be sized as a regular fit, a tight fit, or an oversized fit. Some designers use men's T-shirt blanks for women's T-shirt designs. The standard fit varies from company to company; designer to designer.

Designers may want to bring a sample of an actual T-shirt with them in their portfolios and ask whether the interviewer wants to see a sample of their work. Some T-shirt designers have their own silk-screen studios, and some designers are fully vertical, so they design and produce their own T-shirts. The vertical designer would bring a T-shirt on the interview to show the quality of the T-shirt blanks, as well as the quality and feel of the ink. It's also possible to send a design to a company that does silk-screening blanks. The design can be transmitted electronically as a JPEG or another file. Individuals and groups who are not professional designers often have T-shirts produced this way for conferences or organizational gatherings for advertising or group identity souvenirs.

The concerns for the functional needs of the consumer include the following:

+ How will the garment be worn on your consumers? Do they want a big, baggy fit or a close-to-the-body look?
+ The color palette for the T-shirts can coordinate in your portfolio with a denim collection, a sportswear collection, or any of the categories in the book that have a natural link to your T-shirt collection. T-shirt blanks can be dyed to meet your color palette to coordinate with a sportswear line. Each manufacturer of T-shirt "blanks" has a different set of pre-dyed, in-house colored blanks in stock or made to order. Customers can request colors dyed to match their palette by meeting the manufacturer's minimum quantities per color. T-shirts can be garment-dyed and then washed by some T-shirt suppliers. T-shirts can also be destroyed, distressed, or bleached, or have an added acid-washed finish, depending on the manufacturing source.

+ The T-shirt fabrics should be chosen for their end use. Cottons, poly-cotton blends, eco-fabrics, nylon, and perspiration-wicking fabrics are some considerations.

+ Hardware and trims can be added to T-shirts. The added cost to the garment at retail may hinder sales in certain markets. T-shirts can be ripped, torn, or slashed, and held together by safety pins for added effect.

The graphic layout and illustrations of the T-shirt portfolio should show the lifestyle of the clients and how they wear their T-shirts. Are the garments tucked into high-waisted jeans or worn untucked and baggy? How far away from the body does the T-shirt hang? The attitude and gestures of the illustrative figures is an important selling feature to the portfolio presentation. Many T-shirt designers work exclusively in CAD programs to design the T-shirt graphics. These designs are very easy for the reader to look at during an interview. T-shirt portfolios should include fashion figures wearing the T-shirts either in a cropped layout or in a full figure. The figures can include sportswear and accessories along with the graphic artwork.

T-Shirt portfolio page. *(Nicemonkey / Alamy)*

TECHNICAL DESIGN PORTFOLIOS

Technical design portfolios can be gender- or age-specific, or they can be mixed gender and/or mixed age.

Technical designers may have fashion illustrations in their portfolios. The primary focus of the portfolio is a clear message of the designer's technical skills. The portfolio showcases individual pages that are manufacturer's instructions for how to produce the garments, which include flat drawings, technical flat specification sheets, production and sewing details, and line sheets.

The flats are drawn in exact proportions to the way the garment would look on a flat surface. The proportion of the width to the length of each element exactly matches the specs of the sewn, finished garment.

Flats are developed with different methods of drawing by hand and by CAD programs. Many designers create their own flats from guidelines set forth in technical design textbooks. There are also flat template textbooks that the student designer can trace. Many companies have their own flat templates and want their designers to work with these templates upon being hired.

Some designer's use a slightly stylized flat sketch, which shows a little movement with the fabric. Most flats do not show fabric movement. Any extra lines or style curves added to the garment can be interpreted by the factory as a style detail, a dart, a seam, or an insert that was not intended to be there. Some designers use stylized, "moving" flats for presentation boards, and then develop technical flats for the factory sheets.

The portfolio can have a stylized edge, but the specification sheets need to be precise, accurate, and all-technical. One to two introduction pages of the collection can include stylized fashion illustrations, mood images, color references, and/or textile swatches. The stylized pages can be as follows:

+ A stylized cover/mood page including an overview of the collection's mood, color, textiles, and silhouettes.
+ A flat-sketch rendering of three to six styles drawn on a line sheet for the merchandising, sales, and product development teams. Each style is listed with the style number, style name, season, size range, and fabric content.

The technical pages are usually formatted in a word processing program on a company's flat specification sheet. If you don't have experience in the industry, you can create your own flat specification sheet. Each page has an area within the page that states the style number, style name, season, fabric content, size range, sample size, and date. The flat sketch of the front and back garment is also included on each page.

The details should be entered into the correct fields on the spec sheet by a computer program. If you are handwriting any of the specifications or descriptions, most designers use all capital letters (no lowercase), similar to an architect's blueprint design sheet.

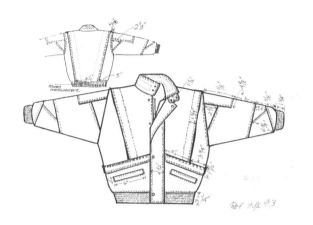

Product Information Sheet		Season:	Style:	Date:
Description:				

Front View		Womens	Mens	Sample Size **Medium**	Size Range: S, M, L, XL

Back View	Print or Color Designation

Materials Sheet	Collection:			Date:		
	Season:		Style:		Style Name:	
Fabric/Trim	Description/Location	Quantity	Color	Width/Size	Fabric content	wt/guage
Shell Fabric						
Lining						
Pkt Lining Insulation						
Findings						
CF Zip						
Pocket Zip						
Zip Pulls						
Pkt Zip Pulls						
Pant Legs						
Cuffs						
Collar						
Drawstring						
Others						

Spec Sheet/Tops	Collection:			Date:		
	Season: Fall 2000	Style:		Style Name:		
		S	**M**	**L**	**XL**	
Chest Width (1" Below Armhole)						
Body Length Front (Hi Shldr to Bttm)						
Body Length Back (Hi Shldr to Bttm)						
Armhole Straight						
Sleeve Length (From CB)						
Shoulder Width (Seam to Seam)						
Back Neck Opening (Shldr Seam to Shldr Seam)						
Back Neck Drop (from imag line)						
Front Neck Drop (from imag line)						
Bottom Opening Relaxed						
Placquet Length						
Placquet Width						
Collar Height at CB						
Collar Height at CF Point						
Cuff Opening						
Pocket Opening						
Front Zipper Length						
Hood Height						
Hood Width						

An example of a simple tech pack, which is the directions for each garment sent to the sample maker or factory by the designer to explain how the garment is to be manufactured. This acts as an agreement document between the factory and the company, specifying size measurements, materials, details, and trims the garment must meet in final production. The designer first sketches a rough flat drawing of the front and back view of the garment for her tech pack. She then finalizes the drawing using a French curve, a ruler, and a fine-nibbed black marker in a precise rendering (Top left). This garment is drawn by hand. Many designers draw their flats in CAD programs; some still draw the garment by hand, scan it into a CAD program, and finalize the sketch using the computer. This designer adds to this drawing the flats measurements of the pockets and seaming details (top right). A basic product information sheet is page 1 of a tech pack. The designer will fill out the information on this page with the season, style number, date, description, etc. and will cut and paste the flats drawing onto the page. Many designers work in a computer program that would electronically cut and paste the flats drawing to the production information sheet. On page 2 of the tech pack (Bottom left), the materials sheet, the designer fills in the information for the factory to make the garment. Next is an example of a spec measurement sheet for a garment (Bottom right). The designer gives the flats measurement of each detail listed, first in size medium for a prototype. Once the sample prototype comes back from the factory and the designer fits the garment on her fit model, she will make the necessary changes and/or comments back to the factory for the final production specs. At that point, the designer will grade the garment for small, large and extra-large sizes on the spec sheet. Most companies have electronic tech packs with sophisticated programs that link the designer's changes from her studio directly to the factory to expedite the production time. *(Author's collection)*

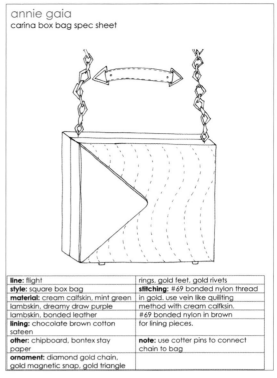

line:	flight	rings, gold feet, gold rivets
style:	square box bag	stitching: #69 bonded nylon thread
material:	cream calfskin, mint green	in gold. use vein like quilting
	lambskin, dreamy draw purple	method with cream calfksin.
	lambskin, bonded leather	#69 bonded nylon in brown
lining:	chocolate brown cotton	for lining pieces.
	sateen	
other:	chipboard, bontex stay	note: use cotter pins to connect
	paper	chain to bag
ornament:	diamond gold chain,	
	gold magnetic snap, gold triangle	

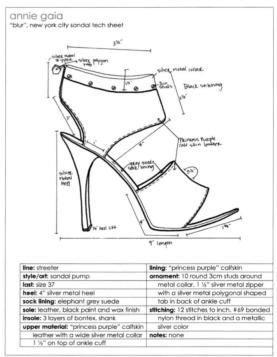

line:	streeter	lining: "princess purple" calfskin
style/art:	sandal pump	ornament: 10 round 3cm studs around
last:	size 37	metal collar. 1 ½" silver metal zipper
heel:	4" silver metal heel	with a silver metal polygonal shaped
sock lining:	elephant grey suede	tab in back of ankle cuff
sole:	leather, black paint and wax finish	stitching: 12 stitches to inch. #69 bonded
insole:	3 layers of bontex, shank	nylon thread in black and a metallic
upper material:	"princess purple" calfskin	silver color
	leather with a wide silver metal collar	notes: none
	1 ½" on top of ankle cuff	

This accessory designer's portfolio pages are stylized and detailed. She shows mood, materials, colors, silhouettes, and flats in her book for this collection. Note the pages that show the silhouettes in spec detail. *(Courtesy of Annie Kee Gaia)*

Description: Running Jacket	Gender: Women's

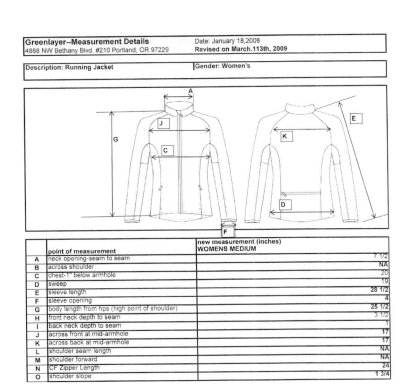

	point of measurement	new measurement (inches) WOMENS MEDIUM
A	neck opening-seam to seam	7 1/2
B	across shoulder	NA
C	chest-1" below armhole	20
D	sweep	19
E	sleeve length	28 1/2
F	sleeve opening	4
G	body length from hps (high point of shoulder)	25 1/2
H	front neck depth to seam	3 1/2
I	back neck depth to seam	1
J	across front at mid-armhole	17
K	across back at mid-armhole	17
L	shoulder seam length	NA
M	shoulder forward	NA
N	CF Zipper Length	24
O	shoulder slope	1 3/4

collar height is **2 1/4"**
length of pocket zippers: 6"
length of back zipper: 9"
length of mesh at lower sleeve panel = 5"

Greenlayer-Product Detail Info Sheet
4888 NW Bethany Blvd. #210 Portland, OR 97229
Date: Oct 28th, 2009

Style #: 120S8W	Gender: Women's	Event:
Description: Long Bra Top	Silhouette: Fitted Tank top	

	point of measurement	new measurement (inches) WOMENS MEDIUM	Requested Measurements 1st sample	Revised
A	neck opening-inside edge of binding to inside edge	7	X	
B	strap width(including binding)	1 1/4	X	
C	front armhole to imaginary SS	8	1/2	
D	back armhole to imaginary SS	14	- 1/2	
E	side seam	13	X	
F	front neck drop (HPS to bottom edge of binding)	5	X	
G	back neck drop (HPS to bottom edge of binding)	2 1/4	X	
H	waist	14 1/2	X	14
I	bottom opening	16	- 1/4	
J	width at widest part of racerback	2 1/2	X	
K	front chest width: 1" below armhole	15	X	
L	side seam on inside mesh shelf bra liner (including elastic)	4 1/2	X	
M	body length (HPS to bottom)	20 1/2	1/4	

Additional comments:

take in at waist- 1/2" total (1/4" tapered to nothing at both sides)

move back princess seams in toward CB at bottom hem by 2" (Center Back panel will measure 5 1/4" at hem)
change the angle of back pockets to be higher at back princess seam, lower at SS
**change top back pocket to be mesh, make top edge foldover with 2NDL and 1/4" elastic so that it draws in the back pocket

Technical design portfolio pages. *(Courtesy of Doranne Westerhouse Awad)*

The pages that show the garment details are one style to a page, so the designer will pick the top four to six styles per group to show the individual pages as follows:

+ One style per page, showing the front and back view of the garment. The back view can be 5 to 20 percent smaller than the front view.
+ Sewing instructions/production pattern page.
+ Production spec sheet with all flat measurements of the flat widths and lengths of the garments.
+ Enlarged detail page showing exact placement and technical layout of the specifications of garment details—snaps, top stitching, length and widths of pockets, yoke details, grommets, buckles, buttons, belt loops, tabs, darts, waistband, plackets, closure details, and so on.

As a student designer, you may or may not have courses offering degree programs available in technical design at your college. It would benefit any designer from the couture category through children's wear to take a class in technical design.

The graphic layout of the portfolio can depict the lifestyle of the client for the portfolio. The spec sheets may be placed on top of a graphic layout, so the interviewer can see the spec sheets as a manufacturer's instructions, without any style implications.

URBAN STREETWEAR

Urban apparel is a growing market. The urban apparel designer portfolio can be gender- or age-specific, or it can be a combination of both.

The appearance, attitude, and mind-set of the urban apparel designer can be of equal importance to the portfolio presentation during an interview.

The precursor to the surge of urban apparel's popularity was a line called Cross Colours, which was formed in 1989 but is no longer in business. Cross Colours was launched under the premise of "clothes without prejudice" and was based around African-American youth culture. The garments were themed around large blocks of color, namely black, red, yellow, and green, and the line became known for its message T-shirts—"Stop the Violence," "Educate 2 Elevate," and "Peace in the Hood" being just a few of the slogans. This paved a visual path for the insurgence of urban apparel.

One of the most insightful approaches that Cross Colour's founder Carl Jones took was to interview young people from within his company and outside on the streets. He had them critique his work so he could make it better for them. He is quoted as saying "it's amazing how young kids can talk about color and fabric. After all, they set the trends."

One of the most influential designers to come out of the Cross Colours design team was Karl Kani, who created his own label. He is known as the originator of urban apparel and had no formal training in design. He paved the way for urban apparel designers to take the same type of business chances he did, and many new designers and companies were formed modeled upon his success.

Another seminal influence on urban apparel is the early 1990s rap/hip-hop music and African-American music moguls' designer labels. As rap music popularity grows, so does the music audience and the apparel's customer base. Today rap music and the desire to dress like the stars reach urbanites and suburbanites of many cultures across the globe, including Caucasian, Hispanic, and Asian cultures.

Visionary rap artists Russell Simmons's Phat Farm and Sean Combs's Sean John are designer brands of apparel and accessories based on their music labels' popularity and successes. Sean Combs (known as "Diddy" as a performer) had set out to "bring entertainment to fashion" in creating his fashion house. Simultaneously, as these artists created higher-priced lines, entrepreneurs joined the market with clothing priced for the mass markets, such as FUBU (For Us by Us), Mecca, Roccawear, and Ecko/Marc Ecko. During the surge of popularity of these lines in the 1990s, streetwear, music, and club wear began to powerfully influence designer labels and mass market designers. The grunge look popularized by Marc Jacobs was taken from the trendy Seattle garage and indie music bands that urged many designers to explore alternative areas of influences and to interpret them in a literal sense for the audience that wanted to "be" the music.

As the urban apparel consumer base grew, so did its influence on streetwear, surf wear, and designer apparel. Now urban design and rap music influences many categories and has spawned many cross breeds of streetwear. Ralph Lauren, Calvin Klein, Tommy Hilfiger, and the Gap are just some of the labels that have interpreted these trends for their jeanswear business.

The fusion of entertainment and music with fashion can give a line some staying power (perhaps over 10 years), but because of a fickle fan base, apparel lines come and go with the popularity of the given entertainer or "hipness" of the brand's image. The consumer in this category is always looking for the next new thing.

The functional needs of the consumer include the following:

+ How the garment should work on the body for rappers and wannabes. These consumers want to walk and talk like their idols, so the garments have to work for dance moves and lifestyle demands. The look of the head-to-toe apparel and accessories is very important to this consumer. The attitude of the clothing should match the mind-set of the trends in entertainment and have street-credibility.
+ The color palette can range from subdued to very loud colors, depending on the niche the urban or street line has carved out.
+ The fabrics' durability and wearability are often highly functional, and often work-wear related.
+ Hardware is an important brand message in this category and is often ostentatious.
+ Graphic layouts and illustrations follow the entertainment trends. The designer has to follow through with the right themes to compete in this arena. The fashion figures and added graphic treatments to the page should follow the way the "real world" of entertainers and wannabes fashion their bodies and their "cribs."
+ Urban garment trends change at a rapid pace, and the designer must keep on top of what's happening with their consumer on a grass roots level.

Urban apparel portfolio page. *(Author's collection)*

OBJECTIVE: To execute a specialized fashion portfolio that meets the client's needs.

1. Identify your specialized category and customer.
2. Interview a typical customer of the specialized category with the box "Informed Needs of the Client."
3. Shop the retail market for five competitive brands within this chosen category.
4. Make notes of price points, silhouettes, style differences, selling floor display styles, brand imaging, textiles, colors, and hardware choices of each brand.
5. Test the competitive brands by trying on the garments in the store dressing room, and

mimic the movements that the client would be performing in this clothing. Observe the full range of motion in the mirror to see how the garment should function. If you do not fit the target market—for example, if you are designing active sportswear for the opposite gender—have someone try on the garments for you, and observe how the garment functions on your model.

6. Either informally or with the list in the box "Informed Needs of the Client," ask friends who wear these types of garments about what they demand of their clothing.

OBJECTIVE: To evaluate your design capabilities for a given category through experimentation.

1. Identify your specialized category and customer.
2. Complete Exercise 5.1, "Get to Know Your Specialized Client."
3. Complete a trial or prototype layout of your specialized fashion category. The illustrations and layout completions can be in state of "prototype," which means less formal and not refined.
4. Evaluate your prototype. Make a list of the pros and cons you observe of your collection presentation.
5. Evaluate your prototype for competitiveness within your market on the rating form that follows.
6. Complete a garment or garments in prototype form to see whether the ideas function for the consumer.

Prototype Layout Rating Chart

Answer these questions, and then rate your layout on each segment on a scale of 1–10 (1 being the lowest and 10 being the highest). When you have rated each segment, add the six ratings together and divide by 6 to determine an average rating for your layout. Did you meet your objective with a 6 or higher? Take note of what you would like to change for the next time you design for this specialized client or for another specialization.

Mood

Did I select a "mood" or theme that can enhance the look of my collection for the client? Is it too dark, moody, somber, peppy, exaggerated, and dramatic for the end-user? Is it "played out" at this point in time, or is it just slightly ahead of current trends to make it highly salable for next season, when this collection will be sold at retail? Has this interpretation of themes been done too often by my competitors?

My rating _____

Color

Do my colors suit the client's needs for the specialty area they will wear this for? Are the types of color (hue, saturation) in line- with my competitor's type of colors? If they are drastically different, will my client wear them? Am I using color in the way this market reacts to how it accentuates the body (for instance, if you are blocking color on the body, is it drawing attention to the wrong parts of the body, making the waistline, backside or thighs look larger?) Am I using color in a color blocking, solid, balance of basic colors to fashion colors similar to the competitive lines at retail?

My rating _____

Textiles

Can my client perform in these fabrics? What fabrics do my competitors use—and how do mine compete with the standard? (For instance, you've designed a knit hat line, and the competitors all use 100 percent cashmere wool, but you've chosen a 50-50 percent acrylic/wool blend. How and why would your hat stand up to the competition and why would the client switch fibers when the standard of 100 percent cashmere works for them? An answer to this could be you are trying to provide the same warmth by lining your hat and offering it at a lower price that your customers have told you they want. A few clients have tested your prototypes and found the hat design performed well for them.) Are the weights of the fabrics and gauges I have chosen going to hold up to wear?

My rating _____

Silhouette

Are these shapes and construction following the standards of the competition, but shaped and built a little better? (For instance, you designed a T-shirt for the urban market, and you found that your clients wanted it to be 2 inches longer to complement the silhouette of their baggy low-rise pants. When you added the extra 2 inches to the silhouette, you also researched a slightly lighter weight knit jersey that would not cling to the pants when the shirt is longer.) Do I think the company I've designed this collection for is capable of manufacturing the garments with the details, stitching, linings, trims, and so on that I've suggested?

My rating _____

Layout

Does my layout speak to the niche market I am aiming for? Is this a presentation that could lure an interviewer to want to hire me,? Do I believe this presentation would lure a consumer to buy my goods at retail, in a catalogue, Internet, or mannequin in-store display similar to my layout?

My rating _____

Branding

Does my line have a branded look to it for its chosen market? Should it have a distinct look of mood, color, textiles, silhouette, or layout that makes it read like the brand I've designed it for? If it is for a hypothetical new brand, how does it stand up against the competition?

My rating _____

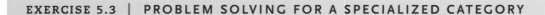

OBJECTIVE: To adopt a method of infusing performance, function, and practicality into the designs of a specialized category.

1. Choose a specialized fashion category.
2. Study the functional details of the given category for its clients.
3. Sketch your ideas using market and client knowledge developed in Exercises 5.1 and 5.2. Experiment with ideas that can meet the client's needs, paying special attention to the exact performance features that your client needs:

a. Your garments need to move on the body as described in the category.
b. The color palette, fabrics, and hardware must perform for the task at hand.
c. The layout and illustrations depict the energy of the specialization, and the lifestyle of the consumer.

REFERENCES

http://www.sginews.com/gifs/SGI_apparel_2003pdf, July 14, 2010.

http://wwww.kleinfeldbridal.com/images/dresssearch/previews, July 14, 2010.

http://www.theknot.com, July 14, 2010.

Kathryn Hagen: Fashion Illustration for Designers, Upper Saddle River, NJ: Pearson Prentice Hall, 2005, pages 262–267.

http://www.philiptreacy.co.uk/bio.swf

http://www.kangol.com/html/retrospective.asp

SUCCESSFUL LINE BUILDING FROM A TO Z: THE PORTFOLIO PROJECT

OBJECTIVES

+ Develop the concept for the portfolio.

+ Edit the contents.

+ Finalize the contents and order of presentation.

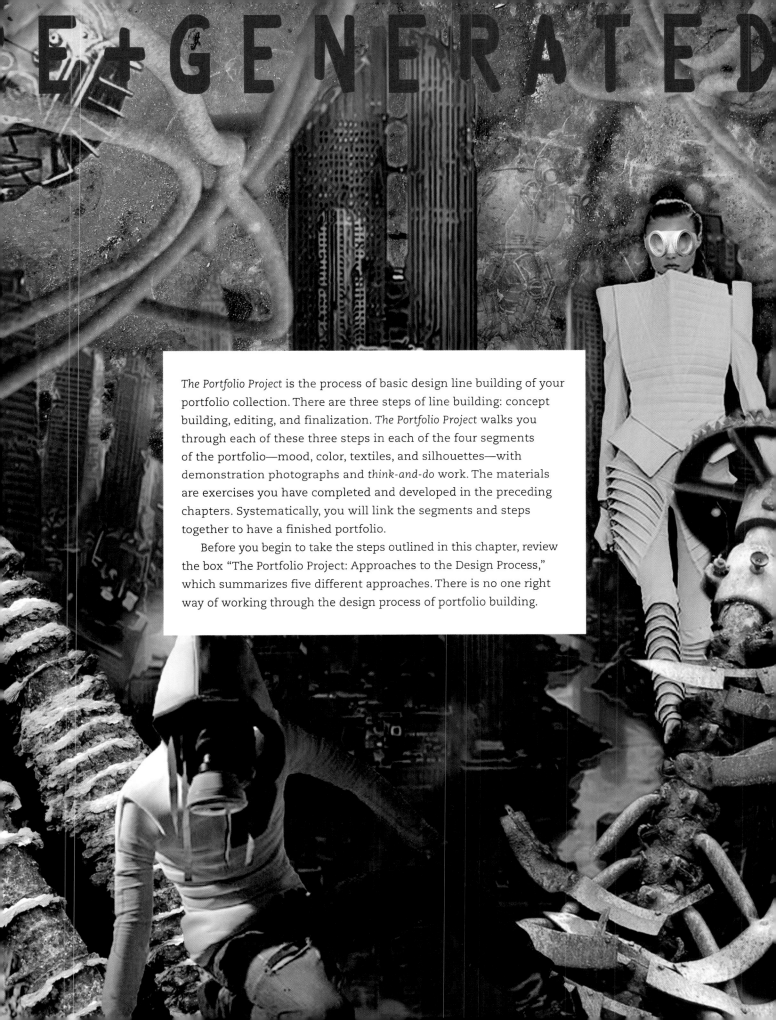

The Portfolio Project is the process of basic design line building of your portfolio collection. There are three steps of line building: concept building, editing, and finalization. *The Portfolio Project* walks you through each of these three steps in each of the four segments of the portfolio—mood, color, textiles, and silhouettes—with demonstration photographs and *think-and-do* work. The materials are exercises you have completed and developed in the preceding chapters. Systematically, you will link the segments and steps together to have a finished portfolio.

Before you begin to take the steps outlined in this chapter, review the box "The Portfolio Project: Approaches to the Design Process," which summarizes five different approaches. There is no one right way of working through the design process of portfolio building.

THE PORTFOLIO PROJECT:
APPROACHES TO THE DESIGN PROCESS

Many people have the mistaken impression that being creative and being systematic in solving a design problem are mutually exclusive. However, a conscious, systematic, and orderly approach does not have to be linear. And even a basically linear approach can allow for changes along the way to the solution of a design problem.

Take the time to evaluate the approaches to the design process that follow. Based on the book, *The Universal Traveler* by Don Koberg and Jim Bagnall, these are choices you, as a designer, can apply to the completion of your portfolio or any other design task. Koberg and Bagnall identify five basic approaches to creative problem solving:

1. *Linear Process* Step-by-step logical sequence; being cautious of not getting ahead of yourself. Well-suited to large, complex, team projects.
2. *Circular Process* Starting at any stage and advancing to the others in turn. Ideal for lengthy projects (like college programs, summer jobs, contracts, etc.).
3. *Feedback Approach* Moving forward while looping back to reconsider previous discoveries. Important when caution is imperative.
4. *Branching Paths* Allowing specific events and the interrelation of separate stages to control progress.
5. *The Natural Pathway* Awareness of all stages concurrently, but emphasis on one or two steps at a time; like viewing seven open boxes in a row, each one ready to receive additional data and thereby modifying your overall thinking accordingly.

These authors compare the Linear Process to to a mule train, "with each unit responsible for pulling the one behind it," and the Natural Way to a horse race, "where all units progress independently; where only one unit is 'out in front' (i.e., in focus) at any given moment."

ORGANIZATION OF THE PORTFOLIO PROJECT

With the five approaches in mind, you're ready to consider the organization of the Portfolio Project in detail.

PHOTOS AND THINK-AND-DO EXERCISES

Each development step of the four segments is explained in how-to photographs of a designer performing the task at hand. And each of the four segments' steps challenges you to create your portfolio images by undertaking the think-and-do exercises as you read through the text.

SEGMENTS

The Portfolio Project is divided into four working segments, each with three steps. See the visualization and a further explanation in the box "The Four Basic Phases of Line Building."

1. Mood

a) Conceptualize: work with free association.

b) Edit: use critical thinking and the "Designer Filter."

c) Finalize: commit the images to the page.

2. Color

a) Conceptualize: work with free association.

b) Edit: use critical thinking and the "Designer Filter."

c) Finalize: commit the images to the page.

3. Textiles

a) Conceptualize: work with free association.

b) Edit: use critical thinking and the "Designer Filter."

c) Finalize: commit the images to the page.

4. Silhouettes

a) Conceptualize: work with free association.

b) Edit: use critical thinking and the "Designer Filter."

c) Finalize: commit the images to the page.

Review the four working segments of the portfolio project as described here in a grid formation. Each of the four working segments will follow the same three steps for its development.

THE FOUR BASIC PHASES OF LINE BUILDING

The four basic phases of line building—the mood, color, textiles, and silhouettes—are explored each time a designer approaches a new season. The phases are revisited many times during the design implementation, refinement, completion, and production of the line. The first ideas are hardly ever just put onto paper or made into a garment without refinement. During the revisiting, it is important to reference ideas in your sketchbook to see whether your initial concepts are going forward the way that you would like to—or the way that you envisioned them. You may have a new vision that does not match your designer sketchbook idea, but checking in on the idea stage before you finish the line can only help your portfolio images. The four phases are spelled out below in simple terms.

Mood/Concept   The concept of a movement, or inspirational base.

Color   The color story of the line, usually two to eight basic colors for each line.

Textiles   A collection of fabrics that work well together for a line that meets manufacturing needs of yardage consumption. Usually two to eight basic fabrics per line.

Silhouette   The shapes and actual garments for each collection. Usually the portfolio will have 8 to 16 ensembles per collection (head-to-toe figures or croquis displayed in silhouettes).

MATERIALS

The four segments and three steps are developed using the following materials:

+ Previously completed materials
+ The Idealized Final Portfolio (Exercise 4.3)
+ The Designer Grid (Exercise 4.4)
+ Previously developed, ongoing work-in-progress materials
+ The Creative Chaos Sketchbook
+ Retail market focus reporting
+ Illustration, layout, and finalization evaluations

As you work through the segments and steps, you will link the four segments together in a portfolio page-flow story. Chapter 7 refines the portfolio statement.

GETTING STARTED

Chapter 6 is an exercise in building the final portfolio presentation. You will get started by walking through the steps of creative line planning concurrently with building your presentation.

GATHER

To start the portfolio project, gather the previously completed materials as listed at left. Work on Exercise 6.1 to prepare the workspace.

+ Study the different ways of preparing the designer grid shown on page 206, demonstrating four different scrambled approaches to creating your line.
+ Keep your Idealized Final Portfolio (Exercise 3.2) transparency overlay on your desktop or on your bulletin board for reference.

Bring these materials to your workspace:

+ The sketchbook or journal
+ Retail market reports
+ Illustration, layout, and finalization evaluations
+ Art supplies previously purchased
+ CAD programs, such as Photoshop and Illustrator

The materials list will grow to include color and textile swatches and silhouette/flats materials as you go through the portfolio project in this chapter.

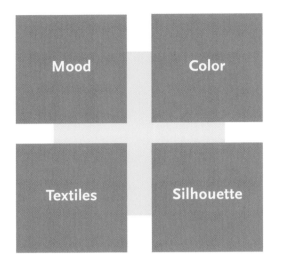

An example of the four segments laid out on the designer grid following the sequence of the Chapter 6. You will develop the four segments simultaneously. You can display your ideas in each segment, and interchange the ideas as you see fit.

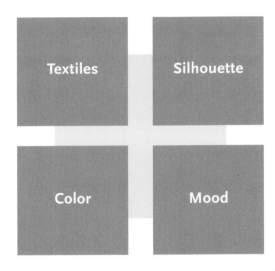

An example of the four segments laid out on the designer grid in a different sequence from that of Chapter 6. In this sequence, the design is *textile driven*. The designer works on selecting the textiles as the first segment of design inspiration. The color, mood, and silhouette ideas spring from the textiles. This designer lays out the textiles on the page in the "first" position, as all her thoughts will leap from there. She works with a belief that the textiles dictate the mood, color silhouette, function, and fit of the collection. Other designers may use the color, mood, or silhouette as a springboard for all decisions. Still other designers will scramble this sequence in their own unique way. Each of these methods works to achieve design results. Experiment with each method. You might find yourself using different sequencing for each design line you create.

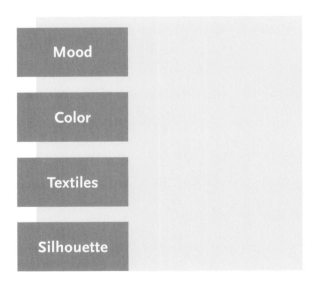

Your designer grid can be "stacked," as in this example. You can view your collected ideas in a row horizontally and view the collection vertically. These four segments can be scrambled in any sequence you choose (the same as the scrambled example in the at the top right figure).

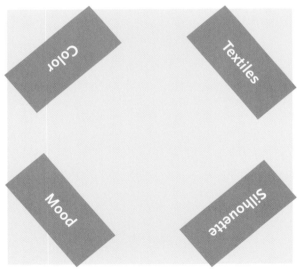

This figure represents the scrambling sequence of working in a circle. It is also an abstract representation of how you can jump back and forth from any of the methods shown in these figures to achieve the same results. The other option you have is to work using your own methods of segmenting and sequencing on a board or page. You might find yourself automatically categorizing your work naturally.

OBJECTIVE: Work with the Designer Grid Method to organize the segments of the Portfolio Project.

1. From Chapter 3, Exercise 3.3, take your completed designer grid and think about different ways you might put together your collection. See the views at left and the photographs demonstrating the various methods.

2. Set up your workspace to design the portfolio collection with the designer grid for the concept, edit, and finalization steps of your portfolio. The designer grid is used for each segment of mood, color, textiles, and silhouette design.

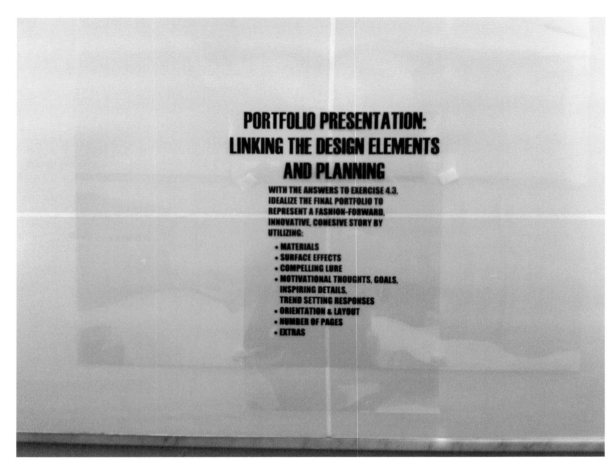

**PORTFOLIO PRESENTATION:
LINKING THE DESIGN ELEMENTS
AND PLANNING**

WITH THE ANSWERS TO EXERCISE 4.3,
IDEALIZE THE FINAL PORTFOLIO TO
REPRESENT A FASHION-FORWARD,
INNOVATIVE, COHESIVE STORY BY
UTILIZING:

- MATERIALS
- SURFACE EFFECTS
- COMPELLING LURE
- MOTIVATIONAL THOUGHTS, GOALS,
  INSPIRING DETAILS,
  TREND SETTING RESPONSES
- ORIENTATION & LAYOUT
- NUMBER OF PAGES
- EXTRAS

Working with the transparent overlay of the idealized portfolio with your concepts of the design collection, you can walk through the design process of creating your dream portfolio with the end-result visual close at hand.

DECIDE ON YOUR COLLECTION FOCUS

Based on completed market research outlined in Exercises 3.1, 3.2, 4.1, and 4.2 and review of Chapters 4 and 5, decide on the client focus for your collection(s). Decide the number of design collections you want to present as you work through the Portfolio Project.

If you plan to work on more than one collection, all of the collections should have a visual connection and purpose for being in your book. The purpose should serve your ultimate client with one design focus. Don't plan to create multiple collections in one book for catchall areas of the markets.

Decide on a season for the collection presentation. The season choices are Spring, Fall, and Holiday. Holiday is an in-store shopping time of late November through January, and it is a strong season for the swimwear, resort, cocktail dresses, and evening wear categories. The season you design for will drive the choices for each segment of the design process. Multiple design collections can be individually designed for different seasons.

Chapter 7 will help you finish putting the collection(s) into the book with final refinements.

UNITE THE SEGMENTS

Mood, color, textiles, and silhouette sections are outlined as separate segments for learning purposes. Remember to work on the segments as one design project, not as separate projects. Each segment is presented in the three separate steps of (1) concept building, (2) editing, and (3) finalization.

The title of this chapter, "Successful Line Building from A to Z," refers to a method of having "a lot of balls in the air at once," much like a juggler keeping eight balls in the air while maintaining balance and control.

Although the line building steps are spelled out in a linear fashion (steps A through Z, or numerically), you will need to work on the elements all at the same time, and each decision will affect the design decisions you make in all of the different areas listed below. The creative process needs to have freedom to flow through these channels as the designer conducts it. You are designing the pattern of decisions to create your portfolio.

Think of the image of the entertainer spinning plates. When attempting to spin eight plates on tall sticks all at the same time, the entertainer has to start somewhere in the line of plates. You can start at plate number 1, 8, or any plate in between. Once you start spinning one plate, it is a quick move on to the next plate to start that spinning, to start spinning the other six plates, and to keep them all spinning at once.

STEP 1: CONCEPT BUILDING

Concept building (Step 1) for each segment is broken into the following sub-steps:

+ *Study the examples.*   Examples of work are shown and discussed to help you make decisions about your portfolio work.
+ *Do the math.*   A format to help you calculate the number of presentation pages you will ultimately have in your portfolio per segment and collection.
+ *Read the FAQs.*   Review the question and answers from designers.
+ *Get inspired.*   Review examples of student work during their transitional stage of conceptualizing the collection, editing, and finalizing their work.
+ *Think and do.*   Make editorial, layout, and critique decisions to put your work on the page.

Concept building of mood, color, textiles, and silhouettes is best approached with an open mind. Thoughts flow freely and openly during the concept phase of each segment.

In each segment of concept building, start with a clean slate. Throw away old ideas that may be irrelevant; build upon past success stories that are relevant. Throw away self-doubt. It could inhibit you from stretching your ideas further.

Glide through the path of deliberate chaos collecting with the following reminders:

+ Use the massage method. Plan well in advance of designing the portfolio line by posting inspirational items on a bulletin board without the thought of designing a line. Each day that you look at the information, reposition the images in order of visual importance to what moves you to design the portfolio line. As you work on each segment, implement a gentle evaluation of your work over hours, days and/or weeks. Keep the information on your Designer Board; step back and look at the segments as separate entities and/or as a group. Evaluate how the segments relate to one another conceptually.

+ Think in terms that may be tangled, messy, foggy, vague, aggressive, fearless, or mixed up.

+ Brainstorm with inherent confusion, scrambled thoughts, and no apparent path.

+ Spark your instinctual concept-building thoughts by abandoning neatness or order in the compilation of materials.

+ Limit judgmental thoughts about the mood, color, textile, and silhouette conceptual information. You can use critical thinking skills in the editing process (Step 2) to examine your work.

+ Expand your thoughts for each segment of line building. Use the branch method by writing your initial idea(s) or key words for a mood concept, color collection concept, textile concept, or silhouette concept. Next, make a list of associated words or thoughts that bring deeper values to support your concept. Start with a picture or a word. Scribble the building concepts around the picture or word much like the branches on a tree.

+ The factors that follow play a leading role in developing your concepts, as well as refining the portfolio. These factors should be *referenced*. They should not be part of a *critique* of your work in the conceptual stage:
  - The retail market report(s)
  - The idealized final portfolio goals
  - Illustration, layout, and finalization goals

MOOD/CONCEPT BUILDING

Designers tell their collection story with mood boards in their studios and mood pages in their portfolios. There are endless possibilities to collect and select mood images, to be inspired by mood concepts, and to represent mood concepts on the portfolio page. Some designers may want to photograph a mood board made in a large presentation format (40 inches x 30 inches) for a corporate meeting and include the photograph in their portfolio in a formal presentation style. Other designers may have photographs of their less formal, conceptual mood boards from their studios, which they can include in a formal layout of a portfolio. See the presentation boards on page 213 for examples of presentation mood boards used in meetings that can be photographed for portfolio presentations.

The mood concept pages are represented by the images on the page of your inspirational story. Mood boards or pages can represent your inspiration from many different angles. Following are various scenarios of mood development:

+ An inspirational mood story that drove your color, textile collection, and designs (silhouettes)
+ The color, textile collection, and designs that drove the inspirational mood story
+ The mood images and inspiration might be *drawn from*
    ■ The color selection
    ■ The textile selection
    ■ The design (silhouettes) collection

The color concepts, textiles selection, or design selection might individually or collectively drive the mood inspiration.

These mood boards were part of a corporate design and sales strategy meeting to consider showing them to buyers interested in placing orders for the design collection. The designer used large boards for impact. Everyone sitting at the table or in the meeting room (2 to upwards of 25 people) needed to see the board clearly. Boards like these can be used for multiple purposes after the meeting, such as being displayed in the manufacturer's showroom for buyer's weeks or in a trade show booth. For meetings and displays, a mix of horizontal and vertical boards is acceptable, as the viewer doesn't have to flip the portfolio around to view them.

Photographs of such boards, reduced to the size of a portfolio page, can be included in a designer's portfolio, or the designer could show a series of mood boards on one page.

The details the designer used for visual interest include the following:

In the figure above:
- Lining the back of the board with burlap with exposed fiber fringe on the outside edges
- Backing chosen images with foam core boards and layering them onto the board for added 3D interest
- A variety of interesting sources for the images
- Homespun, rustic lettering for the title to complement the mood images
- Tropical palm fronds
- Textural paper layering

In the figure to the left:
- Adding brown packaging paper to the back of the board
- Keeping a margin of white around the photo images to create a postcard effect
- Ripped edges of chosen images
- Attaching a beach bag, flip flops, earthenware vase, dried grasses, blue jeans, and a travel journal

View Examples

To *begin* your portfolio mood pages, view the examples to the right for a visual understanding of the effects of mood pages. (We will refer to the mood image pages in your portfolio as *pages* from here throughout the rest of the text. While you may develop *mood boards* for live presentations and for inspiration in the studio, for the purposes of the portfolio, the moods will be represented on mood *pages*.)

Do the Math

Mood pages in the portfolio can be presented in many combinations. In concept, visualize the number of mood pages you will produce. You will decide on the final presentation as you work through the design process. Combinations include:

+ One mood page
+ Two mood pages
+ Combination pages of mood and color on one or two pages
+ Combination of the mood, color, and textiles onto one or two pages
+ Combination of mood and textiles onto one or two pages
+ Incorporating mood images throughout any pages of your collection in backgrounds, borders, etc.

If you are including multiple collections in your portfolio, the mood pages for the different collections don't have to be shown in the same format.

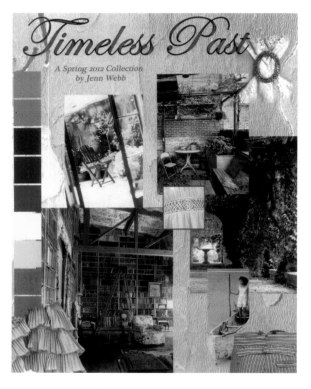

Two examples of portfolio mood pages. A CAD mood page for a contemporary intimate apparel collection (top). The designer collected images from magazines and online sources. She chose a soft background color and used Photoshop to assemble the pictures. She used a romantic script for the title and added a definition of the title. *(Courtesy of Katie Choquette)* In the second image, (bottom) the designer scanned images from a book and online sources into Photoshop to manipulate into a mood page for a women's misses sportswear collection. She features a textured background, her color palette swatches, and garment and trim details. *(Courtesy of Jenn Webb)*

Q & A ABOUT MOOD PAGES

Question: What is a mood page or a concept page?

Answer: A mood page is a page in the portfolio that shows your inspiration. It can be free-form, eclectic, or abstract or highly organized, like a graphically designed page. The layout and format are an integral part of the images you have chosen. They set the mood and create interest for the viewer to investigate your portfolio further and read on. The mood page should entice the viewer's curiosity to turn the page to see more of your collection. Similar to a movie trailer or poster for an upcoming movie, the images for the mood page makes the viewer want to see more.

Question: Do I have to do mood pages in my portfolio?

Answer: Yes, you have to create mood pages. They are an important part of the collection, as they showcase your conceptual thoughts, which should also be reflected in your color, textiles, and final silhouette illustrations. Job interviewers will judge your follow-through capability from your mood pages. They show how you interpret current trends. The designer who hires you wants to know how you see things and just how capable you are at telling this visual story to your audience.

Question: What images are supposed to be on a mood page?

Answer: Show images that have given you reason to create your line. If you haven't worked from images for your concept, look for images that support your silhouettes, colors, or textiles and that pull the line together in your design vision.

Get Inspired

Designers work in many different ways to finish their portfolio collections. Inspiration and images for the portfolio pages can be collected after the collection is fully illustrated. It is most common to first gather information and inspiration images, and then design the collection.

For inspiration, review the figures on the facing page. See how each designer finds a distinctive conceptual "voice" in a unique manner.

Implement, Think, and Do

Exhaust your market and trend research sources, and gather inspirational pictures to bring forward your collection image. See the source lists in Appendices A and B. In addition, you may collect information that seems to be obscure (toys, plastic items, rocks, marbles, etc), eclectic, or "out there."

Keep in mind your chosen pictures are an example of your communication skills. The images will be an example of your

+ Taste
+ Conceptual direction
+ Ability to set a mood or reflect a theme
+ Interpretation of trends
+ Sense of the market or target consumer

The interviewer will scrutinize your work for these important cues about the following:

+ How you think and process information
+ How visually compatible your mood pictures are with your colors, textiles, and designs.

Consider some basic "don'ts":

+ Don't limit your resources to fashion-only magazines and websites.
+ Don't quote from a popular, overexposed advertisement. It is generically recognizable and will be viewed as lifted from someone else's work—that is, unoriginal.

+ Don't fixate on a singular theme during the initial concept-building phase. As an example: if flowers inspire you, don't just gather photos of flowers. Go out on a limb and expand your research. Support the floral trend with pictures of fields in bloom, pastures, rain forests, historical or botanical floral references, scientific flower research, and so on. Another example is to take the initial concept, such as "I love Christina Aguilera and I want my line to be hot like her" as an initial concept, without expanding this statement. Without broadening your research and changing your mind-set, your final collection will seem forced or contrived. The collection will read as predictable or passé. Instead, if Christina Aguilera is your *ideal*, then place your favorite likenesses of her in the "idealized final portfolio" file. Maybe you will use her influences for:

■ A hot page layout
■ Figure/croquis/ pose development
■ A color palette that leads with lipstick red or porcelain skin
■ Silhouettes that refine and shape the body
■ Borders and page treatments that look like her CD cover, stage set, or body shape.

If you find a large 3D object inspiring, take a photo and print a copy for your reference. For example, if you have been inspired for years by the heirloom-quality afghan that your great-grandmother crocheted for you, place several prints of the afghan in your mood, color, textile, silhouette, or final packaging file. As your collection unfolds, an element of the afghan might find its place. Don't leave the afghan on its special shelf in your closet. Keep it in your visual field as you design something further than your initial thought.

Examples of different designers' mood processes and mood pages: In the first figure, at the top left the design studio keeps a large bulletin board propped up against the wall. The design team post trends and inspiration onto the board with push pins throughout the concept development segments of designing their collection. The review and editing processes are ongoing and constant. Each designer can add or edit out materials on the board at any time prior to regularly scheduled design concept, editing, and finalization meetings.*(Courtesy of Plugg Jeans)* In the sample board from Target's Go International collection, (bottom), the designer shows images and color to build his concepts *(Courtesy of WWD)* In the sample board from Francisco Costa for Calvin Klein, (top right), shown on the front page of *Women's Wear Daily*, the designer works his inspiration from extensive textile research. *(© Avital Aronowitz)*

Place in the Ready Position for the Next Step

Place all of the items, sketches, doodles, and words on your designer grid. Look at the images as they relate to one another. Ideas that initially may have appeared to have no relation to one another might be linked visually by shape, scale, color, texture, and so on and can translate into a common theme or a theme developed by deliberate juxtapositions.

Play with the images on a board, a piece of paper, or a tabletop. Think about how the mood images tell a story. Conceptually visualize how the images create a story for you to follow into a color, textile, and/or silhouette story. Ask yourself the following questions:

+ Do the images inspire me conceptually to create a collection?
+ How do they look together as a conceptual collective statement?
+ Is my concept message strong enough to carry the line through to completion?
+ Did I collect images that tell me only color, textile, or silhouette information? Do I need to look at more influencers and gather more information?

If the images are too large or too small to be used in your portfolio, begin to visualize resizing the images for the portfolio page. If you visualize your images being changed, contemplate how you can better conceptually communicate your ideas by manipulating the images:

+ Resize the image.
+ Blur the entire image, the edges, or the middle portion of the image(s).
+ Colorize an image or many images.
+ Change the images to show only silhouette, positive/negative, x-ray, or a basic black-and-white picture.

+ Change the images to sepia tones.
+ Add textural elements, textiles, colors, or silhouette schematics to the theme.
+ Distort the image(s).
+ Burnish, deconstruct, cut, destroy, or splice the images for a theme emphasizing your statement story.
+ Use the images as a background texture, and search for elements that create the mood that can be pasted on top as a layer on the page.
+ Consider how a background or border treatment might emphasize the image story.

Develop a mock-up of the page with the original images. If you are still developing the segments of your design process, make copies of the images and paste together a prototype of the mood page. Search for trend information within the images for color, textile, and silhouette design.

If you find more than one theme, you can save the discards for your next collection.

Reflect conceptually about the results your pictures represent:

+ The retail market report(s)
+ Your idealized portfolio goals
+ The plan for your illustration, layout, and finalization goals

As you develop the next three segments, keep the elements on the designer grid for editing purposes. You can edit the elements at any phase during the process of line building. Search for trend information within the images. Review their conceptual relation to the mood information.

In the top photo, the designer is working on concepts for a contemporary sportswear line. The inspiration comes from the commercial retail and advertising market. Her work is driven by interpreting market trends and pushing them forward to "hit this mark" as in Exericse 2.3. *(Author's collection)* The designer represented in the bottom left photo begins her process of building a collection using pushpins on a bulletin board to display her design inspiration clippings and sketches. Her mood images, color, textiles, and silhouettes are all developed simultaneously. Her designer "grid" is a blend of all of her ideas, which need not be delineated by the traditional grid method. She works in the "Natural Pathway" design process outlined in Point 5 of the box "The Portfolio Project: Approaches to the Design Process." *(Courtesy of Jane Henry)* In the bottom right photo, the designer is developing an avant garde line of women's sportswear for her final runway project as her senior college thesis. She works by doodling and cutting and pasting Internet images into her sketch book. *(Courtesy of Jenn Webb)*

COLOR CONCEPT BUILDING

Color is a powerful element, as it weaves all of the design factors together into a collection. It will set the tone and emotional mood of the garments.

Color can be researched and gathered based upon the designer's intuitive feel. The initial feel may be influenced by market research. During the color concept phase, you may collect color without thought to any other segments of line development. You may be considering the mood, textiles, and silhouette concepts to drive or influence the color selections.

Typically, a designer completes color market research and then develops the color palette concurrently with the mood, textile, silhouette, and trend and market research. It is critical that the color palette be compatible with the mood page expressions. The color palette plan must support and work well with the textures, surface treatments, and print stories you are simultaneously developing.

In the conceptualization phase, it is up to the designer to strike a balance between instinctual color selection and color selection based on market research. You may also balance instinctual color feelings with the processing of market direction, the visualization of the ideal portfolio, and/or the process of designing the line.

View Examples

Study the color page example to the right and on page 221 to get a basic visual imprint of portfolio color pages.

The designer displays her color palette on the fabric swatch portion of the portfolio page. She colorizes her silhouette flats and shows the cropped figure along with the graphic image for the garments. *(Courtesy of Lindsey Russell)*

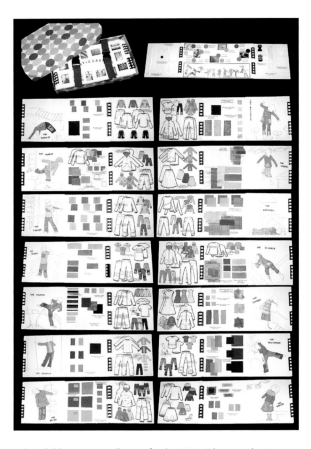

In her children's wear collection for the CFDA Educational Initiatives Portfolio Competition, this student designer covered a portfolio box with a statement circular print that also represented her color story. Each page was hinged with plastic hardware so the viewer could open up the color and illustration page to see the flats and how they related to the color and silhouette. *(Courtesy of Lindsey Russell)*

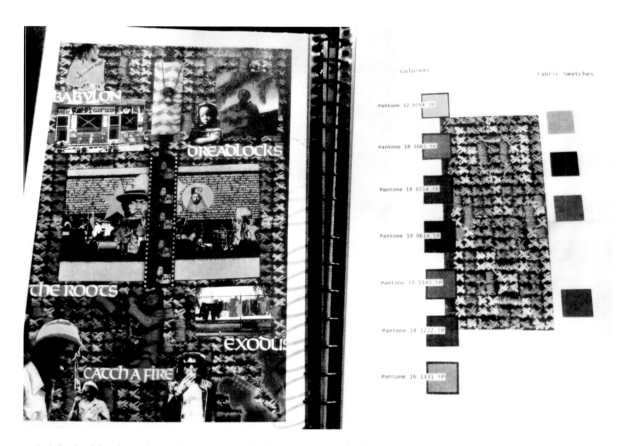

In the left side of this photo, the mood page is setting the dramatic sequence for the viewer by exciting the eye with color and texture. The facing color page reinforces the mood with a definitive color palette. The colors are referenced to the Pantone Color system, with file names printed on the page. The textiles are uniformly presented on the same page, a continuum of the design aesthetic from the mood page presentation. *(Courtesy of Ithwa Huq-Jones)*

Do the Math

Based on the extensive research you have completed for the basis of your portfolio, conceptualize how many colors will be in your collection. Visualize the basic color story on the page(s) in the following combinations:

+ One color page
+ Two color pages
+ Combination pages of color and mood on one or two pages
+ Combination of the color, mood, and textiles on one or two pages
+ Combination of color and textiles onto one or two pages
+ Incorporation of color images throughout any pages of your collection in backgrounds, borders, and so on

If you are including multiple collections in your portfolio, the color pages for each collection don't have to be shown in the same format.

Get Inspired

Study the color presentation in the formative stages in the journal pages to the right.

Color inspiration can come through passive observation of your surroundings, as well as from color matching systems (Pantone, SCOTDIC, Munsell); see Appendix B and the color forecasting services listed in Appendix H.

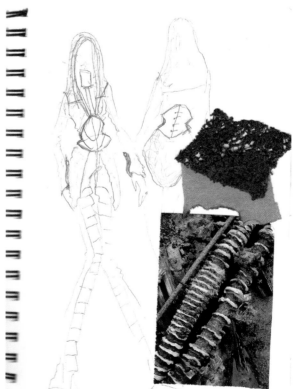

The designer paints color swatches in her journal as she sketches silhouettes and pastes inspirational photos with her work to develop a color palette. *(Courtesy of Jenn Webb)*

Q & A ABOUT COLOR PAGES

Question: Do I have to research color trends for my portfolio collection? I designed a line for the school fashion show, and the colors I showed must have been perfect for my portfolio collection, because the audience applauded.

Answer: Yes, you will need to research color trends to expand or validate your color ideas, depending on your research results. The school runway show was a different venue from your focused portfolio collection geared toward a specific client or consumer. After research, you very well may decide upon your runway colors or variations of them. The research will help you understand the cycle of fashion colors for your chosen market.

Question: Why do I see the same colors in many design categories from budget to better designers when I shop the stores? Am I reading this correctly, and how does this happen?

Answer: Designers combine interpreted forecasted color service information with intuitive color feelings to create their color palette for the season. The Walmart designer and the Calvin Klein designer might interpret color from the same color services. Upon closer inspection, you will see that Calvin Klein's brown for the season is not the same brown as Walmart's for the season. One brown is tweaked for the better market in a particular hue or tone, and the other is tweaked for the budget customer. It is important to look at color tone/hue/depth/saturation from line to line, and teach your eye to see the differences in color from line to line and market to market.

Implement, Think, and Do

Access the color forecasting services listed in Appendix H , if these are available to you. Read through the Basic Guide to Attending Forecast and Color Trend Services' Presentations in Chapter 2.

Apply the retail research and idealized portfolio goals to your work. Realize that at this conceptual stage, the collection is just being developed, and the research and goals need to be looked at from a conceptual standpoint. Later, in the edit and finalize steps, you can evaluate and refine how this research and goal setting is applied to your work.

Evaluate the colors in concept form:

✦ Implement a preliminary evaluation of your color choices as they relate to the mood, textiles, silhouettes, and packaging ideas.

✦ To develop a fashion-forward sense, review the current trend information you have compiled. For more trendsetting color, change or rework your colors to be ahead of the market, anticipating the next trend. Ask yourself these questions:

- Are my color choices a repeat of what I am currently seeing in the stores? If so, review trend information and reformulate your colors to reflect the incoming colors.
- Do my color choices carry a similar weight in saturation or hue?
- Do the colors support my trends?
- Will my colors be appropriate for the textile, prints, and surface treatments I am forecasting?
- Do my colors support or detract from the silhouettes I am sketching?
- Do my colors work for my market and season? Are they too manly or feminine or too sophisticated? If so, adapt the colors to a softer, deeper, or medium tone of the color you originally predicted.
- Am I seeing shades of (for instance) green for two seasons now? Do your green choices look the same as versions that are already out there? Tweak the color to the next shade of muted, clearer, lighter, or deeper shades to better address the trend of the color. Your green needs to be of the same color value as the incoming trend category for the shelf life of your portfolio.

Here is an example of adapting to incoming color information: You want to design a black and white collection. You see it throughout marketing in commercials, ads, movies, clothing, stage productions, etc. You question whether this is overdone. Review your concepts of mood, textile, silhouette, and packaging, and evaluate how your collection will be viewed as the next version of black and white, not the current use of the two colors. The treatment of the mood, textures, shapes, and packaging could give your black and white statement the newness it requires for the market. If you continue to question whether your color choice is correct, have a second and a third color solution to the problem (e.g., gray and beige, brown and pale yellow). Continue to develop all areas of the collection, and keep experimenting with color combinations that make sense by adding color to your rough sketches. Critique the color combination you think is most effectively pushing your line forward.

Keep in mind some basic don'ts:

- Don't overwork or overanalyze color selections, especially in the conceptual stage. Your instinctual feelings need to be considered as you play with the color. Keep some of your first ideas on the board during the conceptual development.
- Don't choose your color palette based on the markers you have in your art supply box. Your favorite color makers aren't indicators of a fashion trend.

Place Colors in the Ready Position for the Next Step

Place all of the color swatches, renderings, yarns, obscure objects, printouts, and so forth, on your designer grid. As you develop the next two segments and place elements on the designer grid for editing purposes, you will be able to refer to the mood and color materials already on your grid. You can edit any of the elements at any phase during the process of line building.

dried up dye looks like rust

Two examples of color development shown on the designer grid as Step 2, with the mood concepts in place. The top photo shows color ideas on a page. The designer collected yarns, swatches, Pantone color swatches, and color direction from Premiere Vision's color forecasting presentation in Paris, France and threw all the color onto a large board to evaluate her feeling of color information. She spent time taking color on and off the board to see which colors help support the design direction of the mood and trends she had established as important for the misses contemporary consumer. *(Author's collection)* The bottom photo shows the designer's development of color through dyestuffs experimentation in a conceptual stage of carrying forward her mood of avant-garde runway fashion. *(Courtesy of Jenn Webb)*

TEXTILE CONCEPT BUILDING

Many designers are *textile-driven*, which means they are inspired purely by the fabrics they see. The fibers, fabrics, and trims become their concept inspiration, and they build the mood/concepts, color, and silhouettes solely based on the way that the fabrics speak to them. They feel the fabrics (both figuratively and literally), and this launches the conceptual process. Other designers may work in a way that the textiles moderately drive their decisions. For some designers, textiles may be the last segment of the concept or finalization of a line.

There is no right way to be inspired by textiles—or any of the other design segments, for that matter. It is customary to research the concepts of mood, color, textiles, and silhouette in a wheel or circular motion; revisiting each segment as you design and collect ideas.

View Examples

Many fiber companies offer trend presentations and overviews of fabric companies' fabric selections. These presentations can help ignite the concepts for a designer's vision.

Fiber companies can be one of the best windows into the fashion trends for the season. A fiber company may inspire you to visit one or many of the fabric companies being showcased at a presentation at a trade show or in the fiber company showroom. Many fiber companies have trend presentations in their showrooms for potential clients. The employees of the fiber mills represent the fabric sources they are exhibiting. They will assist you with any questions you might have, and they will give you fabric companies' contact information and fabric details. The presentation may also spark your interest in other fibers you need to include in the mix of merchandise for your collection. Take notes to visit additional fiber mills.

Do the Math

Textile pages can be combined with the other segments of design, or you can show the textiles as a separate page(s).

In many portfolios, the designer will show the textiles swatches on two textile pages. The old-school presentation style showed the illustrated figure, the swatches of fabric, and the flats on one page. This is no longer a set formula, but designers tend to show their textile swatches on the illustration pages in addition to the separate textile pages.

The number of portfolio page choices is the same as listed in the "Do the Math" bullet points for the conceptualization of the mood (page 214) and color (page 222) segments.

If you are including multiple collections in your portfolio, the textile pages for each collection don't have to follow the same format.

Q & A ABOUT TEXTILES PAGES

Question: My fabric swatch represents the fabric I am using in my illustrations, but the swatch is brown, and I am showing my illustrations in a turquoise blue. Can I still use this swatch?

Answer: Yes, you can use the swatch for reference on a textile page. Don't paste it on a page where you feel the color fights with your illustrations, color, or mood. If you are labeling your fabric swatches with titles and fiber content, add the phrase "for quality reference only" *if* this does not fight with the visuals on the page. You can also dye or color with paint or marker over a swatch that is white or beige to match your portfolio illustrations. Although it is not necessary, some designers prefer the look of a closer match of color swatch to illustration. Another choice is to render your own "swatch" of the surface treatment in the colorway(s). These paper swatches, rendered in the medium of your choice, can be mounted along with the fabric swatches and/or illustrations, mood, or color pages.

Get Inspired

One way to get inspired by your fabric swatches or fabric samples is to work with a mock-up method to evaluate your fabric or surface-printed fabric on a silhouette you are planning it for. Here are a few mock-up methods you can try to see whether your choice of fabrics works on the illustrated page and/or on the body:

✦ *Mock-up illustration swatch/flat sketch/fashion figure.* Look at the fabric's surface and decide how you are going to render it on the page in the silhouettes. You can start with just rendering a *swatch* of the fabric, or render the fabric directly onto a silhouette. One of my favorite ways to play with this mock-up illustration method is to use my rough flat sketches. You can do five or ten renderings on a page of one flat shirt and develop different versions of the fabric surface. You can play with different rendering media: pencil, colored pencil, marker, watercolor, gouache, acrylic, pastels, charcoal, CAD system, and so on. If you want to mix media, here's your chance to play with the different media to accomplish your goal without overwhelming yourself with switching your rendering style. You may find as you play, that you discover a rendering method that works for you that you hadn't previously thought you could achieve. Look at the scale, size and texture of the fabric you are rendering on the page. Your scale on the page can be true to life as the scale would be when worn on the body. You can choose to make your scale exaggeratingly large or small; color intensity can be true to life or exaggerated to meet your ideals; and you can experiment with blending media. Working outside of your normal path could lead you to make a stronger visual statement than you originally conceived.

✦ *Mock-up squint.* Place two fabrics on a board with the fabric for the top of the garment on top with the fabric for the bottom of a garment below it. Step back and squint as if to imagine this mock-up as the garment. Looking at the board in the mirror (or by just looking at it/squinting at it) can give you a perspective on the appropriateness of scale, color and texture of the fabric for the garments you conceptualize.

✦ *Mock-up of wrapped, taped, or pinned fabric sample.* This method requires at least ½ yard of your chosen fabric. If you have a smaller amount of yardage, you can still play with the fabric with this method; however, it might be less telling than a larger amount. Using yourself, a friend, a model, or a dress form, wrap, pin, or tape your fabric on the body in the shape of your design silhouette. Test how the fabric functions for the particular motions that you've intended for the garment. Is the fabric too restrictive for the body to raise an arm or move a leg in the silhouettes that you have planned? Does your fabric have enough stretch for the intended fit and for your target consumer? Do you need to cut your fabric on the bias or the cross-grain to achieve a different affect on the body? Is the pattern too large or small for the design impact you are seeking?

+ *Mock-up a sewn garment.* You can use yardage of your actual fabric(s) to cut and sew a quick mock-up sample of your silhouette(s). You can also use a similar or less costly fabric to see how your fabric selection would work. Muslin is a good choice. If you feel you need to add a mock-up of the texture or print on the muslin, you can add this to the goods before you cut and sew the garment. The garment can be sloppily sewn or it can be expertly sewn. This is your mock-up garment, and it's up to you as to how much time you have to complete this task. Ask yourself the questions outlined above as you step back and evaluate your garment(s).

When you've completed your mock-up method(s) and evaluation, problem-solve now, and reconfigure your fabric selection or your silhouette direction.

A mock-up sketch of rendered fabrics on planned fashion illustration figures. By playing with fabric and color rendering style and medium, the designer makes decisions about the mood, color, textiles, and silhouettes. *(Author's collection)*

Implement, Think, and Do

Research textiles and prints using the same exhaustive possibilities as the research for mood and color concepts. Reference Appendices A and B for sources. Research illustration and rendering methods for fabric treatments, surface effects, and how fabric affects the silhouette on the illustration page. Refer to Appendix B for sources. Apply the retail research and idealized portfolio goals to your textile concept work.

Evaluate your fabric selections to decide whether they are conceptually portraying the data from your retail research and whether they are conceptually supporting your idealized portfolio goals. Examine the concepts with the following questions in mind:

+ Are my fabrics too bulky, lightweight, transparent, opaque, heavy, delicate, or rough for the concepts, colors, and silhouettes?
+ Is there enough structure, or will the fabric flow sufficiently for my designs?
+ Are my colors able to be dyed in these fibers?
+ Are the fabrics too sophisticated, too juvenile, or too risqué for my end-use consumer?
+ Do I need to show lining fabric(s), and should the linings have texture or print interest?
+ Can I choose a grouping of these fabrics, textures, and prints that will work together in a collection? Do I need to expand my search?

Place Fabric Swatches in the Ready Position for the Next Step

Place the fabric swatches on the designer grid, and view the selections with the mood/concept and color segment samples. Remember, you can edit any elements at any phase of the process of line building.

In the first designer's grid, (at the top) the textile swatches support the market-driven collection. The swatches and fabrics are from market research at trade shows. The designer has added two garments from her closet for reference of a type of tribal print and texture she saw in the market. She'll shop the print market to find a fashion-forward print, and she will work with the factory to develop a textural knit in this feeling when the line goes into (pre)production. *(Author's collection)* In the second designer's grid, (bottom left and right) the designer works in her sketchbook to continue her design thoughts as a story. She plays with fabric swatches, silhouette ideas, and mood images to develop innovative silhouettes. She is working on all four segments at once, as there is overlap of mood, color, textiles, and silhouettes in each segment. The designer grid acts as an abstract guide for this textbook presentation. *(Courtesy of Jenn Webb)*

SILHOUETTE CONCEPT BUILDING

In theory, your sketchbook has many silhouettes and collections that your are developing or have developed in an on going, free-flowing pattern. The sketchbook also has, in theory, fully developed line collections from the past and/or the current focused portfolio collection. Silhouettes for the portfolio collection may be developed with the influence of all the concepts you developed in the mood, color, and textile segments. The silhouettes are formulated with the two guides: Chapter 2, page 57, "The Designer's Basic Guide to Retail Shopping," and Exercise 3.1, "Decide on Your Portfolio Design Direction."

Some designers fine-tune their silhouettes during the concept step by first completing their illustrated fashion plates, followed by completing the mood, color, and textile pages. Some designers might complete their illustrated fashion plates in line form and then fill in the color and textiles after they complete the editing step for mood, color, and textiles. Other designers will wait until they edit or finalize their illustrations to fine-tune their silhouette choices. Some designers massage the silhouettes continually through each step. There are no rules as to the best design sequence to develop silhouettes.

Many designers work on the silhouettes *after* they have developed a distinct mood, color, and textile direction. After the designer plays with these elements on the designer grid, the silhouettes become the last cog in the wheel of the design of the collection. The mood, color, and textiles speak to the designer, who will then draw or drape the shapes that work into this vision that he or she sees from the grid. In this silhouette/concept segment, the designer's research into dream/ideal illustration and layout styles can strongly influence conceptual ideas and decisions. Review one example of a designer's sketch method in the figure on page 233.

Retail market research should strongly influence the development of silhouettes in the concept stage. The focus of the collection in shape and form is designed with a specific customer and a specific channel of distribution in mind. The designer may have sketched a line *without* a specific market focus. The next step is to incorporate the market research information into the silhouettes by changing them in shape, details, color, surface treatments, or textiles with the customer in mind.

In the concept process, consider the following:

✦ What stores or distribution channels do I see these garments hanging in?
✦ Are the silhouettes trendsetting for the market I've identified?

A designer's focused attention to building a collection through silhouette development. She develops her collection as well as her beginning ideas for portfolio layout and illustration as she sketches her design concepts as outfits. *(Courtesy of Cat Craig)*

View Examples

To influence your silhouette designs and illustration style, research the illustration influencers listed in Appendix I. On page 235 are examples of illustrators and historic references.

Do the Math

The number of illustrated fashion plates per collection can range from 6 to 16 pages. The variables are (1) the number of ensembles per design collection, and (2) the number of fashion figures you are placing on the page. Here are some configurations for your consideration:

+ Design 12 to 16 ensembles (head-to-toe garments) per collection.
+ Decide on your orientation (horizontal or vertical placement on the page).
+ Decide on the number of fashion figures you want on each page: one fashion figure per page (a technique used mainly for evening wear, gowns, bridal, and voluminous statement pieces), or two, three, four, or five fashion figures per page.

While there is no rule as to what configuration works best, it will be best to take into consideration how the garments will fit on the page with your illustration style. Some designers like to add volume to exaggerate the silhouettes, while other designers like to elongate the figures (even further than they have already elongated them to the 9½-head fashion figure) so the silhouettes might take up less width on the page.

The number of figures per page can vary. Or you can make a strong statement by keeping to a fixed formula, for instance, two figures per page for all pages, for all collections.

Consider how the pages will turn in your book, as each page (with the exception of the first and last page of your book) will have a facing page with the binding of the book in the middle, so each left-hand page must relate to the facing right-hand page as one continuous image or "spread." The first eight pages of the illustrations will need to relate to one another in a story format. Later on in the editing step, you will work to have the illustration pages relate to the mood, color, textiles, and flats pages in a story format. For instance, if you have 16 ensembles planned for your collection, you might deem the 16 fashion figure pages to read:

First left-hand page: 2 figures
First right-hand page: (facing first left-hand page) 3 figures
Second left-hand page: 3 figures
Second right-hand page: (facing second left-hand page) 1 figure, with a textile and color section
Third left-hand page: 2 figures
Third right-hand page: (facing third left-hand page) No figures, textile and trim section
Fourth left-hand page: 2 figures
Fourth right-hand page (facing fourth left-hand page): 3 figures
As with the mood, textiles, and color pages, it is OK to mix the four segments of mood, textiles, and color together in any format of storytelling that is effective.

Illustrations by Rene Bouet-Willaumez (top left and right) (*Courtesy of Fairchild Archives/Rene Bouet-Willaumez*) and Richard Rosenfeld (bottom left) (*Courtesy of Richard Rosenfeld*), and an illustration for Victoria's Secret (bottom right) (*Courtesy of Victoria's Secret 2011*) show a variety of styles focused on different market segments.

Consider Showing Multiple Design Collections in Your Portfolio

If you have more than one collection in your portfolio, it is not necessary to follow the exact same formula of storytelling for each collection. The collections shown in your portfolio should tell a *consumer-focused* story. For instance, you would not design two collections of women's sportswear, and then include a third collection of unrelated fashions, such as men's formal wear.

There are exceptions to every format. The examples are endless for widening a focused portfolio to address various related markets. If your interest is to broaden your collection focus, work on the conceptual research for each design category at the same time you design the main portfolio collection. Visualize and plan the approximate number of collections you want to include in your portfolio and how they can relate to each other. For example, if the women's sportswear company you are designing for also has a toddler division, you might consider adding a toddler collection so that you could also be considered for a position as toddlers' wear designer. In this case, a collection for toddlers *would* be relevant to the target customer for your women's sportswear collections.

Begin to think about the drama you want to create as page turners (discussed later in the section on editing), but the basic concept is to lead the reader through a buildup of mystery or excitement so the reader will *want* to turn the page. A poorly planned layout of silhouettes, mood, color, and textiles adds up to one boring portfolio.

Additional illustration pages can include the following:

+ *Fashion plates* Plan to have an additional one-, two-, or three-page sequence of all 12 to 16 illustrated figures of each collection, showcasing the entire line as one fashion sequence. Many designers trace or use a CAD program to cut and paste duplicates of their illustrated fashion figures to group these figures together. The figures should not be physically cut and pasted together. They need to be seamlessly illustrated in a group fashion on the page(s). The fashion pages are *usually* shown as the last pages of the collection. This illustration layout is very important to show the energy you have created for the consumer surrounding your line and is critical to the interview process. Here is an example of how to show a fashion spread of 12 to 16 figures:

- One page: Show all of the figures on one page, either horizontally or vertically.
- Two pages: Show all of the figures on two pages, vertically. Connect the figures with gestures and/or props, movement, and background so both pages appear as one.
- Three pages: Show all of the figures on three pages, either vertically or horizontally, using a foldout of the polypropylene sheets. Tape the third page to the second page, so that the third page becomes a continuum of the second. Connect the figures with gestures and/or props, movement, and background so all three pages appear as one.

+ *Flats pages* Flat sketches are the final schematic drawings of your silhouettes, which include front and back views. The flats can be completed only after you have finalized your silhouette illustrations. Each flat must reflect the exact silhouette that your stylized illustration suggests. Just as architectural blueprints tell a builder how to construct a building, the designer flats tell the factory how to construct the clothing.

Sufficiently plan where your flats will be placed in your book. Allow space on the silhouette illustration page(s) if you plan to place the flats on those pages. Put a conceptual plan in place for the flats to be shown. Here are some possibilities:

- Show flats on one to four separate flats pages.
- Show flats on the same page as the fashion plates.
- Incorporate the flats on the page(s) with mood, color, or textiles.

While any of these options work for portfolio presentation, it is customary to show very detailed sketches of your flats on separate pages from the mood, color, textile, and silhouette pages. When the flats are on a separate page, the reader can concentrate on evaluating your garment construction talents. Many times, the designer pages of mood, color, textile, and silhouette are best shown in a creative manner, and the flats are shown as detailed sketches for manufacturing. Again, the presentation style is up to the individual designer.

Get Inspired

Review the portfolio presentations in Chapters 4 and 5. Review the inspirational websites and references listed in Appendix C.

You may still be toying with the exact focus of your portfolio collection or assortment of portfolio collections, based upon your personal creative process. As you browse through the collections, visualize furthering your portfolio goals. Make sketches and notes about the goals you would like to achieve. Combine these goals with the idealized portfolio goals you have outlined. There could be an overlapping of ideas from your initial goals.

Question: Why should I research other illustrators for my portfolio? Doesn't that mean I am copying someone else's style?

Answer: No, you won't copy someone else's style. If you do, it would be too easily recognized by a viewer. You can, however, be strongly influenced by an illustrator or layout. The influence can help you know what to design or what not to design. It can reveal to you how to fit your designs on the page using a different style of drawing.

Question: Why would I look at illustrators when I am busy designing a line?

Answer: Viewing other illustrators' work will enhance your silhouette designs as you process how to draw and stylize from another perspective. It should help you to get your design ideas on the page more quickly. The illustration style and style of the layout go hand in hand with the development of the silhouettes. As you are attempting to interpret a trend as a sketch for your portfolio concepts, you may find that switching to a different illustration style in the concept stage may help you express your design style more effectively.

Many designers have an abundance of ideas in their heads but can't get those ideas down on the page before the ideas disappear! By researching illustrators, you can come up with strategies to express your design ideas more effectively. You might not be sure how to show a back view of a design you have, for example, or how to draw a fluffy tulle accent collar. Finding how other designers express their ideas could trigger a technique to get the idea on the page quickly and without hesitation, so you can design more garments, instead of being stuck on how to

draw it. When you interpret the back view or the fluffy tulle accent collar, use the reference drawing as a model for the drawing technique. Don't copy the design.

Question: What details should I consider changing in my illustration style to work better on the page and to enhance my silhouettes?

Answer: Look at different aspects of the page:

▶ How does the illustrator show multiple or single design ensembles on the page? How is the page using positive and/or negative space to tell the story?

▶ How does the illustrator change the style to reach a different audience? For example, does the illustrator show evening wear with one style, and sportswear with a different effect? What did the illustrator change in order to appeal to a different consumer?

▶ Do you want to draw more fluidly, mechanically, controlled, graphically, animated, or realistically than you have in the past? Which illustrators should you research to find this answer?

▶ Look at line quality; view different effects of pen, ink, marker, brush strokes, and so on of different illustrators to find effects to experiment with.

▶ How do you want to express your design ideas? Research illustrators and periods of historic dress to get ideas about media rendering styles you might want to incorporate into your portfolio collection.

▶ How does the illustrator use graphic design details to show the garments or frame the garments on the page?

Implement, Think, and Do

As in the previous segments, research the same exhaustive lists in Appendix B. Apply the retail research and idealized portfolio goals to your silhouette concept work.

Because you have been following FDP methods, you can apply the illustration changes to your work now, in the conceptual stages of developing your silhouettes.

From the observations you made in the "Get Inspired" section, and the Idealized Portfolio Goals, begin to make changes to how you are sketching and illustrating the portfolio collection.

Review your work, and ask these questions about your concepts:

+ *Silhouettes*   Are these designs my personal best for my portfolio?
+ *Illustration style*   Am I going to work in the same illustration style that I have been comfortable with, or am I adding new techniques? Am I planning on developing a new illustration style, and will it communicate my design ideas for the market I am designing for?
+ *Layout styles*   Have I explored layout styles as I developed my silhouettes?
+ *Design focus*   Are my silhouettes relating to one another as a collection? Is my design focus suitable for my customer?

Place Your Visuals in the "Ready" Position for the Next Step

Place all of your collection sketches, illustrations, notes, doodles, and so forth on the designer grid. You can edit the elements at any phase during the process of line building.

All of your concepts for each segment are now laid out on the designer grid. As you view the work, start to eliminate any materials that aren't immediately relevant. There should be a connecting vibe to all four segments that immediately jumps out at you. The design features that you eliminate can always be added back in as you continue through editing and finalization.

Review these checkpoints to follow the FDP methods of self-correcting:

+ Revisit the designer grid in increments of time: 1 hour, 1 day, 2 days, and so on, to play with ideas or massage the creative process. The collection should have a cohesive message in the concept phase.
+ If a cohesive message does not seem clear during the concept phase, it may be the way the design process works for you.
+ If you project that your presentations will come together through editing and finalization, then continue to work through these stages to reach cohesive completion.
+ If you feel your former final portfolio presentations were lacking focus, work through the concept steps more carefully. Go back through the concepts and see how you could best change your work *now*.

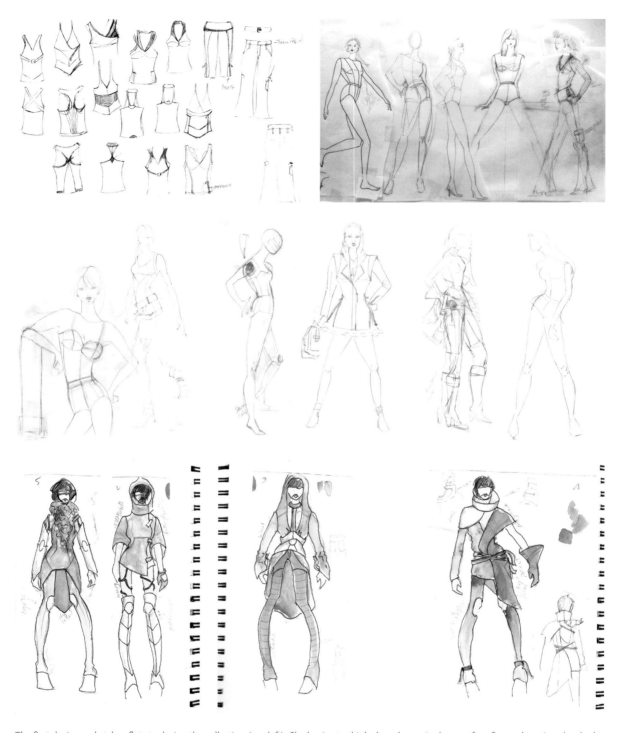

The first designer sketches flats to design the collection (top left). She begins to think about layout in the next four figures by using sketched fashion croquis from her files. She resketches gestures, heads, and attitudes to tell a story of the collection consumer. *(Author's collection)* The second designer begins to broaden her silhouette sketches to fashion figure drawings (bottom row). *(Courtesy of Jenn Webb)*

STEP 2: EDITING

Refer to the box "The Designer Filter" in Chapter 2, which takes the design concepts through an editing process. The process asks you to sift through your ideas to find the best way to communicate them on the page.

Before and during the creation of the portfolio pages for each segment in the editing step, examine how the segments relate to one another. Working with the idealized portfolio goals, retail market information, and layout goals in hand, analyze and evaluate the segments in Step 2 individually and collectively. Determine which conceptual ideas fit best with your portfolio goals. The retail market information influences each editing decision. Layout goals should be considered as you edit your designs. Editing will be to fine-tune the fantasy design collection you put together in the concept phase.

Look at your overall design statement with all four segments laid out on the designer grid. Overview the collection and critique and edit the big picture. Then, go through each segment's edit section to further fine-tune the presentation. Review the big picture with the following list:

- Make a list of the lifestyle activities of your typical consumer. Answer the following questions to evaluate how well your target consumer could wear your garments in the colors, fabrics, and silhouettes that you have envisioned in the fantasy phase of the concept building.
- Visualize a muse or a person that fits the profile of the typical consumer you are targeting.
- If you don't personally know your consumer, speak to or interview the consumer you visualize buying your clothing.
- Add questions to this list that are specific to your consumer.
- Are your garments right for the age group of your consumer?
- Are your garments fantasized in the right shapes for this consumer's typical body type?
- Are your garments appropriately conservative, radical, trendsetting, fun, avant-garde, fashionable, or stylized for your typical consumer?
- Are your silhouettes showing the garments in the right body stances and gestures for your consumer's lifestyle?
- Do your design layout details express a day in the life or your consumer? Look at:
  - Backgrounds
  - Typeface
  - Accessories
  - Hairstyles
  - Gestures
- Will your fabrics, colors, and silhouettes perform for your consumers through most of the activities they enjoy in their lifestyle? Consider the demands such consumer activities as the following will place on their clothing:
  - *Office worker, corporate executive:* Sitting 2–8 hours each day at a desk or cubicle; needing to impress clients; making presentations in meetings; going from the board room to business dinners in casual or four-star restaurants; traveling extensively by plane, train, car, or bus to different markets both domestically and abroad.
  - *Student:* Attending classes full-time or part-time; shuttling between classes, the dorm room, home, and/or work; possibly participating in campus and off-campus life: sports, performance and visual arts, parties in different social spheres.
  - *Mom or dad and family shopping for weekend wear:* Following a flexible schedule for weekend events including sporting events, picnics, barbeques, workouts in and outside of the gym, coaching sports, driving children to events, walking the dog, family dinners, formal or semiformal evening attire for events or dinners in better venues. In addition, moms, dads, and/or families shop for *recreational weekend wear*, which is transitional clothing that can go from brunch to shopping, long walks, lunch, errands, family events, the movies, or out to dinner, and so on.

- *Children*: Evaluate the age group you are designing for and make a list of the specific typical lifestyles.
- *Urban collection consumers*: Fully visualize the urban consumer's typical day and what garments are purchased. Visualize how the garments are worn in a head–to-toe look from hair to makeup, jewelry, nails, belts, hats, footwear, and other accessories. Be sure your garments function for the way the consumer stylizes this head-to-toe look. Can the garments be put on over typical hairstyles or makeup of your consumer? Can the shoes be realistically worn with the garments you have designed? Are the colors right for various skin tones?
- *Participants in action sports*: Consider the athlete's performance needs and how the garments will function through full range of motion. Endurance, wicking, thermal, and waterproof fabrics are just some considerations. Will the recreational athlete or professional athlete be able to perform the sport in your garments without interference from poor fit or impractical silhouettes or embellishments? Speak to athletes who perform the sport you are designing for and build into your garments the proper technical details to enhance movement and performance.
- *Consumers of foundation garments*: Are your fabrics, colors, and silhouettes appropriate for the age group you are targeting? Do the drawings show the technical details that you had in mind for your garments?
- *Consumers of lingerie and sleepwear:* Are your fabrics, colors, and silhouettes appropriate for the age group you are targeting? Can you see your typical consumer wearing these garments?

Whatever your design category, be sure to look at how the garments need to function for the consumer.

GENERAL MATERIALS CHECKLIST FOR STEP 2: EDITING

As you edit the concept, colors, textiles, and silhouettes for each collection in your portfolio, you will need the following materials:

- ✛ Portfolio presentation book.
- ✛ Polypropylene page covers.
- ✛ Presentation pages for your choices of media: marker paper, vellum paper, water color paper, acrylic paper, sketch paper, and/or computer printer paper. The background of the pages can be colorized, treated, texturized, multi-colored, deconstructed, and so on during any steps of development. In addition, the background colors of the pages can be white, black, ecru, or any other color.
- ✛ Specialty papers for layout accents (optional).
- ✛ Bristol board for backing each page in your portfolio so the polypropylene pages won't become crumpled or creased. The Bristol board is sized to fit into the polypropylene sleeves— that is, the same size as your portfolio image pages.
- ✛ Drawing supplies: markers, color pencils, pastels, watercolor paint, acrylic paint, gauche, pencils, oil paint, inks, and CAD programs. Experiment with multiple rendering supplies throughout the process.
- ✛ 2D images you've collected for any or all of the four segments.
- ✛ Rubber cement, spray mount, or double-sided tape.
- ✛ Paper cutter and/or scissors and razor knife.
- ✛ Form-a-Line artists' tape for linear trim (optional).

EDIT THE MOOD PAGES

In addition to the materials listed on page 242, follow this materials checklist for your mood pages:

+ 2D images.
+ 3D trim and accessory treatments may be included on the mood page or within the textiles, silhouette, or flats pages. Accessory and hardware treatments include zipper pulls, snaps, rivets, topstitch treatments, belt buckles, buttons, exposed elastics, draw cords and cord locks, and closure treatments, among other items.
+ Metal and plastic trims that you want to include on the page will need temporary bubble wrap or foam core board placed above the polypropylene sleeve to protect the other pages from the impression or bending of the metal or plastic piece. It can be removed just before an interview. Another display choice is to scan and print trim items in your computer program, so that the 3D trims won't create bumps in your book. Plan to duplicate any surface treatments or 3D effects that cannot fit into the portfolio sleeves by scanning the work in the computer or color copier. Remember any bumps, bulges, or wrinkles in the portfolio sleeves can cause bumps on all of your portfolio pages as the pages stack up on top of one another.

Lay out the first version of your mood page or pages. Determine from these pages whether you will carry some of the images onto the color, textile, and/or silhouette pages.

Determine from the mock layout how you should best put the page together. Consider the following:

+ Use the images in their original form.
+ Resize your images.
+ Recolor, texturize, paint, distort, or reconfigure your images using CAD systems, Photoshop, Illustrator, and cut-and-paste methods. If you don't have access to computer programs, the color and black-and-white copier can reduce, enlarge, use halftones, alter brightness and darkness, and blend the photos that you cut and pasted together into one image.
+ Cut, fray, burnish, tear, wrinkle, paint over, or marker images to suit your goals.
+ Experiment.
+ Try many different versions of the mood layout before finalizing.
+ Use neat, precise, professional cutting and pasting methods for portfolio presentation pages. This practice makes for a professional presentation and increases the longevity of the page. Hastily pasted pictures with curled edges aren't suitable for the final portfolio, nor do these curled images have a long shelf life for future interviews.

Assemble your mood page first; then finish the additional portfolio pages, or develop the mood pages simultaneously with the other segments of your design collection.

In the top photo, the designer begins editing the mood images by trying different layouts on the page. In the photo at left, she has adds the color swatches to the mood page to experiment with combining the mood and color pages as one page. *(Author's collection)* The photo at right is the designer's first edited mood page. *(Courtesy of Jenn Webb)*

EDIT THE COLOR STORY

Consider that color is a possible main reason for an impulse purchase of various products, especially apparel and other fashion-related items. Consider color as a way to package your portfolio from start to finish. Your color choices for your portfolio pages are based upon what works for your design collection. The color choices for backgrounds, borders, typeface, and so on can brand or package your image as a designer. From the color of your portfolio case to the pages in it, and the color choices you make for your résumé, there should be a unified feeling or taste to these choices.

Color Associations with Designers and Brands

Color, through marketing and consumer purchasing, can become synonymous with a designer's product or image. There are specific shades, hues, and tones that have consciously or subconsciously become trademarks with consumers. Examine these aspects of color, and think about the price points that have become associated with these products and how your color choices relate to your consumer's purchasing power. Following are examples of colors that conjure up specific brands, marketing schemes, and certain consumer profiles:

+ Clinical lab white: iPod and Macintosh electronics
+ Pigskin brown: NBA basketballs, NFL footballs, MLB gloves
+ Team colors: NBA, NFL, NHL, MLB, international soccer teams, Olympic team's country pride
+ Hermès saddle brown: luxury leather and apparel products
+ Indigo blues, washed denims: high-end jeans
+ basic unwashed denim: Levi's 501 jeans

+ Avocado green: 1970s home design for kitchen appliances and décor
+ Tattoo ink colors: street or urban attire
+ Woodsy greens, blues, burgundies: Outdoor performance or survival gear
+ Neon colors: Performance sporting apparel and equipment, 1980s runway apparel, Stephen Sprouse's designs, Marc Jacob's remix of neon graffiti, Betsey Johnson's apparel lines, Andy Warhol and Andy Warhol-esque artwork, Peter Max artwork
+ Grey heather: Norma Kamali's sweatshirt collection from the 1980s
+ Primary red tartan plaids: Alexander McQueen's collections
+ Black and white with black leather: Karl Lagerfeld, Chanel
+ Cardboard brown: Bloomingdale's shopping bag and the Bloomingdale's shopping experience
+ Aqua blue: Tiffany products (sometimes this color is referred to as Tiffany blue)
+ Clean brown and ecru: Henri Bendel's unique boutique-like shopping experience
+ Shades of lavender: shopping at Bergdorf Goodman, a high-end shopping experience
+ Basic red and white: Macy's customer, merchandising, and product selection and Target's main marketing colors
+ Primary yellow: Shell gasoline
+ Nautical colors: Ralph Lauren, Nautica, Gant Shirts
+ Cheese orange: Cheez Whiz, Pepperidge Farm Goldfish crackers, Nabisco Cheez-It Crackers

Keep in mind how color can be a driving force of the packaging of your portfolio. Each collection's color story can help brand your merchandise (color in relation to branding is discussed further in Chapter 7).

Consider these branded colors as you pan through your color swatches. Think about hue and degrees of saturation and how your colors might fall into a certain consumer mind set of product taste. For instance, if you are putting together a "preppy" collection, look closely at the color red that you select. Is it too team-driven? Does it look like a color for a Major League Baseball team? If you are looking to up your preppy look with a trend toward team sports, then this red works well as a choice. If not, research preppy color palettes, and determine which shade of red will be the next trendsetting color for your collection.

Create a group of colors that best supports your mood, textiles, patterns, and silhouettes. At the same time, your color palette should set a *direction* for the market you are designing for. The market will be for 1 year or 18 months from now, so consider how appropriate it will be for the season. Think of the anticipated consumer need for the themes you are generating. Anticipate the consumer need for the particular shades, hue, and saturation of each color within the color palette.

The potential interviewer will read your color palette for originality, market savviness, and color selections that relate to one another and to the consumers' need.

As you arrange the colors on the board, experiment by moving colors from group to group. Switch colors that aren't working. Anticipate the inspiration your colors will create for your client and in-store presentation of your collection in a year. Reject or add colors that need to be tweaked. Evaluate your colors multiple times to establish the proper balance of hue, value, and saturation as they relate to your garment, textile, and mood statement.

Materials Checklist for Color Pages

The following materials checklist relates specifically to your color pages:

+ 2D samples: cuts from paper, printed computer colors, cutouts from magazines, paint chips from the hardware store, wallpaper books, and other sources that you can repurpose.

+ Renderings of swatches in paint, magic marker, ink, pastel, and other media.
+ Specialty papers from craft stores cut into color or pattern tabs.
+ 3D samples, including but not limited to yarns, fabric swatches, fibers, embroidery threads, and vintage clothing swatches.
+ Even though this page(s) is for a color statement, you have choices as to the background color of your page—white, black, or any color—and the page can be weathered or distressed and/or have mood images as the background (preferably halftones or quartertones of the original images—any stronger tones could clash with your color swatches). Strongly consider and play with color choices as the background of your color page by laying out the colors on top of the choice(s). If the background reads stronger than the color statement, you've done a disservice to all of your color research. This is too distracting to the reader.
+ Pantone Reference Book or Web Reference, or a universal color system, such as SCOTDIC or Munsell.

As you are going through the editing process, or when the editing is complete, prepare the yarns, swatches, and paint chips to be mounted on the boards. If you have ten colors and are editing to five, this is a good time to formally mount the colors. Stepping back and looking at the colors as they are mounted can help you edit the colors.

Color Identification and Matching

As you formulate your color palette, you have an option to do any of the following:

+ Name your colors, and label the colors with names in your portfolio.
+ Match your colors to a universal color system (such as Pantone), and label the color numbers in your portfolio.
+ Show your color swatches matched up to a universal color system (such as Pantone) by mounting the Pantone color references next to your initial color swatches. You can use the tabs from the Pantone book, use computer printouts of color tabs, or order fabric swatches from Pantone to show a larger swatch of the color.

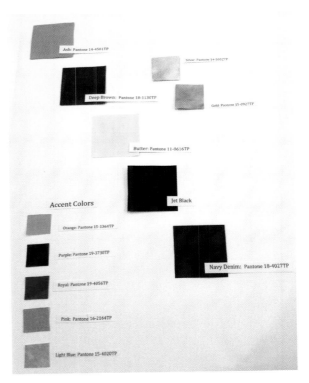

In the top photo, the designer matches the colors to the Pantone color book and labels the colors with the Pantone reference numbers. She uses simple names for the colors so a buyer can visualize the color when placing an order from the name of the color. The bottom photo shows the designer's editing of the mood and color images as she begins to develop two pages in a portfolio book that will be facing one another. *(Author's collection)*

Naming the colors yourself is one way of "romancing" the colors for the viewer. Color names can be fun, entertaining, somber, or telling, but most of all, they can be a professional way to tell your color story. The names chosen can be pulled from your inspirational research. The color name should be one or two words. The color name should not confuse the reader. It should conjure up a visual sense of the color. For instance, if you name a shade of gray "Cement," it should be relatively close to the shade of cement. The reference to cement should be part of the overall theme. If you are creating a back-to-nature mood, then "cement" certainly won't be the right color name; "thunder" might be more appropriate. The color name "cement" would be better married to an urban or utilitarian-bent collection.

Showing the Pantone reference color numbers and/or Pantone color swatches is another option. You can show these on the same page with your color story or on a separate page. It is not necessary to show Pantone samples; however, posting the Pantone reference numbers demonstrates your understanding of the manufacturing process.

Once you're employed, the company or designer whom you work for will have its fabrics dyed to match the Pantone color swatches or other universal color system that your company uses each season. This helps the manufacturing process move more efficiently than asking a dye house to match a random swatch of color. The Pantone (or other universal color system that your company works with) number comes with a formula for the dye house to match the color on the selected fibers. The process is similar to mixing paint to match a paint chip in the hardware store. This method helps ensure that your wool sweater designs being manufactured in China will match your linen jacket designs being made in Turkey. Both factories will receive the color information from the universal color system about the amount of dyestuffs they should use to achieve a match to your color in the chosen fibers.

Assemble and finish your color board now or when your creative process is best sequenced. Review the relationship of the colors to each segment on the designer grid. As with the mood concepts, try mocking up different versions of the color board before completing your presentation.

EDIT THE TEXTILE SELECTIONS

Editing the textile pages can be a daunting task. Many designers want to use many different fabrics for one collection.

Manufacturing Constraints on Textile Selection

Designers need to consider the manufacturing limitations and projected market placement of the product.

+ For basic ready-to-wear designed for distribution in common retail channels, the fabric selections need to meet minimum yardage requirements. The goods must be cut and sewn to achieve an acceptable profit margin. Too many fabrics planned for tiny inserts of garments won't meet manufacturing minimums. The collection statement will seem scattered and poorly planned. In the real world of the industry, the designer will have help from the merchandiser and raw materials manager in culling the fabric choices to best meet these manufacturing needs and still keep the designer's vision strong and salable.

+ Dye lots are considered during this process. Each color chosen for each textile may need to meet a substantial yardage minimum. The designer will have to consider this requirement. The textile and color choices go hand in hand with the reality of constructing the designs.

+ For smaller companies, haute couture, and better designer markets, the price points of the textile choices are crucial. The better the designer label, the more leeway the designer may have to choose luxurious and/or expensive fabrics. Some of the better textile houses may have smaller yardage and dye lot minimums, as they cater to the luxury market. They may charge a premium for smaller yardages of goods, which the high-end designer houses may be able to support. For small start-up companies, these choices can make or break the launch of a line and may hinder or halt the longevity of the product line.

You have identified your market distribution channel for your design collection. With this in mind, carefully edit your textile choices to meet the real-world expectations of cut-and-sew yardage minimums for your market. In general terms, plan realistically. Plan to illustrate your collection using the fabrics in multiple garments that relate to one another on the page from a design perspective. As you edit the fabrics, plan the silhouettes to meet realistic yardage usages. Too many fabrics shown in one collection can indicate a complete lack of direction.

Marketing Considerations in Editing the Textile Pages

Plan how your customer will be buying your separate pieces from your collection. The consumer will want to buy separates in the same fabric to mix and match outfits to work with one another.

In the concept phase, you fantasized about the fabrics you wanted to work with. In the editing phase, your task is to narrow your fabric selections. A realistic approach comes into play. Edit the collection by evaluating your decisions based upon:

+ Retail shopping information
+ Trend information
+ Your ability to render the textiles in stylized illustrations

Reference the questions posed in the textiles/concept segment. Dig deeper into the questions as though you are about to have your portfolio collection produced for the retail market. Make the decision to eliminate fabric so the garments can be manufactured. Your illustration goals should include showing that your creativity and imagination have the capability to turn your designs into a reality.

As you edit your textiles, consider the following:

+ The manufacturing process and minimum yardage usages for each fabric. Plan to use the fabric in enough silhouettes in your design collection.
+ The taste of your consumer. What fabric blends will sell in your market?
+ The price per yard of the fabrics you are presenting. If you are showing swatches of very expensive fabrics for a moderate-priced line, be prepared to explain (when asked) in an interview that you plan to have the manufacturer weave or knit a "takedown" version of the expensive fabrics in a less expensive fiber(s) or fiber blend(s).

As you place your fabrics on the designer grid, visualize the fabric for each silhouette. If there aren't enough silhouettes or cut parts to support the use of the fabric for your market, then eliminate some of the swatches. In addition:

+ Evaluate the fashion-forward strength of your fabric choices.
+ Look carefully at the fabrics to achieve the proper balance of textures, weight of the goods, and end-use performance abilities of each fabric.
+ Look at the balance of heavy-weighted fabrics to lightweight fabrics. How they are used within one garment? Can you realistically construct a garment using these fabrics together in one garment? Can you realistically balance the lighter weight fabric on the body when worn with the heavier weight fabric?
+ Consider how your customer would wear this fabric.
+ Is your customer going to be comfortable in this fabric, and can it perform in the environment where it will be worn? Think of the end uses your customer has for these garments. Put yourself into the shoes of your ultimate consumer, and think about how these fabrics have to perform. Your consumers have a lifestyle, and the fabrics need to work well for their needs. For instance, in bridge lines for business wear, is the fabric too thick or heavy to wear in the office all day? Is it comfortable enough for the consumer to sit in a meeting, travel on a plane, pack in a suitcase, go from the boardroom to a dinner? For sportswear and recreational attire, ask yourself, "Are these fabrics wash-and-wear? Can the consumer get in and out of a car with these fabrics? Can the consumer look stylish yet function in these fabrics? Will the fabric "give" enough for everyday activities?"

- Use dry-clean-only fabrics for a consumer market that supports these fabrics. Many consumer bases in the moderate to budget market will not purchase garments that need to be dry cleaned, as dry cleaning is expensive and not a possibility for these consumers.

Mock up the fabric layout in different ways before deciding on the final version.

Materials Checklist for the Textile Pages

In addition to the general materials checklist, have the following at hand for editing your textile pages:

- Fabric swatches. If you don't have this on hand, check the Internet for companies that will send you swatch samplers (for no cost, or a minimal fee) to enhance your presentation. If you don't have access to wholesale or industry-level fabric stores, use the Internet for fabric swatches.
- Mock-up painted or rendered fabric swatches if you don't have the actual fabric swatch in hand
- Scotch Magic Tape, a ruler/straightedge, pen.

The designer uses a fabric print as the background of the page. She decides to show mood and silhouette trend images to demonstrate the plan for the function of the fabrics on the body and on the end-consumer. *(Author's collection)*

Lay out the swatches for portfolio presentation. Keep the layout boards ready for further editing through the silhouette, flats, and summary portions of the editing process.

As explained in the concept segment, you have an option of including your textile swatches on your mood pages, color pages, and/or silhouette pages. Play with the textile swatches in mock layouts. Place the swatches in different configurations on the textile pages. Place the swatches in mock layouts on the color and mood boards. Cut the smaller versions of textile swatches, and view how they work with your illustrations. You may opt to show the larger textile swatches on the textile pages and the smaller swatches on the illustration pages with the silhouettes.

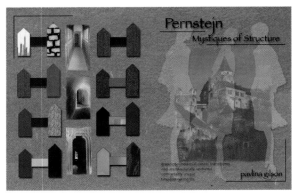

Examples of two final fabric presentation pages in a designer's portfolio. The top photo shows the mood, fashion illustration, flats, fabric swatches, and flats with the fabric and color added. The designer hand-drew the fashion illustration and drew the flats in Illustrator. She scanned in the fabric textures and made "swatches" with an added shadow effect to make the swatches look like they were pasted to the page. She used pattern fill for the figure and colored flats from the actual fabric swatch in Photoshop. She manipulated the mood image to a halftone or washed-out version of the original image to use as a background for the entire board. In the bottom photo, the designer drew little towers for her fabric swatches which were taken from her design theme/architectural castle structures. She scanned in the actual fabric and pasted it into the tower shapes in Photoshop. She used Photoshop for the background images as well. *(Courtesy of Pavlina Gilson)*

EDIT SILHOUETTES AND FLATS

The silhouettes and flats in your presentation may be in the rough form, semi-completed, or fully rendered and completed. It is, again, different for each designer as he or she works through the creative process. As you are editing the collection illustrations, look at how you are proceeding to attain your portfolio goal. Check the overall presentation:

+ Are historic references applied to the illustrations?
+ Are illustration style goals beginning to actualize?
+ Are layout style goals planned and beginning to take shape on the page?

Consider the overall line presence your collection will have at retail:

+ Did you apply your retail market reports to your work?
+ Does your line follow through for a focused distribution channel?
+ Are the silhouettes calling out to a targeted consumer?
+ Are the ideas trendsetting or yesterday's news for your market?

Review the overall format of the collection(s):

+ Do your ideas work with the "do the math" plan?
+ Do you have multiple design collections or just one?
+ Do you have a plan for a multi-figure spread?
+ Do you have a page-turning drama in mind to lay out here in the editing process?
+ Do you have a plan in mind for the flats presentation?

LINK THE SEGMENTS

Editing the silhouettes and flats segment will naturally lead to linking the segments of mood, color, and textiles to the silhouettes. Review your transparency overlay to help you develop an idealized version of your portfolio as you are finishing this last step of editing and reworking your silhouettes and flats.

At any step during the concept and editing process, you may have laid out only one segment on your designer grid to work on, or you may be working on all four segments at once.

With the design silhouettes and/or flats in front of you, edit the collection to relate items that work well together on one body. Look at the relationship of the outfits to one another, and make decisions as to which outfits would be best shown on the page grouped with another figure. Specifically, consider the following:

+ Think about which figure poses best show the silhouettes' details. Should the back view be featured, or the front, three-quarter, or side view?
+ How do each figure pose and each outfit work best on the page? Should any of the figures be shown as single figures on the page with flats, mood, and color swatches? Should all of the figures be shown in groups of two or three, or should each page be a different configuration?
+ Are you repeating a figure pose? Are you mirroring a figure pose?
+ Can the concepts be superimposed onto the background or graphic touches be added to the page to enhance the presentation?
+ Can background color be infused either manually, with color paper, or with a CAD program to help boost the page's presentation?
+ Should the concept/mood pages be the only place for mood images to be presented in this (these) collection(s)?
+ Is the mood image page compatible with the mood of your shapes and garment details?

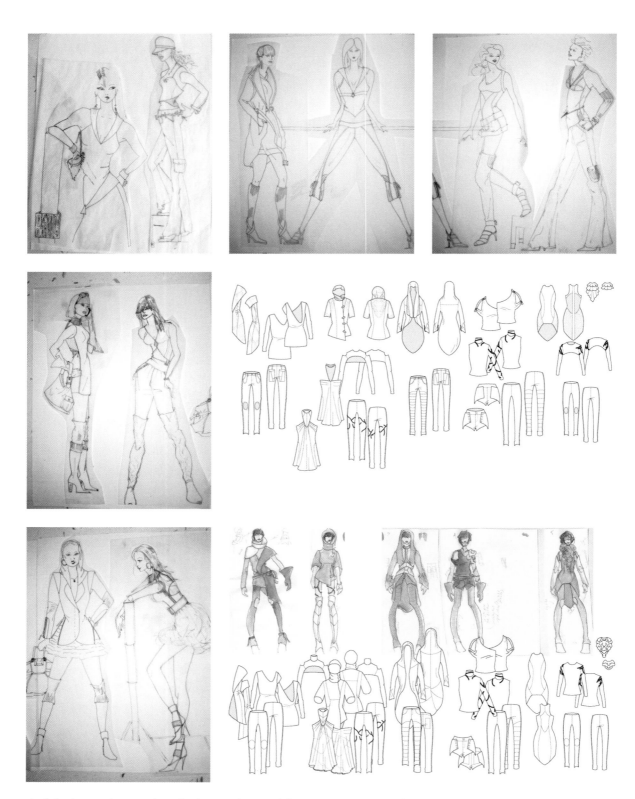

The fleft column and top row shows the designer's layout and illustration planning as she finalizes her silhouettes. She uses a cut-and-paste croquis method to reposition the figures on the page. She balances the outfit collections on the bodies in the poses on the page for overall presentation of the collection's attitude. *(Author's collection)* In the photos on the right, the designer shows her flats development for the editing step. *(Courtesy of Jenn Webb)*

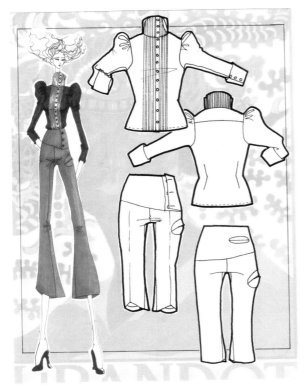

The designer planned his elongated fashion figures to be interacting on each pair of facing pages throughout the collection. The uniform poses (with slight variations of gestures) and the hair and soft border detail help to pull the eye to the clothing on the page. On the flats page, the designer used a soft tone of the mood images as a background "wash" for overall mood setting. The flats are the main focus of the page, and the fashion illustration reinforces the silhouette. *(Courtesy of David Bermingham)*

- Are you rendering color and textiles to match your color references properly? Did you render tones of color that accurately match your color projections? Are your rendered colors consistent from garment to garment and page to page?

- Are the textile surface effects exaggerated, subdued, or realistic, and do they give your collection the attitude of the consumer and garment shapes?

- Are your colors working well together in the outfits you've planned, and do they flow from the first figure through the final figure in the collection?

- Are your textiles represented in swatch form and/or rendered in swatch form?

- Do you want textile swatches on each page to reinforce your ideas?

- Are you rendering textiles as the fabrics would work on the body?

- Are your figures holding the garments on the body the right way, and do they best show the details of the garments?

- Are your garment shapes on the body the right proportions to your design thoughts?

- Do the flats match your garment proportions and details? For your designs to be credible, the flats need to provide exact specs for achieving the look of the garments as shown on the bodies in your silhouettes. Scale, proportion, shape, seaming, darts, stitching details, hardware, and so on need to function and be able to be manufactured or sewn.

- Do you visualize your garments functioning on a hanger on a retail selling floor? If the garment can't be shown on a hanger, it can't sell (unless you are an haute couture designer).

- Do the garments function on the body for the end use you have designated them for?

- Have you drawn the seams, seam stitching details, darts, hardware, and silhouettes accurately on the body and on the flats?

- Do the textiles and their surface treatments move on the body as they would in real life?

Lady Fabergé is the fusion of exaggerated silhouettes, embellished details, and elegance. Lady Fabergé embodies the grandiose and opulence of the Fabergé Imperial eggs and embraces the classic feminine figure.

Here is an excellent example of mood images telling a story that is followed through in detail with the designer's collection. *(Courtesy of Jane Henry)*

- Are your figures interacting and inviting the viewer onto the page?
- Does the flow of your pages tell a story?
- Do your layouts show a good use of negative and positive space within each page? Do facing pages naturally connect and flow?
- How have you used static and/or action poses? Do you need to add, subtract, or change any figures within the page?
- Do you have a consistent graphic message to your work?
- Are the pages clean and neat? Are the flats clean and neat?
- Is your collection message coming through on the page as you step back and look at the collection?

LAYOUT CHECKLIST

Consider the following points as you lay out your mood, color, textile, and silhouette pages:

- Plan for a title page (optional).
- Layout of a sequence of pages for a dramatic and effective presentation.
- Layout of the sequence of collections you are showing in your book.

IMPLEMENT, THINK, AND DO

Place all of the pages of each collection into the polypropylene sleeves and insert the pages into the binder of your portfolio in the sequence you have planned.

Step back and evaluate your goals and critique your work, and make all of the further changes you deem necessary. Seek advice from your trusted sources to help with the critique if necessary.

Reference your evaluations of your professional goals for rendering and drawing. Within your evaluations from previous chapters, you were challenged to realize your personal best balanced with a realistic time frame for completing your work. Don't make too many changes that will make any portion of the presentation look contrived or overworked. The book should look "in the moment" and have a somewhat spontaneous flow to the page presentations.

Edit your styles and presentations now to show your garments in the best light. You can make revisions directly on the original pages of your collection. If you have time to mock up the changes on separate pages, put the revisions next to the original pages. Critique your work and evaluate which version(s) would best tell your story.

Rearrange the sequencing of the pages. Compare and contrast the sequences to determine which story best represents your work to the prospective interviewer.

In Step 3, you will completely refine and complete your portfolio statement. Review the two completed portfolio projects outlined in this chapter in the figures on pages 258–260.

Above and on page 259, the designer's combined color and mood two-page layout, textile page, and layout of a ten-figure page presentation for a misses contemporary portfolio collection. [Author's collection]

The designer's final portfolio presentation of her avant-garde runway thesis collection. She told her story from beginning to end with the mood page, (top left) the thesis statement with five figures, (top center) and separate fashion plates for each outfit (top right and center and bottom). She chose one outfit per page as her presentation format and included a fashion illustration, color, fabric, flats, and her runway models on each page. This is the first collection she shows in her portfolio. She feels it is the strongest collection and represents her as a designer. She starts her portfolio with a cover page with her name and info on a photo with rusted metal. The next page shows the mood board, and the intro page faces it. She shows four collections in her portfolio. She switches the second two collections in and out of her portfolio depending on who is interviewing her. They are more general sportswear portfolios and are smaller presentations of two collections. Her last collection is a strong collection for Liz Claiborne sportswear. *(Courtesy of Jenn Webb)*

STEP 3: FINALIZING AND COMMITTING

In Step 3, refine the final statement of each collection you chose to show in your portfolio. You will link the four segments of mood, color, textiles, and silhouettes in one fluid review.

As you assemble the portfolio with the final refining touches, remember your portfolio presentation can change as needed. You can add, subtract, and/or revise your portfolio before each interview you go on. Evaluating your portfolio before every interview is highly advised, even if you don't anticipate needing any changes. Before every interview, sit down and view your portfolio as if you were the interviewer. Peer into your work as if you were the person doing the hiring. What makes your portfolio stand out to *you*? Perhaps these self-observations can be used in an interview when the interviewer asks you "why should we hire you for this position?"

Following are some discoveries you want interviewers to make when they look at your work:

+ You really know the market you're designing for.
+ You did your research thoroughly.
+ You are up to the minute with current trends and how they should be interpreted for the given market.
+ You are a devoted and hard worker (the focus is shown in the rendered finished page).
+ You are open to new ideas and concepts.
+ You have sound technical knowledge.
+ You can communicate your ideas intelligently in your visuals without a lot of verbal explanation.
+ You are innovative in your approach to design.
+ You have a strong sense of color.
+ You have a strong sense of textiles and /or surface effects.
+ You are a strong designer of garment shapes.

IMPLEMENT, THINK, AND DO

Lay out your portfolio collection in the sequence you have decided upon. Review the multiple collections you are showing for their overall effect. Is there a link or natural segue between collections?

Be sure the mood pages have their respective feelings as separate entities. Each mood board for each collection should have an individual layout and evoke a completely different feeling for a new collection theme. If the collections are specific to one consumer base or distribution channel, be sure each collection can stand on its own and not demonstrate a boring redundancy. If there is too much repetition from collection to collection, you will appear to be incapable of creating prolifically from season to season.

Review your color presentations of each collection. Keep your color presentations to five to seven colors for a collection, with additional accent colors for piping or trim color details, prints, hardware, and graphic placements on the garments. As in the mood presentations, use a sharp eye to remove any extraneous colors or redundant statements. If you color statement appears weak or needs to be perked up with accent colors, add the colors to your presentation pages. Add the accent colors, if necessary, to the garment illustrations.

Review the textile presentations of each collection. Be sure the number of fabrics you are showing is realistic for the manufacturing of the collection. Make revisions as possible within your time constraints. It might be a project for after your interview if you don't have time to finish all of your changes.

Within the time limits, if there are new changes you can make by scanning in and perfecting your work in a CAD system, make those changes now.

Review the layouts of your illustrations in relation to the mood, color, and textile statements. Review the need to add or subtract color tabs, fabric swatches, or mood references to the silhouette pages. You can also assess whether the color, fabric, or mood pages could use references from any of these segments to better link the collection storyboards together.

There can be distinct differences in the illustration styles from collection to collection if this is your forte. Some designers like to show their drawing diversity, or their different markets or ages of target consumers from collection to collection. This can be effective if the overall feeling of the book is naturally interesting and builds upon your strengths from start to finish.

Review the sequencing for how you are telling your story. Are you

+ Opening with a bang, closing with a bang, and linking all items in between the beginning and the end?
+ Opening slowly, building up to your best work?
+ Opening with your best work, and winding down to your less interesting work?
+ Remaining steady and constant throughout?

Review your layout touches on the page. If borders are overpowering, or if you need to add in borders to the page, make the changes now. Look through your pages and touch up any smudges of color, erase leftover pencil lines, and reprint any bent or wrinkled pages from a CAD program. Smooth any pasted photos, colors, or textile swatches that aren't affixed perfectly flat on the page. Trim any hanging threads. Recut any pages that aren't fitting into the polypropylene sleeves properly. The page margins should line up neatly with the edges of the polypropylene sleeves.

Your portfolio is now ready to represent you as a designer if you've followed the steps of the concept, edit, and final evaluation process.

BUILDING ON THE PORTFOLIO PROJECT

OBJECTIVES

+ Build on the Portfolio Project collection to adapt your portfolio to job interviews and other presentations.

+ Establish that your idealized portfolio goals were actualized in the Portfolio Project.

+ Refine the layout details.

+ Develop page turners for the completed Portfolio Project collection.

+ Finalize sequencing for the Portfolio Project collection.

+ Develop branding packaging options.

+ Review additional inclusions from past collections.

+ Keep fluid through portfolio building, now and as a lifetime task.

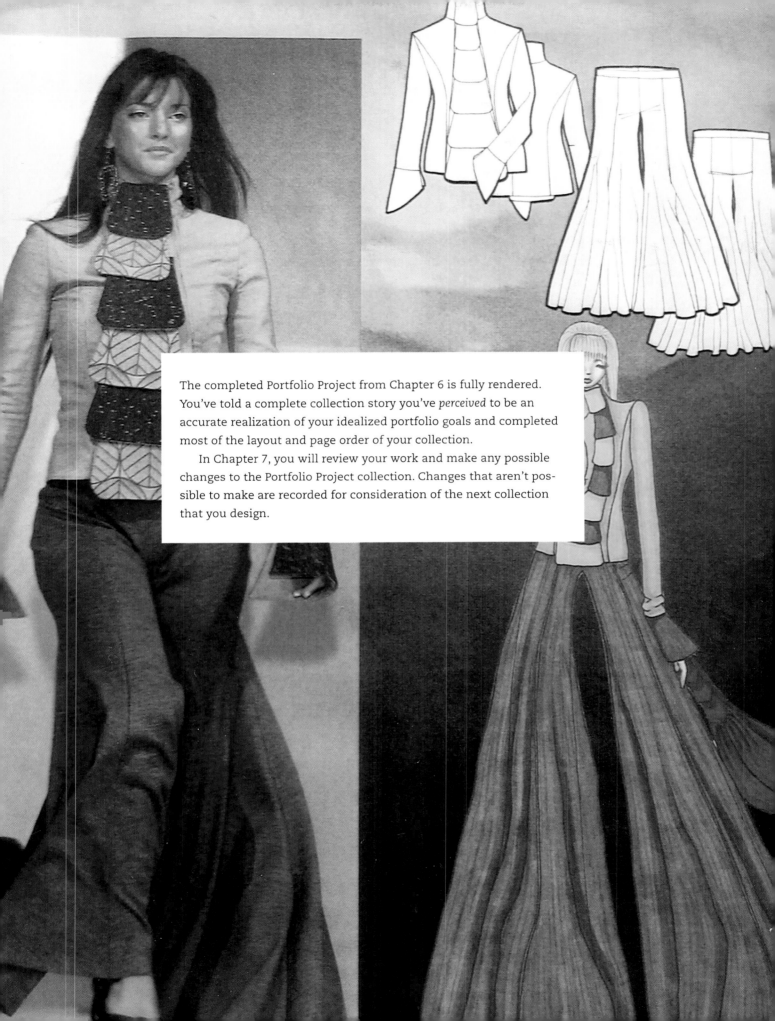

The completed Portfolio Project from Chapter 6 is fully rendered. You've told a complete collection story you've *perceived* to be an accurate realization of your idealized portfolio goals and completed most of the layout and page order of your collection.

In Chapter 7, you will review your work and make any possible changes to the Portfolio Project collection. Changes that aren't possible to make are recorded for consideration of the next collection that you design.

REVIEW OF IDEALIZED PORTFOLIO GOALS

See Exercise 7.1. The conclusions from your review can be used to refine the current portfolio collection(s). Alternately, make observations from this exercise, and make changes on your future collections. Changes for future collections are discussed in detail later in the chapter.

Re-review your final layout. Can you add more details, or do you need to take some details out? Check the layout of each page and the story that the collection tells from start to finish. Make changes to your layout details to enhance the story. Self-critique the details in the finalization process, and/or ask a colleague to critique with you.

Typical enhancements that you can make include the following:

+ Use background page colors that set a stage for your work.
+ Add "shadows" of gray or a light wash to the silhouettes.
+ Check the layout of silhouettes on the page for spacing, balance, and flow. Make appropriate changes by adding silhouettes to the page or completely replanning the page with a better presentation.

+ Check your texture renderings; add or emphasize texture details to the renderings.
+ Check your line quality of the illustrations: add, subtract, or emphasize silhouette details with bolder strokes. Erase or re-render over-emphasized details.
+ Check faces and hairstyles for changes that might be needed. The faces or hairstyles shouldn't overshadow your apparel design statement. Add details, erase, or re-render overemphasized details.
+ Add any accessories that might appeal to your customer.
+ Finesse your finishing touches with border details using hand-rendering, CAD printout, or prepackaged graphic artists' line tape.
+ As options, add logo designs, hangtags, or packaging suggestions.

OBJECTIVE: Based upon your work style, how far along you are in completing your portfolio project, and what collections within your book you choose to apply this exercise to:

▶ Become more capable of realizing an objective point of view in a self-critique.
▶ Establish whether the idealized portfolio goals were actualized.
▶ Make changes to the current portfolio project and/or peripheral collections.
▶ Establish changes you will make in the future for furthering the idealized portfolio goals.

Materials

▶ Portfolio Project collection in the polypropylene sleeves
▶ Portfolio
▶ Peripheral collections to be reviewed if completed
▶ Completed Exercise 3.3, "Idealize the Final Portfolio"
▶ Completed Exercise 3.1, "Decide on Your Portfolio Design Direction"
▶ Notebook, paper, pencil or pen, sketchbook

Assignment

1. Lay out the Portfolio Project pages flat on a desk for review by taking them out of the portfolio.
2. Lay out the peripheral collections to be reviewed individually or as a continual story (your choice).
3. Go through your initial responses to Exercise 3.3, "Idealize the Final Portfolio." Evaluate your final portfolio to decide whether it represents what you perceived it to be.
4. Write down your new observations.
5. Write down any new goals you may have.
6. Make changes to the portfolio, or use the new observations and new goals for your next design collection.
7. Review Exercise 3.1, "Decide on Your Portfolio Design Direction."
8. Observe and critique how your portfolio collection meets the consumer's taste, price range, distribution channels, and age group projections that you established.

9. Write the answers; take notes about ways to improve for your next collection.
10. Make changes to your current Portfolio Project.

The opening pages to the designer's portfolio collection. This title page showcases her fabrics and mood. She created a patchwork quilt with precision cut fabric swatches. She briefly states her story in two sentences, as required for her senior class project. One image reflects her mood on a background of green shades which became the final backdrop of each of the fashion plates for this collection. View her work in Steps 1 through 6 to see how she arrived at the final illustrated fashion plates and multi-figure fashion plates.

Step 1: Three pages of journal rough sketches from the concept stage of developing the collection. The journal sketches are a precursor to the design of the portfolio pages. She works through the illustrations and page layout simultaneously with the construction of her garments for her senior fashion show.

Step 2: Two pages of first final sketches of the fashion plates. The illustrations help her visualize and make construction changes to the collection.

Step 3: One page of final sketches for the fashion plates. She will work through many different background and layout ideas before arriving at her final layout.

Step 4: Two pages of fashion plates of the final portfolio. She used Illustrator and Photoshop to create the page with a background of hombre greens, the flats, the illustration, and a photo from her final runway presentation.

Step 5: Two pages of the "first final layout" of the multi-figure collection page. She worked on creating a balanced layout of mood and texture as a background for the illustrations, multi-figures, and flats.

Step 6: Two pages of the "final layout" of the multi-figure collection page. The designer changed the page to be cleaner and more streamlined to highlight the details of her illustrations and the flats. The hombre green background remained a constant for each fashion plate in the group. (*Courtesy of Rebecca Sheehan*)

OBJECTIVE: To assemble your portfolio pages in a logical sequence that shows an interviewer what your strengths are as a designer and your design focus.

You can sometimes have time to change the portfolio sequencing or number of collections or add a new collection specifically for an interview. Other times, your book should be ready and waiting to show to an interviewer at a moment's notice. For basic, on-the-fly interviews, your portfolio should always be ready to go, prepared as follows:

1. The Portfolio Project should be the first collection shown in your book.
2. Decide which peripheral collections will be in your portfolio case.
3. Decide the sequencing of the peripheral collections.

As you schedule specific interviews, consider the viewer. For each interview, you can change any of the collections or any number of collections you will be showing. The ultimate outcome of presenting your work is to sell your suitability for the position to the interviewer.

Time permitting, add a design collection if you have an interview in a category of design that you haven't represented in your book.

Materials

▶ The Portfolio Project collection
▶ Artwork: Logos, hangtags, packaging, hardware, in-store design concepts
▶ In-class collection illustrations
▶ Past work from former jobs, if applicable
▶ Student fashion show photographs
▶ Press coverage: Internet, newspaper, and periodical clippings, if applicable
▶ Awards: photos or illustrations of collections, if applicable

Length

Consider the length of the interview.

Breadth

Consider approximately how many pages you want to show during the interview.

Balance

Consider the balance of:
▶ Hand-rendered work
▶ Computer-driven images
▶ Hand-rendered work combined with computer-driven images
▶ Combinations of mixed media for interest

Approximately 75–90 percent of your portfolio illustrations (not including the mood pages, the color pages, or the textile pages) should be illustrated fashion plates, and 10–25 percent of the portfolio can be flats drawings. This equation can be balanced by your illustration/presentation style. Some designers are very strong in flats drawings, and they can balance their flats to fashion illustration plates to a 50–50 ratio.

Focus

The focus of each collection should be defined and clearly obvious to the interviewer.

Linking

Link the pages within each collection, defined by a unifying layout method.

Storytelling Styles: Sequencing the Pages within the Collection

Adjust the order of each collection, considering the same segments and steps that you followed for the Portfolio Project. Sequence the pages for additional collections, taking into account the storytelling styles described in Chapter 6 on page 263 and on page 282.

Opening

Consider the options for the opening pages of the portfolio described on pages 282–283. Decide whether to open with a blank page or to have a cover image page, whether to include a copy of your résumé and/or business card, and whether to include a logo page. For each additional collection presented in your portfolio, make the decisions about opening page and logo page. Of course, you would not include your résumé and/or business card at the beginning of any pages for additional collections. Weigh the pros and cons on pages 282–285 to help you make your final decisions.

EXPLORING BRANDING AND LOGOS ON THE PORTFOLIO PAGE

A trend today in marketing and design is branding oneself, one's design collection, or the marketing of a design collection. Whether we as designers agree with this trend or not, it is a definite part of our culture and influences the way we approach design and the way we approach packaging our designs on the page for our portfolio. Depending on your market direction, you can package your styles with a brand or logo message. We are passively reading or viewing packaging and/or branding of any salable item in today's market. Whether it is the plain green or generically packaged merchandise at a store, or a simple Internet home page, each item has an identifiable look or branding stamp to it. Some examples are in the list that follows. Try to imagine whether you could identify whom or to what company these brands belonged if the name of the brand were stripped from view. With today's marketing and packaging standards, if you didn't see the product name, you would most likely be able to identify the brands that follow:

+ Google, Yahoo!, or AOL's home page. Each of these companies has decided on a look for its page and carries it through to appeal to their its consumer.
+ Mac or Apple products.
+ Chanel, Louis Vuitton, Christian Dior, Gucci, Burberry, Tommy Hilfiger, Victoria's Secret, Pink, Juicy Couture, and/or The Gap merchandise. If you saw their merchandise in a blind study (wherein you wouldn't know who the designer was), you most likely would know exactly which company or designer they belonged to without seeing the logo or inside

label. Similarly, if you saw their marketing ad campaigns without their designer name on the page, you could guess which designer they belonged to. If we had access to their designer's portfolios, we could most likely take an educated guess as to which fashion plates belonged to which brand.

Another way of visualizing branding and how it can change your approach to your portfolio layout or collection designs is to think of your favorite performing artist. He or she may have a signature look that has developed, evolved, or been deliberately planned. Visualize the following artists, and you can easily imagine, in your designer's eye, the portfolio collection you would design for their branded image. You can apply this signature approach to how you visualize your customer and eventually design the portfolio page:

+ Paul McCartney
+ Madonna
+ Michael Jackson
+ Victoria Beckham
+ Steven Tyler
+ Beyoncé

BRANDING YOUR PORTFOLIO

Your portfolio can take a decided branding point of view to your presentation. Each of the series of collections in your book can have one particular way of showing your merchandise that makes it identifiable to you. Or each collection can have a different approach to the page. Techniques to brand a collection or presentation can be any one or combination of the elements listed below. Some designers have a very strong point of view, and these elements become strongly obvious on the illustrated page as their branded signature and are consistent through each page in the portfolio:

+ Your signature illustration style
+ Your signature layout style
+ Your approach to shapes, cut, or dimensions of the garments themselves
+ Your approach to color or pattern
+ Your approach to choosing particular types of textiles
+ Your logo: the design of the logo, the shape of the logo, the subliminal suggestion the shape of the logo may take on, the color of the logo, the placement on the garment, the placement of the logo throughout the illustrated page, and so on
+ A company or designer logo you are designing for currently, or for a particular interview, showing your grasp of the company or designer's brand

The trend and these elements can then be translated on a sliding scale:

+ Merchandise and portfolio pages that have a full, all-out, in-your-face branded stamp
+ A less obvious approach to the merchandise and the page with suggestions of some of the elements listed above
+ Quiet or subtlety applied elements

You might add pages to your portfolio to display drawing of packaging designs and/or extraneous logo-driven items:

+ A schematic drawing and color layout of clothing labels for inside or outside of the garment
+ Plastic, paper, cardboard hangtags for the garments or accessories
+ Signature hardware closures that may or may not have an embossed surface logo, but have a brand image to their quality or shape (rivets, snaps, buttons, and so on)

Above and page 275: An example of a designer's signature illustration style that is easily identified as his. The first multi-figure fashion plate is for a CFDA Educational Initiatives competition. He added a title to the collection, Ghosts, and a logo on the bottom right corner. His illustration style for his sketch plates is similar to the Ghost collection style and carries through both men's and women's collections. The sketches in his sketchbook have the same illustrative style, and his flats are detailed with a stylized flair. Each of these examples has the designer's look stamped on it, whether it be planned or spontaneous. He can choose to develop his entire portfolio collections in this style or work on collections in different styles based upon his point of view and idealized portfolio goals. *(Courtesy of David Bermingham)*

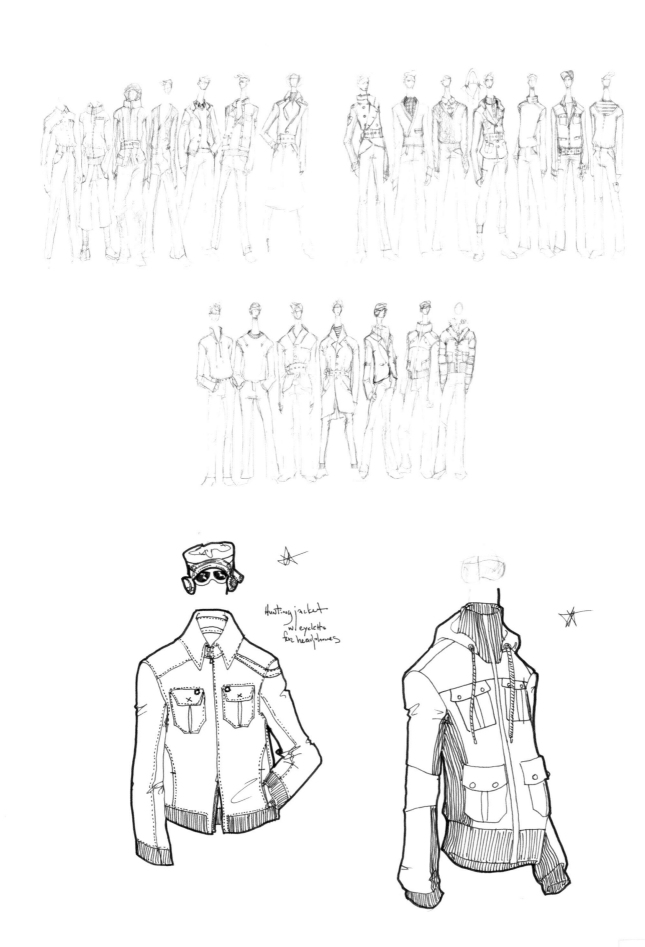

Hunting jacket
w/ eyelets
for headphones

LOGO-BRANDED MERCHANDISE ON PORTFOLIO PAGES

Some branded portfolio collections are logo-driven by the placement of the logo on a garment and/or the illustration layout page. Your portfolio collection(s) may be planned to include branded logo merchandise. These circumstances include, but aren't limited to:

+ A scheduled interview with a company that exclusively sells merchandise that has the company or designer logo on every item.
+ A scheduled interview with a company that is seeking a designer who can update or radically change the logo design direction if requested by the interviewer or can suggest adapting the logo to the company's vision for a new direction.
+ A directional portfolio statement where the designer developed his or her own company logo and has plans to manufacture and sell the garments.
+ A designer with strong graphic-design skills who wants to showcase a collection of logo-driven merchandise with multiple logos or one logo that drives the entire book's design direction.

Logo-driven merchandise is vital to the sale of some categories of design. Performance active wear, accessories, jeans, denim collections, footwear, luxury branded apparel and accessories, and urban streetwear are some categories of design that have logos that are integral to the product image. In these categories, the product designs and the consumers who wear them identify their image by the logos.

The design of the logo is as important as the scale, size, and placement of the logo on the product. A designer working for an apparel company with an established corporate logo will use a graphic layout that the company provides for all garments he or she may be designing. The layout design of the logo cannot be changed without corporate and legal approval. The loyal customer base depends on the logo being the same stamp for years or decades.

The scale and size of the logo can be reworked as long as the designer works with the proper parties within the corporation for approval. These include the merchandising, marketing, sales, and legal departments.

The placement(s) of the logo is part of the attitude image of the garment. Some logo designs are placed on the left chest, the center front of a garment (sometimes in large scale), the center back, the bottom left hem, or the left pocket seam. The logo may be used as an overall print by repeating and resizing it as a surface treatment.

Design, size, scale, and placement of the logo on accessories is legislated by the same parties within the corporation. The placement of the logo may vary greatly depending on the product line. Again, similar to branded garments, the logo drives the sale of the merchandise.

The taste of the merchandise and the logo need to be married to one another. The design of the merchandise and the logo play off of one another, and sometimes deliberately compete for the consumer's attention. The consumer who purchases logo-driven merchandise identifies and wants to live up to the image of the person(s) in the marketing campaigns. For instance, the average runner may identify with the Olympic champion portrayed in a Nike running ad.

In your portfolio, you can show a suggestion of a logo on your figure illustrations. The artwork for the logo can be shown on separate page.

For scheduled interviews with a particular company, you may add your logo to the already designed portfolio collection to appeal to the interviewer. You may have interviews, for instance, with Reebok and Nike. In that situation, you might want to keep copies of your work without the logos drawn on them, then add the Reebok or Nike logo to the page for each particular interview.

An example of an illustrated fashion plate for a logo-driven collection. (top (Courtesy of Tim Hamilton) The multi-figure groupings of branded merchandise in the photos can inspire your concepts for the designs and merchandising of a logo-driven collection. The composition of the photo of men's, women's, and children's preppie designs can serve as a model for a layout that combines genders and age groups on a single portfolio page. Notice that the garments are all closely related and easily identifiable as products of the same brand (center) (Courtesy of WWD/Thomas Iannaccone) The photo of a young contemporary sportswear collection demonstrates that men's and women's garments can be shown together to read easily as a branded collection (bottom) (Courtesy of WWD/Thomas Iannaccone)

An example of logo embellished hardware for a designer's collection. The artwork, photos of the artwork, or actual samples and/or samples of the hardware can be shown in the portfolio. If the actual samples are being shown, it would be best to keep the samples mounted on a separate page from the portfolio pages. The hardware will make impressions, bends, and wrinkles on the flat portfolio pages, an unacceptable situation in an interview presentation. The designer could also keep the hardware in a separate envelope or case to show if the interviewer needed to see it. The preferred method is to photograph the hardware and show the logo placements on the individual types of hardware in the original artwork layout. [a-d] (Courtesy of WWD)

LOGOS ON HARDWARE

One important or dominant area for placement of logos is on garment hardware. The logo can be words, or just a symbol of the design house's name, or philosophy.

Hardware can also be a way of branding a designer's look without putting a logo on it. By choosing materials that are consistent with the designer's collection image, hardware types, uses, and placements can become a signature look for a designer. A simple example of this is a designer who uses safety pins to hold shredded garments together for a line of punk clothing that may exist or eventually become the designer's signature. Another designer may choose a high-end (artificial or real) horn button for use on every garment, and every garment is closed with a button(s). The button becomes synonymous with the designer's brand. The consumer knows from afar which design house the garment belongs to and can therefore promote the brand with a "look" of a high-end hardware item.

Following are some hardware composite materials to consider and research:

+ Plastic
+ Rubber
+ Polished metals: brass, gold, silver, copper
+ Burnished metals: brass, gold, silver, copper
+ Enameled metals: dyed to contrast or match the garment color
+ Magnets that create an invisible closure
+ Glass
+ Abalone
+ Shell
+ Pearl
+ Horn (artificial and real)
+ Ivory (artificial)
+ Crystals

Hardware details are as follows:

+ Zippers
+ Zipper pulls
+ Rivets
+ Snaps
+ Buttons
+ Grommets
+ Nail heads
+ Hooks
+ Draw cord locks
+ Chains
+ Belt buckles

Samples of hardware details that can be researched for sizes, colors, design, and so on, to be placed on garments to create a signature, or for a designer to add a logo to. *(Courtesy of WWD)*

Hardware can add a signature look to a designer's collection, even without a logo. *(Courtesy of WWD/Kyle Ericksen)*

OTHER GARMENT DETAILS THAT CAN FEATURE LOGOS

Following are some additional details that can be branded or have logos added to them:

+ Shoulder seam, vent, and neck seam tapes
+ Elastic waistbands and elastic trim inserts

As you review your portfolio presentation, consider the consumer base you are designing for. Add details that would lend themselves to your target consumer, if necessary.

Designing a planned collection for an interview with a logo-driven company may be approached in a few different ways, each possibly leading to several reactions on the part of the interviewer.

+ Design the garments showcasing a new take on the existing logo.
+ Use the logo in a new design placement, different from the cultural norm.

The interviewer may welcome these approaches as a refreshing portfolio presentation. But there is a possibility that the interviewer may object to the logo being used outside the cultural norm. To address both potential reactions, you can design the garments as two mini-collections. Show one part of the collection using the existing logo, and the second part of the collection with the various original takes on the logo as described above.

Interview scenarios for this approach:

+ The interviewer perceives that you gave the company a choice. You appear to be flexible, with a range of design skills.
+ The interviewer perceives this as a mixed-message statement. You appear to be incapable of making a design statement or to be unsure of your convictions.

In any of these scenarios, it is important to explain in as few words as possible why you used the logo on the garments in the way that you chose. As you design any changes or alternatives to logos, put yourself into the mindset of your ultimate consumer. Ask yourself, "Would my customer wear this product?"

The best case scenario for designing a specific collection for a company would be to design the collection *after* the first interview. Many times, the designer is asked to design a presentation board collection after the first interview to be seriously considered for the position. At that time, the designer could ask the interviewer for the specific looks to be designed and whether the logo can or cannot be modified.

SEQUENCING THE PAGES WITHIN THE COLLECTION

As you adapt the portfolio prepared for the Portfolio Project to presentation for job interviews, competitions, or any other situations where you would be using it to represent yourself as a designer, consider the sequence of pages. Make sure they tell your story in a logical order. Also consider adding pages to show your sense of branding and packaging. Once you've revised the portfolio, you can consider adding sections for additional collections.

STORYTELLING STYLES

Solidify the page-turning sequence of the Portfolio Project. Review the order of presentation for a style that dramatizes your story. Following are some choices (introduced in Chapter 1 in preparation of a temporary portfolio):

✦ Open with your best pages; close with your best styles, and show great style in between.
✦ Open softly; build up to a climax with a dynamic ending.
✦ Open softly; build up to the middle as a climax; and wind down to a soft ending.
✦ Open softly; build up to the middle as a climax; and wind up to a dynamic ending.
✦ Open with a bang; build up to the middle climax; wind down to a soft ending.
✦ Open with a bang; build up to the middle climax; wind up to a dynamic ending.

INTRODUCTORY PAGES

The opening pages of your portfolio make a general statement about you as a designer that should prepare the interviewer for the presentation of the collection or collections that follow. Consider the options in the following table:

Content of Page	Pros	Cons
First page (blank)	Since this is the first page in the portfolio, it is acceptable to have a blank page.	The interviewer wants to turn the page to get to the collection right away.
Résumé and business card	• Reviewer can ask questions about your past experience and accomplishments. • Acts as a catalyst for discussing your talents. • Dresses up the opening page. • A solution to "How do I start my portfolio story? I don't want a blank page." • Serves as contact information. In the event that you lose your book, the finder can call you to return it.	• The reviewer has asked for your résumé already; it is in his or her hands, and you've already reviewed this information. It's redundant. • If you have very little experience, this just highlights that fact. • If you've made poor choices of résumé paper, it distracts rather than adds to your talents.
Cover image page	• Immediately showcases your talents. • Great opening for the designer who is talented in layout packaging. The right page doesn't reveal too much but does emphasize your packaging skills.	"Lets the cat out of the bag" too soon. The reviewer may want to see your collection story told more slowly.
Logo page	Showcases your branding communication skills.	The reviewer has your résumé and doesn't want to look at a logo page that is fantasy-driven.

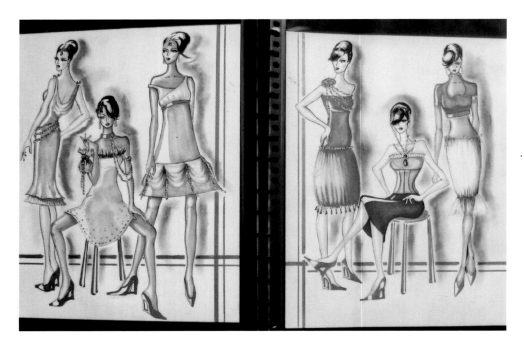

In-class student illustration as last pages in the portfolio. The student showed her best sportswear collections in a logical sequence, and then included some of her best fashion plates at the end of the book for her exit interviews and for the first year or so out of college. *(Courtesy of Ithwa Huq-Jones)*

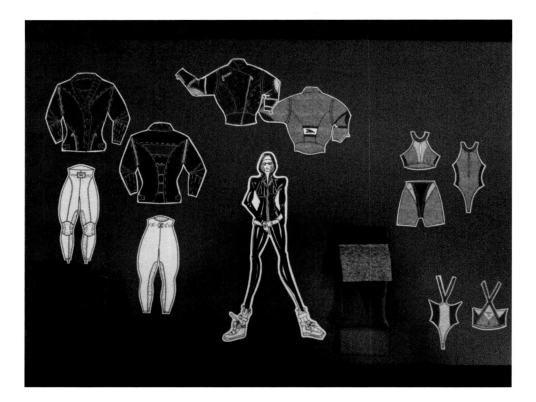

A 20" x 30" presentation board for a corporate design meeting, which was professionally photographed and printed to fit into a 14" x 17" portfolio. *(Author's collection)*

ADDITIONAL PAGES

In addition to the opening pages and the presentation of your Portfolio Project collection, you may decide to include other collections based on work done for your fashion design courses or, once you've begun your career, for previous employers. You may also include promotional materials, such as photos of fashion shows in which you've participated, press coverage of your designs, and information about awards or other recognition of your work.

In-Class Collection Illustrations

Look at your in-class collection illustrations or past illustrations as possibilities for an additional collection to show in your portfolio. If there is a short collection story that can be shown, this could be a next collection in your book. Remember to keep a break or cover page or blank page between the two groupings.

If this is your while-in-college portfolio, or first exit portfolio from college, the in-class illustrations don't necessarily have to relate to the portfolio project, but they should be your best student or past work. The interviewer understands you have collections or work from college that should be included to show your range of work. While this may contradict the basis of having a strong, consistent portfolio message, the need to show this work is understandable and is part of what the interviewer might expect from a student or recent graduate. The in-class illustrations, however, should be edited and well thought out and presented in a concise, logical manner. As the student and recent graduate portfolio evolves to include newer collections, weed out this student work and make room in the book for more refined collections.

For the full presentation of the portfolio while you are in college and when you graduate, review the student work with a college advisor and/or instructor. The reviewer can best guide you as to and where and which fashion plates would or would not work in the presentation.

silk and carbon fiber stability dress

Two images from a winner of the CFDA's educational design competition. The designer photographed his work and presented it in the portfolio with his illustrations. *(Courtesy of Shawn P. Reddy)*

Past Work from Former Jobs

Some students and recent graduates may have jobs or internship positions during their college years. Here are some guidelines for including this work, as well as a guideline for future portfolio building in the next 5 to 10 years.

Illustrated fashion plates from products you developed with another company can be shown in your portfolio, as your opening statement or second or third statement. Dynamic presentations from start to finish are concise. Edit your work and choose only the best pieces. If there is a best-seller item, be sure to show the illustration. If the opportunity arrives during an interview, you can explain its relevance. The collection(s) can be 1 to 12 pages in length.

Fashion presentation pages from work for past companies make excellent presentation vehicles, if they are the actual garments that you designed. If not, be sure to present the work in your portfolio only as your artwork, not as your designs. These pages will show the interviewer your on-the-job presentation skills.

Large-sized boards can be photographed by a professional studio and reproduced in the size of the presentation in your portfolio. The photographs can be scanned into your computer program and printed in the size of your portfolio. The boards can also be color-copied and reduced to a size to fit into your book. Present a maximum of 12 boards.

Flats presentation boards that you have composed can be reproduced in the same manner to show in your book. Present a maximum of six such pages. Tech packs and schematic drawings used to communicate to factories can be shown. Present one to four pages total.

A seasoned designer's portfolio pages featuring press coverage in *Women's Wear Daily. (Author's collection)*

FASHION SHOW PHOTOGRAPHS

Many designers have professional-quality photographs taken from student fashion shows, fashion competitions, or nightclub fashion shows. In the past, these photographs weren't shown in the portfolio. These garments were considered complete fantasy, without having much relevance in the real world of design production.

Today, the photos can be shown as one (or some) of the last pages in your book. Alternately, compose a small 8½ inches wide by 11 inches long by 1 inch thick bound notebook with these photographs encased in polypropylene sleeves or a small ITOYA plastic notebook. If the interviewer seems interested, these can be shown.

The photos should be professional quality, and four photos shown within the portfolio would be the maximum number to display. The photos should be seriously scrutinized by a professor or advisor before you put them into your book. Sometimes the stylization of student shows can be exactly that, *student work*. The interviewer cannot draw a logical conclusion about your talents from these highly personalized or fantasy-driven designs, created for a different venue from that which you are interviewing for.

These photographs can hinder your hire, rather than help your portfolio presentation. Speaking to an advisor within your school is the best way to make this decision on a case-by-case basis.

PRESS COVERAGE: INTERNET, NEWSPAPER, PERIODICAL PUBLICATIONS, AND FASHION AWARDS

If you have press articles featuring your work in photographs or the written word, do include these in your portfolio. If you are highly experienced and have a library of press photographs, you will need to edit the information for presentation in your portfolio.

Awards should be cited in your résumé. Photos or illustrations of collections that won awards can be in the back of your book. If you have a prestigious award within the industry, for instance, a CFDA award or scholarship, this should be on your résumé, and the presentation of the garments might be best suited as the first or second collection that you show in your book. Again, meet with a faculty advisor as to the proper placement in your portfolio.

KEEP THE CHANGES FLOWING: NOW AND AS A LIFETIME TASK

The sequence of the pages is crucial to the way the portfolio will be read. The reader wants to feel the pages of each collection are linked in some visual way. The separate collections need to segue into one another in a non-jarring manner. The reader understands there may be multiple collections within the book. The most important and relevant collection to the interview should be shown first. Usually the Portfolio Project is most important to the interview and should be shown first, especially when you are beginning your career. If you needed to customize or rearrange your portfolio collections based upon a particular interview, then do so.

As you go on different interviews, you may want to rearrange your book for each particular reader. Some designers compose more than one book for this purpose. Designers change, eliminate, or add pages based on the feedback from the interviewer.

As you build and grow your career, the portfolio needs to be constantly updated with new ideas. It's important to update the portfolio at least every 3 to 6 months during your fashion career. There may be reason for you to interview at a moment's notice. Assemble the work in polypropylene portfolio covers and decide on the sequencing of any new work. Put the work into your portfolio case, not on a shelf or in a drawer. The case should be ready to go. Follow this checklist as you work in the industry:

+ Rework current portfolio designs, if necessary.
+ Add new collections.
+ Remove irrelevant or outdated designs.
+ Keep all "discards" on a flat surface, covered in polypropylene covers. You may need these fashion plates or boards in the future.
+ Photograph or keep copies of all boards or flats that you've designed within a company.
+ Keep copies of press coverage of any of your designs in polypropylene sleeves.

Chapter 8

THE DIGITAL AND WEB-BASED PORTFOLIO

OBJECTIVES

+ Understand basic digital and Web portfolio terminology, formats, and visual presentations,

+ Complete a digital or Web-based portfolio by using specialized instruction manuals, online tutorials, and college-level courses.

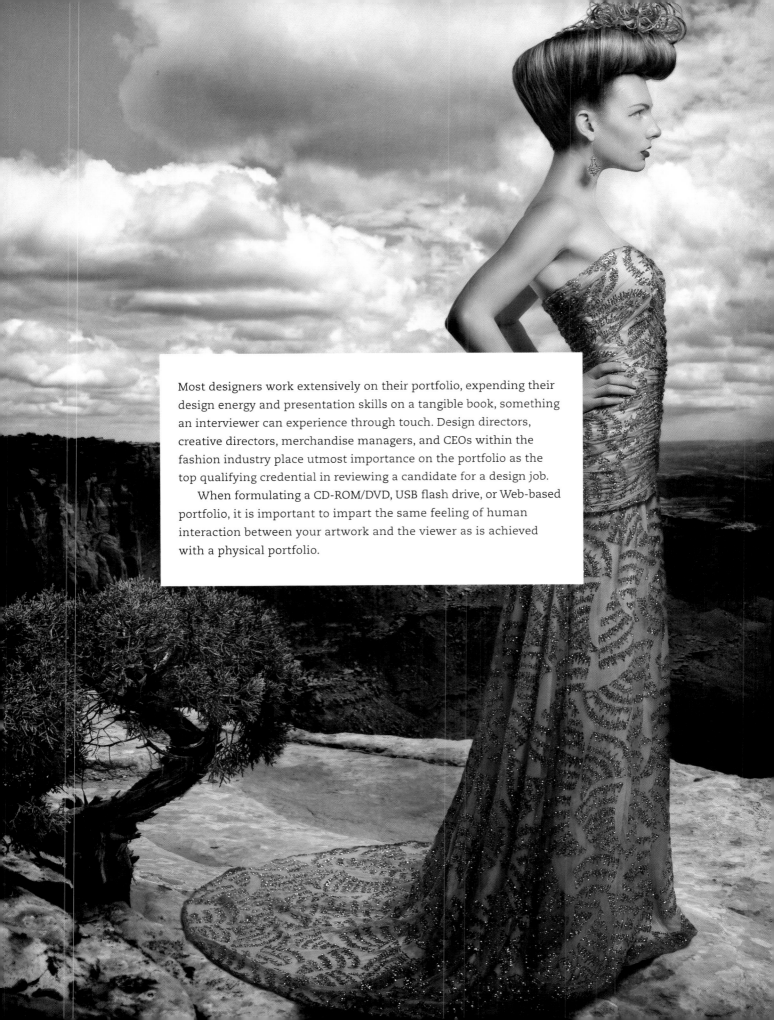

Most designers work extensively on their portfolio, expending their design energy and presentation skills on a tangible book, something an interviewer can experience through touch. Design directors, creative directors, merchandise managers, and CEOs within the fashion industry place utmost importance on the portfolio as the top qualifying credential in reviewing a candidate for a design job.

When formulating a CD-ROM/DVD, USB flash drive, or Web-based portfolio, it is important to impart the same feeling of human interaction between your artwork and the viewer as is achieved with a physical portfolio.

THE TACTILE "OLD SCHOOL" PORTFOLIO PRESENTATION

The book can, obviously, be held and touched. It is an interactive experience conducted by the interviewer. Holding the book on a tabletop in his or her own office, the interviewer can feel the designer's creative work. This process helps the interviewer evaluate the designer from an intuitive and analytic perspective.

The interviewer can start at the beginning, middle, or end of the book. The viewer is in control of the interview and of the approach to the book. Interviewers evaluate the feedback and/or vibe they get from you as they ask questions. The page-turning of the book lends a momentum and a pace to the interview as the interviewer investigates the level of your design ability. What you say in words is fully integrated with what is on the pages.

Step back and think about the tactile and interactive experiences of creating a fashion collection. Remember that your audience (the fashion professional or consumer) needs to touch what could be the next "in" merchandise, fiber, or silhouette. Visit a trade show or a retail store. Observe the visitors. Many designers and merchandisers rush to feel the next great fabric for their lines. They can be seen grabbing at the apparel displayed on the mannequins to feel how the fabric would work for in-store placement with hanger appeal.

Historically, the connection designers make with their initial thumbnail sketches on a piece of paper (or electronic touch pad) is vital. They physically hand off the sketch to the pattern maker, draper, sample hand or factory. The design or product development team brings that vision to fruition. A dynamism and a synergy are created as the design passes through the stages of development to bring the designers' visions into product.

You should attempt to capture this physical energy of the 3D form when putting together a digital or Web-based portfolio. Try to visualize the excitement you bring forward when you've completed a style or a collection. At the time when you share that vision with the creative group, there is a surreal explosion of collective energy that clicks with the design and corporate team. A Web-based portfolio or digital image can prompt that level of excitement with the viewer. The ideas should "have legs" and prompt the viewer to want to see more of your work in the real world. The disconnect between the electronic image and the real world can be overcome by a presentation that creates tension, curiosity, emotion, and involvement.

The digital devices (CD-ROM/DVD, USB flash drive and website portfolios) aren't intended to replace the book. The digital devices and websites add credibility to the claim that the designer is multifaceted and skilled in 2D, 3D, CAD, and digital design. They further market the designer in a competitive worldwide design industry.

Designers and merchandisers are charged to produce quick-turn merchandise, available in-store in a 3-week window display. The integrated design systems used by many companies allows the designer to conceive the design, publish the information for corporate decision makers, and electronically transfer the manufacturing instructions to overseas and domestic factories from the design studio station. This is a complex, sophisticated variation on the hand-to-hand version of the designer's creative process from sketch to final product. It still, however, involves the creative synergies of the design team with the electronic equipment to make the design come to life.

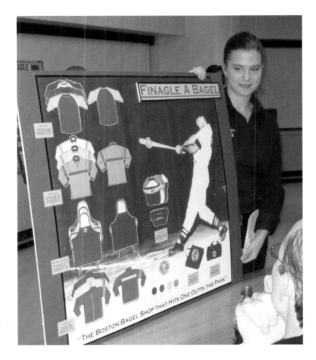

The designer makes a board presentation to the merchandising group, engaging the audience with her board layouts, body language, and professional demeanor. *(Courtesy of Virginia Fretto)*

THE "NEW SCHOOL" PORTFOLIO EXTENSION

The CD-ROM, DVD, USB flash drive, and Web versions of the portfolio give designers a portable fashion venue in which to showcase their work. The CD-ROM, DVD, and USB flash drive can be used:

+ To make a presentation during an interview to one person or to a design team on a projected or large-screen monitor.
+ As a leave-behind piece.
+ To mail to prospective employers or to share files with design firms.
+ To attach files to an e-mail.
+ To store and manage design files.

The Web portfolio gets your name, résumé, and designs "out there" and marketed heavily to the general public, potential customers, and employers. It increases visibility and can help establish a designer who is new to the industry. Anyone can access it anytime, anywhere around the globe. It can represent you and your designs as accessible and projects your desire to be part of the workforce.

Your websites can show your personal style and your professional work. It can give a shout out about your commercial value or readiness to be part of a commercial design market. It can display a strong individuality toward the avant-garde or a made-to-order line of clothing.

See the box "Programs and Devices" for choices of media and programs to consider, with some pros and cons.

Review the terms listed in Exercise 8.1. These are the basic terms and products you can choose from to produce your electronic portfolio. Evaluate your needs and research the programs through online user ratings, personal and professional colleagues' advice, and academic support through classes and study programs. In addition, designers can access a software product's website to view free tutorial videos and step-by-step guides. See the list of resources in the box "Software Online Tutorials and Trial Resources" for the list of product websites. As you navigate the websites, you will find endless tutorial and video examples of how the products are used and what tools are available. Examples of an artist at work are shown, and the computer screen will give you a point-and-click demonstration of an image manipulation. Complete Exercise 8.1 to familiarize yourself with the terminology you will be working with to create your electronic presentation.

The good news is that most designers and students can learn to use these programs effectively and without a great deal of difficulty to create an electronic presentation to support their portfolio.

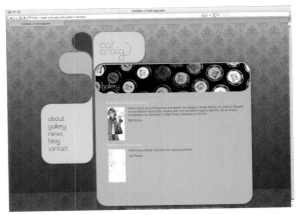

Fashion designer website, page 1 of her gallery (left) and page 2 (right). *(Courtesy of Cat Craig)*

Accessory designer website, home page (left) and style page (right). *(Courtesy of loomlab.com)*

Couture designer website, home page (top) and press page (bottom). *(Courtesy of Jeury Rosario)*

PROGRAMS AND DEVICES

Review of (1) portable electronic devices, (2) multimedia programs, and (3) Web-based portfolio presentation programs.

Portable Electronic Devices

The portable devices listed below can be used to backup your design/portfolio files, as a storage device for your design/portfolio files, or as a display or leave-behind piece for your designs/portfolio presentation.

To choose which device(s) to use:

▶ Consider the size of the device, and evaluate how many design files you will need to hold.

▶ study the K, M, or G sizes in the charts below.

▶ Do the math to determine how much storage size you will need to use. For instance, consider that a basic graphic Photoshop file that is 11" x 17" saved at a resolution of 300 dpi (dots per square inch) is 24 megabytes in size. This means a CD-ROM would give you room for about 26 images of this size on a disc.

What does K, M or G stand for, and what are the size capacities of each?

K or KB	M or MB	G or GB
A kilobyte (K for kilo, and B for byte)	A megabyte (M for mega, and B for byte)	A gigabyte (G for giga, and B for byte)
Size: 1,000 bytes	Size: 1,000,000 bytes (1 million)	Size: 1,000,000,000 bytes (1 billion)

What are the capacity sizes of the storage devices?

Capacity size of a CD-ROM	Capacity size of a DVD	Capacity size of a USB Flash Drive
Size: 700 megabytes	Size: 4.7 gigabytes	Size: Ranges from 64 megabytes through 32 gigabytes

Multimedia Programs for the CD, DVD, or Flash Drive Presentations

Name of Program	Uses for Designers	Comments
PowerPoint Presentation	Present a simple slide show of all of your design elements of collection illustrations, flats, photographs, textile swatch images, color references, and so on, add music and simple animations.	Program is easy to learn. It can be hyperlinked so that the viewer can access them out of sequence. If it is not hyperlinked, it must be viewed in sequence, from start to finish or in reverse order.
Adobe Flash	Create a slide show and video presentation with all of your design elements.	ActionScript, the programming code, is easy to learn. A portfolio presentation can be completed in a relatively short period of time. You can import files from Photoshop, Illustrator, and AutoCAD.

Web-Based Portfolios

A Web-based portfolio gives quick access to potential employers and customers anywhere, anytime, around the world. The viewer can navigate each page at their own pace, and they can jump from page to page at their leisure, in any order they please. It should open with a home page that contains links to other areas of the portfolio.

The portfolio presentation can include a designer's statement or philosophy and résumé. Similar to the portfolio book, you can display multiple collections and subcategories of your design work.

Name of Program	Uses for Designers	Comments
Adobe Dreamweaver	Create a Web presentation with great flexibility in design and design navigation. It features a drag-and-drop-style HTML editor with layout tools.	It works well with Flash and Photoshop. Creation of the layout and menu extension can be done without coding experience.
Adobe Acrobat	It can be used to rework layout-style pages such as QuarkXPress and InDesign into Web links. It converts PDF format (Portable Document Format) files. Designs created in AutoCAD can be imported.	It works well with Microsoft Office Word, PowerPoint and Excel. If you are familiar with page layout software, you can learn Adobe Acrobat. The pages contain index links for viewers to go to other areas of your portfolio.

Additional Software Options

When you are converting your portfolio pages to a digital format, you have three choices of programs: raster-based programs, vector-based programs, and page-layout programs.

▶ Raster-based programs use bitmap graphics, created pixel by pixel, with a screen resolution usually presented in 72 dpi.

▶ Vector-based programs use math to describe points or shapes that make up the image. They are not good for photographs, but they work well with Adobe Illustrator and CorelDRAW for line illustrations.

Name of Program	Uses for Designers	Comments
Adobe Photoshop/raster based program	Offers many color, design, and artist's tools You can add special effects to the pages and work with features like auto-removal of defects from original sketches (eraser marks, pencil smudges, etc.)	Used by many fashion designers on its own or in combination with Adobe Illustrator Learning curve is a bit long to master for a professional-looking presentation Most students can learn the simple basics within a short period of time
Corel Painter/raster-based program	Known as the "natural media painting program" A large range of artist's media and tools are available	Can be more time-consuming to learn than Photoshop or Illustrator
Adobe Illustrator/vector-based program	Offers a large variety of drawing tools, and special effects can be created	Used by many fashion designers on its own, or in combination with Adobe Photoshop Has a powerful drawing program Relatively medium level of difficulty to learn the basics in a short period of time
CorelDraw/vector-based program	A drawing program and a Web design program	Features animation, drawing tools, text tools, textures, patterns, and interactive tools
QuarkXPress/page layout program	Used for commercial media, such as newspapers and magazines Gives great flexibility in placement and layout of designs and text Has an easy-to-understand interface	Some fashion designers may use this for catalogue, flats, and design/merchandising presentations; it may take more time to learn than other programs.
Adobe InDesign/page layout program	The latest version (as of this printing) is CS6, which features creative tools, precise control over typography; ability to create a user-friendly interactive space; and video and audio playback on tablets, smartphones, and computers	

OBJECTIVE: Become familiar with digital and Web-based vocabulary.

The computer terms in this box provide an overview of hardware and software terminology. Whether these computer terms are brand-new or familiar to you, you should become more familiar with them by reviewing the following definitions. As you begin to put your electronic portfolio together, knowing the meanings of these terms will help you move forward with confidence.

Bandwidth   An amount of data that can be sent from one computer to another in a period of time, usually expressed in bits/second. Higher bandwidth results in higher speed.

Bitmap   A maplike pattern composed of dots or squares in a digital graphic image. Each dot or square is assigned a color value from 1–32 bits. GIF, JPEG, and similar files are all examples of bitmap, and can be read by Adobe Photoshop and similar programs.

Browser   A program that allows access to the World Wide Web. Examples include Internet Explorer and Mozilla Firefox.

Cache   The location of temporary memory or data storage. This is separate from the computer motherboard and allows for faster retrieval of, for example, recently visited pages or websites.

Cascading style sheets (CSS)   A system that specifies style formats such as font size, color, or page layering. CSS allows the application of similar formatting to multiple Web pages.

Dial-up connection   An Internet connection via a land-based telephone line, common in early uses of the Internet.

Domain name   The name that identifies an address for a website, usually a company name plus an extension of ".com," ".gov," etc., used to access the website. It is the name that commonly follows "http://www." in a URL.

Freeware   Free software, which may be offered with restricted usage.

FTP (File Transfer Protocol)   Protocol for file transfer between computers on a network.

Gigabyte   1 billion bytes of information, which describes the storage capacity of a given device.

Graphic interchange format (GIF)   A graphics file format that is an alternative to JPEG file format. Limited to 256 colors and used for still images and simple animation. Works well with sharp-edged art (such as logos), and yields sharp black and white images.

Home page   The page to which an Internet browser opens when one logs on to a website.

HTML (Hypertext markup language)   Code that formats Web pages; it is not seen on the screen; it simply gives instructions on page formatting. (If curious, in Internet Explorer, click View, then Source to view HTML.)

Image file formats   Graphics file formats such as GIF and JPEG.

Image map   A graphic with invisible buttons that link to other pages.

Image optimization   Modification of image size, shape, or other property to best display them for presentation on the Web.

JPEG (Joint Photographic Experts Group)   A graphics file format that contains up to 24 bits of color information. JPEG files are larger than GIF files.

Kilobyte   1,024 bytes of data, often simply shortened to "k." Refers to amount of storage information.

Megabyte   1 million (1,048,576) bytes, used to describe available memory of a computer or hard drive.

Multimedia authoring program   A software program used to create digital interactive files, such as Adobe Director and Adobe Flash.

Navigation bar   A bar (subsection of a Web page) that displays links to other pages. Sometimes referred to as a links bar.

Path   The direction to a stored file.

Raster-based graphics   Graphics that have a fixed resolution of dpi (dots per inch). The images are created pixel by pixel inside a grid of pixels.

Resolution   The number of dpi, in images on a computer screen. is The most common size used for conversion to print is 300 dpi, but images online can show up clearly at a lower resolution.

USB flash drive (Universal Serial Bus)   Flash memory data storage device with a retractable insertable tab, which is removable and rewritable. Also called *jump drive, pen drive, thumb drive.*

Vector-based graphics   Design system describing points or shapes of an image using math.

Web host   A company that maintains websites.

Web-safe colors   A set of 216 colors that are most common to browsers and will give the user the same results on different browsers and platforms.

XML   (Extensible mark-up language) A variation of HTML (Hypertext Markup Language); code.

Most software programs have many available online tutorials and trial resources. The best way to find out information about tutorials and trial resources is to go directly to the home page of a software company by typing in its name followed by ".com." Also, search for the company's websites and similar links by going to www.google.com, typing in the name of the software or device, and choosing a website. Below is a very abbreviated list of sites.

For searching for varied sources, from the actual software company to pedestrian demonstrations, go to www.google.com and type in the name of the software or device in question. Here you will be lead to numerous sources, including You Tube demonstrations from students and professionals. There is always something to be learned by browsing through these videos and websites.

Adobe Illustrator.
http://www.adobe.com/products/illustrator.html?promoid=DIOCX
Free trial:
http://www.adobe.com/cfusion/tdrc/index.cfm?product=illustrator
Free tutorials:
http://www.adobeillustratortutorials.com/
Topics include Basics & Tools; Creating Art & Effects; Type, Text Effects & Logos; Web Graphics; and Miscellaneous (for any other topics).

CorelDraw:
CorelDraw products include CorelDraw and PaintShop Pro X4.
http://www.corel.com/corel/
CorelDraw:
http://www.corel.com/corel/category.jsp?cat=cat3430091&rootCat=cat20146

Free trials:
http://www.corel.com/corel/category.jsp?cat=cat4130083&rootCat=cat3610091
Currently offers free trials of CorelDRAW Graphics Suite and PaintShop Pro X4, among others.
Free tutorials:
http://www.corel.com/corel/product/index.jsp?pid=prod3670089&cid=catalog20038&segid=800018
Tutorials include The Curve Tools; Designing for Accuracy; Exploring Corel CONNECT (content organizer); Advanced Graphics with Mesh Fills; Using the Document Color Palette; Pixel View & Enhanced Web Graphics; Photo Effects; Enhanced Image Adjustment Lab: Working with RAW files and snapshots; Creating a Marketing Brochure in CorelDraw; Creating Graphics for a Full Screen PDF Presentation in CorelDraw; Cropping Graphics in CorelDraw; Making Image Corrections Quickly and Easily in Corel PHOTO-PAINT; and many other tutorials.

PaintShop Pro X4:
http://www.corel.com/corel/product/index.jsp?pid=prod4130078&cid=catalog20038&segid=2500058
PaintShop Tutorials:
http://www.corel.com/corel/product/index.jsp?pid=prod4130078&cid=catalog20038&segid=2500062
Offers both written and video tutorials of PaintShop.

Written topics include Introducing the Corel PaintShop Photo Pro X3 Express Lab; Using the Camera RAW Lab in Corel PaintShop Photo Pro X3; Replicating tilt shift photography with Corel PaintShop Photo Pro X3; and Posterization effect.

Video tutorials include Handcolouring, Restoring Faded Photos, Restoring a Damaged Photo, and Restoring a Stained Photos.

DEVELOPING
A PLAN FOR
THE ELECTRONIC
PRESENTATION

Studying basic presentation skills to prepare for the electronic presentation is key to a successful finished product. Here, we review the following:

+ Color
+ Fonts
+ Layout
+ Navigation

COLOR

A Web-based or electronic presentation should use color effectively to tell a story on the page. Background colors, font colors, combinations of colors on the page, and the colors of the collection pieces need to be balanced and synchronized so there is a cohesive statement of both the colors of the graphic details and the garment details.

The color choices set the tone, energy, and pace so that the viewer gets a distinct impression of the designer, the target customer, and the designs. The colors chosen for emphasis on the Web page should sharply define the designer's marketing vision or brand. It is important that the colors are not jarring or erratic in nature, and they should create a path for the viewer to follow. The colors should also help to make the page user-friendly.

The collection designs, not the background, should be the dominant focus. As with the physical portfolio, attention is on the garments. To make the garments stand out, consider how you want to pull your consumer into the page. The figures that follow are examples of several designers' computer-based work, highlighting the use of color and form.

Review the color terms listed in Exercise 8.2 to prepare for creating your electronic image package.

Electronic presentation boards. *(Courtesy of Katie Choquette)*

(Courtesy of Jane Henry)

Importance of
BASE LAYERS:

Laser cut
detail

Interior compression
corset with wicking
(moisture management)
properties, nylon spandex

Belt looped below top
CF pleats; pleats still
remain close to body
due to shaping

Bodice pleated with
stretch mesh inserts
to articulate movement

Very full sweep
at hem

"Chérie" dinner dress,
Dior spring/summer 1947

(Courtesy of Jane Henry)

(Courtesy of David Bermingham)

OBJECTIVE: Review the following color terms for a well-planned electronic presentation.

Develop a plan for a balance of color harmony for your electronic presentation. Review these color terms and apply this knowledge in your decisions for creating a visually strong electronic portfolio.

Analogous colors   Three or more adjacent color on the color wheel. These colors can be called a color family. Example: red-violet, violet, and blue-violet.

CMYK   A model for color that stands for the colors cyan, magenta, yellow, and "key," which is black. They are used in print media, and are mixed to create the full gamut of colors.

Complementary colors   Colors that are opposite one another on the color wheel. Example: blue and orange.

Hue   A name of a color from the color spectrum. Example: Red, green, or blue.

Intensity   The level of saturation of a color. (see Saturation)

Monochromatic   A color scheme featuring variations of one color based upon tints, shades, and different saturations of that one color.

Primary color   A pure hue that can't be achieved by mixing other colors. The primary colors of light are red, green and blue. The primary colors of pigments are red, yellow, and blue.

RGB   Abbreviation for red, green, and blue, the primary colors of light, which can be mixed to create other colors.

Saturation   The level of purity or intensity of a color. Color saturation can be decreased by adding gray, black, or white to the original color.

Secondary color   A color produced by mixing two primary colors, such as mixing red and blue to create violet.

Tertiary color   A color produced by mixing a primary color with an adjacent secondary color on the color wheel

Value   The lightness or darkness of a color. A lighter version of a color has a higher value. A darker version of a color has a lower value.

Source: Based on *The Graphic Designer's Guide to Portfolio Design* by Debbie Rose Myers, Hoboken, NJ: John Wiley & Sons, Inc., 2009, pp. 241–251.

FONTS

The fonts you choose will help bring your design style and personality alive on the page. Evaluate the typeface on a page in a prototype mock-up. Use different fonts to see which ones best represent your design "spirit" and complement the designs on the page. Your choices will set the tone for your designer image and help brand your designs.

+ Use legible fonts. The font and typeface should not just carry the design image throughout the presentation; it should be easy to read. To understand the content of your message, the viewer must be able to read it. Some fonts can be fun to view but difficult to decipher.
+ Strike a balance with the fonts' styles, weights, and combinations with each other. Style, weight, and combined typefaces add visual contrast. Be careful with certain fonts that could make the background path of information more dominant (or eye-catching) than your collection details. By mocking up several prototype layout pages with different fonts, you can experiment to see the effect on the viewer. As with the Portfolio Project, use friends, colleagues, instructors, and family to critique and evaluate the effectiveness of your prototypes to better your product.

+ There should be a rhythm to how the individual pages read, as well as how this rhythm flows from page to page as you scroll through your electronic presentation. Check how your words flow on the page in context. Are the words correctly used and spelled? Is the description too lengthy, too abbreviated? Do the words enhance the collection? If not, make necessary changes. Do the words on the page create a natural rhythm on the page so the viewer can read each paragraph and know what the words relate to? Look at the overall rhythm of the words on the page without reading the words. How does this path of words help the reader understand the products (designs) you are featuring? If the program you are using allows the viewer to page-jump or skip through pages and work in a nonlinear sequence, consider how this rhythm works for the viewer by testing the navigation process. Does the presentation do what you want it to do for your consumer or viewer?

LAYOUT

Layout of the page should be planned for the viewer to have a pleasant experience. Overly complicated and haphazardly planned pages can turn off your viewers and ultimately shut down their interest. Curiosity as to what is next is an important part of the visual effect that you must create with layout for your electronic portfolio.

Once the view of the page or the navigation becomes cumbersome, difficult, or just plain unattractive, you lose your audience. A viewer (or interviewer) browsing through your electronic portfolio can customize the viewing process, much the same as a viewer peruses any website. The interviewer is more apt to point and click away from your work quickly if you don't capture his or her attention.

An interviewer is much more likely to have high expectations of an electronic portfolio presentation than of a traditional book portfolio. We all view the Internet daily, and electronic images that we view are professionally composed to meet a high standard: Capture the viewers and, keep them interested. Interviewers looking at an electronic portfolio may have developed expectations that perhaps are subconscious; they need to be wowed or pulled in, by even student work. Obviously, the interviewer is taking into consideration that you are a student and your work won't look like Calvin Klein's designer website. Nevertheless, the expectations are high.

Specifically, consider the following:

+ Have a planned objective for each page. Make a list of what you want to accomplish with each page. Make sketches of each page layout with headings, subheadings, and design image placement plans. Create a mock-up version(s) of what you want your page(s) to look like in sketch or CAD form, with a plan for color use, fonts, and text content. Work on creating a page structure by checking that your mock-up versions obtain the objective for each page. Use bulleted lists as necessary.

+ Use symmetry. Presentations that are symmetrical through balanced placements of text, designs, and details give the viewer a feeling of calm review that is straightforward and to the point. Add interest to the page by using a variety of fonts, sizes, and colors, and use color placement to create this.

+ Use asymmetry. Asymmetrical layouts can add motion with your work and keep the viewer moving to review each element on each page, as well in navigating through the pages. View the negative space and the path that it creates to keep your viewer from being frustrated by the deliberate imbalance of form that you've created through asymmetrical layouts. Keep the elements less complicated to balance out the asymmetrical pathway.

- Use bulleted lists.
- Keep words to a minimum. Web and electronic wording can cause eyestrain, so the more concise your wording, the better.

NAVIGATION

As you develop your website and/or digital portfolio, perhaps the most complex job you will have is setting up the navigation with a computer program. Choose a system that your level of experience can support. You can update your work or completely revamp the portfolio presentation as you gain more computer knowledge. It's best to get started with a program that you can apply yourself. Know your time restrictions, and be realistic about the learning curve as you decide the best system for you.

When contemplating the navigation setup, be sure that the most important information is viewable on the top of the screen. You don't want your viewer to need to scroll down to see your best work. You can also plan your website or digital presentation *not* to have a scroll feature.

Website navigation can be set up in one of four basic ways: linear, global, hierarchical, or local. Linear navigation Web pages are set up with links that viewers can click on to find collections or information on your website in a straight path. Global navigation gives viewers access to all links on every page of the website, giving them the ability to flow through your Web pages at their own pace and in any order. In this format, the designer places the links in the same position on every page. Hierarchical website setups showcase each section of the designer's work under a separate heading. Viewers can enter a category (such as Lingerie, Spring 2013) that would house a large part of the designer's collections. Subcategories of the designer's work can be listed under links such as Spring 2013 Bridal Lingerie, Spring 2013 Sleepwear, Spring 2013 Loungewear, and so on. Local navigation setups combine features of the global and hierarchical arrangements.

Exercises 8.3 and 8.4 will help you organize your digital or Web-based presentation.

OBJECTIVE: Immerse yourself in a self-guided or academically guided production of the CD-ROM, DVD, flash drive, or Web-based portfolio presentation.

Sketch the layout of your electronic presentation. Execute page-by-page layouts with rough sketches.

Start with the home page, which should include a title or a heading, small section headings and/or smaller subsections. This page should reflect the message of your work. It can be a statement of the design image you want to use for marketing all of your designs, a simple layout page, or something in between. Your design statement or philosophy can be artfully presented. It's best to try many different versions through sketching and using the computer tools to come up with the presentation.

Use boxes, lines, and button designations to create a structure for placing the design illustrations, flats, textiles, colors, surface patterns, photographs, and text.

Write the text or storyline for each page, paying close attention to the word content and how it relates to the collection. Reread, edit, and rewrite your work as needed.

Mock up the work by hand with a medium of your choice (paint, markers, pencils, etc.) in a rough form, to use as a model for your final presentation. Consider the following questions. Write down your answers and evaluate through re-sketching your mock-ups and solve the problems before you put together your final version.

- How do you want the viewer to navigate or view your work? Does your layout accomplish this goal effectively? Have you tried navigating through a similar website or presentation that is similar, and is it user-friendly? Can the user interact with your page the way you foresee?

- How do you use the space on the page to include a feeling of dimension? How are you using color, texture, pattern and contrast?

- How will you proportion the images on the page to achieve balance and harmony?

- Will you use repetition to emphasize certain works, and does this become monotonous or does it look overworked?

- Are your navigation paths obvious to the viewer?

- Is this a quality presentation that meets or exceeds your standards?

- Is your plan for text easy to read through font choices, font sizes, font weight, and actual word content accurate to the garment details you are showing?

- Regarding background color and/or graphics, have you scrutinized your color choices for compatibility with each element you've planned for the page? Do the colors and graphics complement or distract from the matter at hand (your design collection)?

- Does your presentation communicate your ideas? Bounce your ideas off a colleague.

- Is your planned presentation engaging, distinctive, and informative?

- Will this presentation meet your client's objectives?

- Does your layout create movement and rhythm on the page?

- Do your pages work together in a cohesive manner?

- Is there emotion to the presentation viewing?

- Have you balanced positive and negative space?

- Is there too much or too little information?

- Does the page invite movement or seem to have adventure?

- Does the color overpower the page?

OBJECTIVE: Create a PowerPoint presentation for your portfolio.

Preparation

Prepare to create your presentation by planning to select the images best suited to your end goal. As with the preparation and completion of the Portfolio Project, remember to customize the collection images and overall presentation for your audience (i.e., a general sportswear interview, a specialized collection interview, etc.) This discussion is based on PowerPoint 2003.

- ▶ Select the paper and/or electronic images that best represent your work.
- ▶ Improve the images and/or sharpen the edges with an eraser.
- ▶ Scan your images into a scanner, saving them in a unique folder.
- ▶ Choose the resolution for your images.
- ▶ Use software such as Photoshop or Illustrator to rework or enhance your designs.
- ▶ Make changes to color, tones, layout, background effects, and text for an effective slide show.
- ▶ Plan the sequence of the slides to tell a story to your audience.

Create the PowerPoint Presentation

1. Open PowerPoint.
Click on **File**
Click **New... (Ctrl+N)**

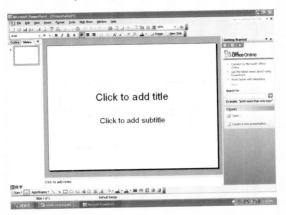

The New Presentation window will open.

2. Click on the drop-down arrow in the **Getting Started** toolbar on the right dialog box.

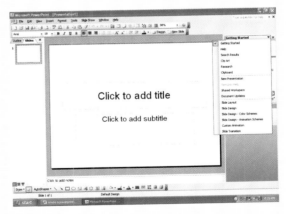

Note that PowerPoint offers many options, from Getting Started to Slide Transition.

3. For now, choose Slide Layout.

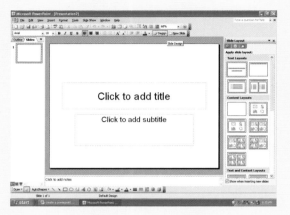

The central portion of the screen shows that slide that you are working on.

4. Type in either box to enter text.

5. If you do not want the second box, delete by placing your cursor on the edge of the box; it will generate four arrows. Click, and hit the Delete key.

6. Click in the remaining box and enter your title, or enter text in both boxes.

Your first slide is complete.

7. To add your next slide, click on **Insert** in the menu bar.

8. Note all of your options here. You can choose **New Slide** or **Duplicate Slide**, which will give you an exact duplicate of your current slide.

9. You can also use the Insert option to insert pictures, diagrams, text boxes, movies and sounds, charts, tables, objects, and hyperlinks within an individual slide.

10. For our purposes, choose New Slide.

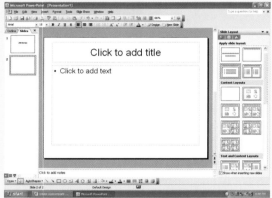

11. Notice that your first slide is visible in the left box, as is your second slide, shown as a blank. This box offers two views, **Outline** and **Slide**. **Outline** offers just that: an outline view of your show.

12. For now, remain in **Slide** view.

13. Like the first slide, the second slide has two text boxes. You can work with this same format or choose a different slide format in the right Slide Layout box.

14. Choose a different format.

Note that you have a new pre-formatted slide. Although these are labeled as text boxes, you can add pictures/images here as well.

15. As before, click on **Insert** in the menu bar, click **Picture**, and click on your picture's location.

16. If you want to add text in this box, do so. To remove the bullets, click on the **Bullets** toolbar button.

17. Continue to add slides. Use Slide Design (click on left toolbar) and other options to format your slides. Don't forget to **Save** as you work.

18. PowerPoint is similar to Microsoft Word, and is similarly navigated. Changes in font, format, numbering, etc. are all available in PowerPoint.

19. When ready, create a slideshow. Click on the **Slide Show** button on the menu bar. Begin with **Set up Slideshow**; **Slide Show** to **Slide Animation** and **Slide Transition** are other helpful choices.

20. To view your slideshow, click on **View** in the menu bar, then on **Slide Show**.

PowerPoint 2010 uses slightly different instructions. But version 2010 also offers video editing features, such as creating a video and packaging the presentation to a CD. You will also be able to Disseminate your slide show or video by using e-mail, saving to the Internet, saving to a sharepoint to collaborate with team members, publishing your slides, and broadcasting your slide show using a created link. For more information on creating a slide show, refer to any of the many books and websites on this topic.

Chapter 9

INTERVIEW INSIGHTS

OBJECTIVES

+ Prepare for entry-level, design-related interviews in the apparel industry.

+ Anticipate questions from interviewers.

+ Follow up interviews with thank you notes.

Throughout the text, you have seen a wide range of portfolio styles and explored various design categories illustrated by a range of design styles. The display of portfolio style choices mirrors the broad range of job choices in the apparel industry for the entry-level and experienced designer.

As a designer fresh from graduation, you might have initial choices with job offerings, have none at all, or have only one job opportunity that comes out of many interviews with many companies. During the process, you may have to adjust your expectations and short- or long-term career goals based upon the economic climate, market trends, and job offers you receive. You may not get a job at your dream design house but may be offered a unique opportunity to work for a dynamic, seasoned professional designer. The job may lead you to the next steps in your career, and may be the proverbial "foot in the door" to gain credibility and experience.

Don't be afraid to take time to learn. It's good to work for other people. I worked for others for 20 years. They paid me to learn.

VERA WANG

Your career path may be altered in a positive manner based upon your flexibility, attitude, and ability to adjust your talents to serve the company's needs. Gaining as much experience as possible as an assistant designer can be an excellent proving ground for you to see how much and what type of work you can produce on a commercial level. It can teach you what you do and don't want in the next job that you pursue.

Become acquainted with some general job search criteria.

+ *Design job descriptions*   Look through *Women's Wear Daily*'s classified section, both online and in the newspaper. The description of day-to-day tasks for assistant designer, associate designer, technical designer, pattern maker, draper, designer, senior designer, and design director vary from company to company.

+ *Design positions for different tastes and consumers*   The design positions are posted for design houses and companies that have specific target customers and tastes. For instance, your refined taste for better products might be very well suited for a design position at Target Stores, as you can reach many consumers with varied levels of spending power seeking well-designed products at a price. Your FDP portfolio of sportswear for the masses can be perceived as well focused on the Target interview as well as the interview with a top apparel brand in the better market.

+ *Employer expectations of a potential employee*
The job descriptions post general day-to-day tasks and prerequisites. Individual employers posting similar ads will have specific expectations of your work, which may vary from company to company. The job descriptions may sound the same in writing, but the employer will have a set way of looking at your portfolio and work ethic and relaying the company's expectations to you. Some employers may be very "loose" about a 40-hour work week and ask that you put in your 40 hours without arriving promptly to work on time. Another employer may use a time clock and demand that you arrive on or before 9 AM, and not leave the studio before 5 PM. One employer's description of "must be able to sketch" may mean rough thumbnail sketches that only the designer can read. Another employer may mean that you must sketch ideas in meetings for a group of corporate managers, which have to be much more refined than a rough thumbnail.

+ *Employee expectations of a potential employer*
You may have certain key expectations of a potential employer. One expectation might be the day-to-day exposure to the design/merchandising/production/sales meetings and chain of command. In basic entry-level jobs, this is not always part of the job description. You can inquire about this when the interviewer invites you to ask questions. The benefits of working for a top designer or a top manufacturing company may far outweigh the exposure, and you will have to measure those pros and cons during the decision-making process upon receiving a job offer.

+ *Employee expectations of their own career goals*
Before, during, and after an interview, you will have expectations of what you will gain by working for the company where you are interviewing. Room for growth, potential for lateral movement, and day-to-day recognition for your work within the company may be important career goals that can be discussed in a first interview if the potential employer is indicating that you are being seriously considered. It is therefore important to listen to what interviewers have to say about their exact expectations of you as the potential employee and what on-the-job skills will be expected of you should you be hired. As you listen carefully, try to formulate questions you can ask (when prompted) that may clarify the meaning of the descriptions. The interviewer may explain further with visual examples or verbal details. It is crucial for both parties that you speak the same language regarding job functions.

MATCHING YOUR QUALIFICATIONS TO THE JOB

Sometimes, you may discover that the expectations the interviewer would have of you on the job are higher than you feel you can achieve. Sometimes, you may be in a place in your career that makes you "ready for the challenge." You may determine that you want to get ahead in your career by working toward these higher expectations. Other times, you can gauge that you don't want to get in "over our head," and perhaps this job is not the best step for you at this time. One way or the other, it is not necessary to come to these conclusions during the interview. It's best to get a job offer by presenting your most positive self during the session. Then, afterward, you can weigh the pros and cons of the job as it relates to your career goals as well as to your current level of ability combined with your projected goals.

Sometimes, taking a job that you feel is beneath you as far as skill level can pay off in the long term. For some designers, working for a prestigious designer "picking up pins" as an assistant far outweighs a job with more design responsibilities for a volume-oriented manufacturing company.

Another deciding factor is the chemistry between you and the interviewer. Sometimes, the working relationship you would have with the interviewer can be the main reason you are offered a job or the reason you take a job. Your long-term and short-term career goals will have to be considered carefully, as well as your gut reaction to the employer when you make your decision based upon a job offer. The first goal is to make the best impression possible on the interviewer, and assess the job description after you get the job offer.

In many companies, the second or third interview may involve a group interview to get acquainted and to be assessed by the design team. The team will be called into a meeting room, and the designers will look at your portfolio and ask you questions about your past experience and what you are looking for in this job, and perhaps why you feel you are the best candidate.

When an interview goes well, many interviewers will ask you to come back in 2 to 7 days with a completed collection designed for their company. When you are asked to put this together, it is best to ask specific questions as to what the design house may be looking for:

+ Tops and bottoms?
+ A particular season and in-store ship date?
+ Price points?
+ Outerwear and accessories?
+ Men's and women's and/or children's collections?
+ Roughly how many styles?
+ What size of board or presentation format?
+ How many boards or pages would be best?
+ Does the presentation requires flats and illustrations, or does the interviewer prefers flats presentations over illustrations?
+ Is logo artwork needed on the garments, and if so, can you get a copy of the logo artwork to use?
+ Does the interviewer expect CAD work only, hand-rendered work only, or a combination?
+ Will you be making a presentation of the designs to a group of people on your next interview or just for the interviewer?

Design houses have different levels of expectations of portfolio presentations based on the designer's experience. Current college students applying for an internship or part-time job might be expected to have student work from school presented as a compilation of their class work. A recent college graduate will be expected to have the collection-focused portfolio he or she has worked on in FDP. Some design houses will expect a design collection (small or complete presentation) designed specifically for their company.

The graduate school portfolio features intensely focused, specific areas of design illustrations using refined techniques. The experienced designer's portfolio would be expected to show an increasing level of work from past employers with press releases, catalogue or periodical feature ads, or sales brochures. The portfolio collections of experienced designers should show only those garments they designed or assisted in designing. Be sure to make clear, when presenting your portfolio, whether the designs you are showing have been produced and what your role was.

Your vision is very important. You should know whom you're selling to, what your marketing and advertising says about you, and whom it's speaking to. Me personally, I don't try to please everyone. I understand who I am selling to and I work towards that vision all the time.

RALPH LAUREN

PREPARING FOR THE INTERVIEW

Practice and prepare for your interview sessions. See Exercise 9.1 to practice a mock interview with a company executive or design director. Prior to your interview prepare a "to do" list. Start with the following list, and add any items as necessary. Be ready for the big day with these items completed:

1. Make a list of key ingredients of the company's image and product line. Memorize and process the information for the interview so you sound knowledgeable when asked questions about the company by your interviewer.

2. Make a list of your professional and personal assets and weaknesses. Be prepared to answer a question about your strengths and weaknesses in an interview by choosing the top two assets and weaknesses you think are most relevant to an employer. Be prepared to explain how you are dealing with your weaknesses to improve your performance.

3. Make a list of what you are currently looking for in a job or an employer. Memorize and process the information so you can assess the job being offered prior to, during, and after the interview.

4. Know your 2-, 5-, and 10-year plan. Many interviewers ask the question, "Where do you see yourself in 10 years?"

5. Practice shaking an interviewer's hand with a classmate or professor. The best handshake is firm, brief, matter-of-fact, and to the point. It sets a professional tone for the meeting.

6. Be prepared for a difficult or challenging interview. When you arrive, if the interview is more relaxed and less difficult than you anticipated, you won't be taken off guard.

7. Prepare for the real interview with the mock interview exercise. You can also ask a friend or relative to help you with a mock interview.

8. Practice pronouncing the interviewer's name. If you aren't sure of the pronunciation, don't guess. The best approach would be to call the human resources department and ask for pronunciation, or call the receptionist and explain you are scheduled to meet with [name, pronounced as best you can], and you want the correct way to pronounce his or her name before you arrive.

9. Wear comfortable shoes and apparel to the interview. Follow basic guidelines for business attire (see the box "Interview and On-the Job Business Attire").

The best thing you can do is go away from this saying, "I can do this too," because it's all possible and I'm living proof.

RALPH LAUREN

10. Be sure to have an index card or your business card pasted to the inside front or back cover of your portfolio case with your name, address, phone number, and e-mail address. If you were to lose your portfolio, you might have a chance that someone would contact you to return it.

11. Prepare your portfolio case with extra copies of your résumé in a folder in the inside pocket of the book. When you arrive at the interview, even if you have sent a copy to the interviewer prior to your meeting, it is best have a hard copy of your résumé ready to hand to the interviewer.

12. Find the correct carrying case for your sketchbook, or insert the sketchbook inside the zipper case of your portfolio for the interview. It is customary to arrive at the interview with *only* your portfolio case. Do not carry a messy or jumbled stack of additional artwork or bags into the interview.

13. Plan to arrive early to the interview to avoid being late. The best advice is to arrive one-half hour early. You can always wait in the lobby or at a local coffee shop if you are extremely early. Being late to an interview is usually a poor way to make an impression on the interviewer. Some interviewers will not meet with you if you are more than 10 minutes late.

If an extenuating circumstance is making you late, call the interviewer at least 10 minutes prior to the interview time to explain your delay. Your excuse may or may not be accepted by the interviewer. If you are driving or taking public transportation, arrange to do a mock trip to the site during the exact hour of travel a week prior to the interview to be sure you will be there on time and to familiarize yourself with the route. Many tall corporate buildings in large cities require that you sign in in the lobby before you can be sent upstairs for your meeting. There may be a line of people waiting to do the same thing as you, and it can take 20 minutes to clear you through the lobby.

14. Plan to go on the interview even if it is not the perfect job for you so you can gain interviewing experience and/or possibly make a connection for another position you might want. During the interview, be interested and engaged because you might find as the interview unfolds, you change your mind and are actually interested in this position.

Adapting your portfolio for interviews at different companies can be a challenge. After all, your portfolio is representing your creative talents as suitable for a design position in each company where you apply. In addition you are being evaluated by the way your dress and act during the interview. Your own dress and demeanor represent you as a professional in the fashion industry, *not necessarily* as the target consumer that your prospective employer caters to.

You might find an interviewer in a young, trendy company to be very conservatively dressed or wearing a hip fashion outfit. However the interviewer dresses, the interviewee is usually expected to be dressed professionally. While some interviewers can look past some of your more trendy choices of dress or demeanor, others have very strict standards for how interviewees should present themselves, and strict interviewers hire based at least in part upon whether an interviewee has dressed in what they consider appropriate.

You should depersonalize your appearance somewhat, especially if you are not in the target market of the prospective employer. This may take some practice, as creative people want to have a touch of their own designer style showing in the way they dress. Little touches of accent colors, small accents of jewelry, and other little touches of personal style added to a conservative outfit go a long way when you are being scrutinized for a position by an interviewer. Later, when you have the job, you can adapt to the company dress code and add accents of your own style into your work wardrobe. For the interview, less is more.

Interviewing with different companies might necessitate research into how you should dress the part of a designer for each initial interview. Research the company, studio, designer, offices, showrooms, and websites to get an insider view of the company. Look at the way the website is formatted. Most design offices, studios, or companies have a given personality based upon their clientele and their design aesthetics. If you have access to the office site, you can go to the location and casually observe what the employees are wearing and take note. You can plan your interview attire to be slightly more formal than the prevailing style if you are applying for a position with a company that specializes in, say, sportswear or activewear.

If your interview is with an avant-garde design company at its studio design offices, you would want to consider dressing in interview attire that is more up-to-the-minute with current design trends than if you are interviewing with a large corporation—for example, for a position developing designs for a private label of a national department store chain.

Here are some guidelines for dressing for job interviews.

Do's and Don'ts for Women

Women's Do's	Women's Don'ts
Do wear a basic business suit in a conservative color: e.g., black, brown, gray. If there is a pattern or texture (tweed, twill, herringbone, stripe, etc.), be sure it is small-scale.	Don't wear loud-colored or patterned suits or blouses.
Do wear a blouse or a conservative knit top in a tasteful complementary color to your suit.	Don't wear a camisole or tank top showing excess cleavage.
Be sure your blouse or shirt is long enough to be tucked into your skirt or drape appropriately over the waistline of your skirt without a gap of skin showing or the tail of the shirt sloppily hanging outside of the jacket.	Don't show bare midriff, ever.
Do wear practical pumps or open-toe shoes in appropriate climates. Keep heel height to a kitten heel or a 2.5" heel. Check the weather on the day of the interview; if you will need to wear all-weather boots to the interview, change into your shoes inside the building lobby or close to the interview site.	Don't wear stiletto heels. Interviewers can think you are dressed inappropriately for a business meeting.
Skirt length should be between the knee and mid-thigh.	Don't wear a miniskirt, ever.
Do keep jewelry to a minimum. Conservative pearl earrings, small diamond or cubic zirconium stud earrings, and no more than two rings, and one toe ring, if you must. Do wear a small bracelet or statement cuff if the outfit calls for it, and/or a small necklace.	Don't wear large hoop earrings; long, dangly earrings; loud, clanging multiple bracelets; multiple string, macramé, or rubber bracelets; a statement medallion (e.g., a large dollar sign)
Do wear nude or conservatively colored legwear.	Don't wear fishnets, or fishnets with cut-up holes and safety pins.
Do have a basic manicure and/or pedicure the day before. Choose a neutral color, and keep nail length fairly short and shaped rounded-square.	Don't have long fake or real claws for nails; paint your nails a loud, flashy color; or add multiple graphic motifs.
Do wax your upper lip, uni-brow, and excessive facial hair.	Don't forget personal hygiene, especially from the neck up.
Do keep your hair groomed and well-kept, blown dry, or simply stylized.	Don't wear a Bumpit, tease your hair, or add unnatural bright colors to your hair. Don't shave half of your head.
Do sit with your legs crossed at the ankles or at the knees. Try not to cross and uncross your legs. Remember you are wearing a skirt, and any movement needs to be refined for modesty.	Don't sit with your legs open. Don't let your skirt ride up past mid-thigh when you cross your legs.
Do wear soft, understated makeup.	Don't wear heavy foundation, loud-colored lipstick, heavy blush, angularly shaped eyebrows, heavy eye shadow, or harsh eyeliner. Don't wear excessive, trashy makeup.

Do's and Don'ts for Men

Men's Do's	Men's Don'ts
Do wear a conservative suit, dress shirt, and tie.	Don't wear a flashy suit, a loud-patterned or -colored shirt, or a funky tie.
Do be clean-shaven or have conservatively well-groomed facial hair.	Don't have a five o'clock shadow and a scraggly beard or mustache, or overly stylized sideburns.

General Do's and Don'ts for Women and Men

Do's	Don'ts
Do wear business attire as described in the tables for women and men.	Don't wear a biker outfit, a hoodie, or a goth outfit.
Do remove headwear unless your religion requires you to cover your head indoors.	Don't wear a hat, baseball cap, or sport visor.
Do wear your eyeglasses or contact lenses if you need them to see clearly.	Don't wear sunglasses indoors.
Do wear long sleeves to cover tattoos. Women may wear pantsuits if they have tattoos on their legs.	Don't show your tattoos if you can cover them.
Do wear deodorant.	Don't wear cologne or perfume. Your interviewer may have asthma or allergies.
Do have freshly manicured or trimmed fingernails.	Don't have dirt under your fingernails or have chipped fingernails.
Do use the bathroom before you leave for the interview, if possible. If you have a long commute to the interview, plan to arrive early enough to use the restroom well before the time of your appointment.	Don't wait until the last minute to use the restroom.
Do turn off your mobile phone and put it away.	Don't wear a Bluetooth device, MP3 player, earbuds, or headsets. Absolutely no texting, e-mailing, Facebook posting, or talking on the cell phone while in the waiting room or during an interview.
Do eat long before the interview. Brush your teeth, and check for food caught between your teeth.	Don't walk into the interview with food, coffee, or bottled beverages. Don't eat spicy or unfamiliar foods the evening or morning before an interview; you don't want to have a bad reaction to something new in your diet. Don't be hungover. If you smoke, don't arrive at the interview smelling like a cigarette (an interviewer may be allergic) or anything else that you smoke.

General Do's and Don'ts for Women and Men *(continued)*

Do feel free to accept a beverage from the choices offered to you.	Don't ask for a beverage if one is not offered.
Do make direct eye contact with the interviewer, especially when answering questions.	Don't avert eye contact with the interviewer. Don't let your eyes wander away from the interviewer or stare out the window or around the room. Even if the interview is not going your way, or if you have lost interest in the job, stay engaged. You might learn something that you can apply to future interviews.
Do maintain a relaxed but attentive posture.	Don't sniffle or excessively touch your face or hair or use other nervous gestures.
Do think before you respond to questions so that you can frame your answers in ways that reflect well on your professionalism. Respond to the specific questions the interviewer poses.	Don't tell the interviewer your personal or professional life story.
Use correct grammar and your professional vocabulary.	Don't use slang or "fillers" such as "like," "um," "you know," or "I mean."
Do listen attentively to the interviewer for information about the job and the company and for a clear understanding of the interviewer's questions for you.	Don't, under any circumstances, interrupt the interviewer.
Do, when invited to ask questions, focus on the job's qualifications and responsibilities.	Don't debate or be contrary to the interviewer. Don't ask personal questions. Don't ask, "How many vacation days do I get?" "What is the starting salary?" or other questions about employee benefits and company policies toward employees. Wait until you get a job offer and then ask the human resources manager.
Do listen for clues that the interview is finished, and then thank the interviewer for his or her time and leave with a clear understanding of what the next step will be.	Don't leave abruptly or overstay your visit.

OBJECTIVE: To be become comfortable with the interview process through mock situations.

1. Review *Women's Wear Daily* online and in print and your college's career counseling service's job descriptions for assistant designers, pattern makers, associate designers, and technical designers. Get accustomed to the descriptions and the experience or background that the companies or designers are looking for so you can write a mock job description for this exercise.

2. Research different companies and/or designers that are in your category of design. You will choose one of these companies to be submitted to your instructor as a mock interview for someone in your class.

3. Set up for the interviews: If the class has students who have created portfolios for different design specialties, the class will break up into the categories of design in which their specialty is the focus. If the class has one category of design portfolios (for instance, menswear), then it is not necessary to break up into categories.

   To create the mock interview situation, each student in each category will need to set up a mock interview for another student as follows:

   a. Each student in each specialty group picks a name of a current design company and writes a job description for an assistant designer for this company on a small piece of paper.

   b. The instructor collects the job descriptions from the students. The instructor chooses pairs of designers (either from within the same category of design or by mixing categories).

   c. The instructor then gives each student another student's description of a job to interview for, based on the category of design featured in his or her portfolio.

   d. Students will take turns interviewing each other in pairs, role-play, the candidate and the interviewer, as outlined below.

4. Each student researches the background of both companies the pair has picked: merchandise mix, sizing, distribution, location of design offices, and so on.

5. The students prepare mock interviews of one another. For each position, the interviewer makes a list of questions for the designer. The interviewer does not share the questions in advance with the designer. The designer prepares for the interview by anticipating the type of questions the interviewer might ask relative to the background of the company and the job description.

6. The interviewer conducts the mock interview as outlined in Step 7. Because all interviews are different and do not follow a standard format, the questions that you ask the interviewee may follow the basic guidelines on page 324, and you may customize the interview to your style of questioning. The role play begins by the potential employee walking into a room set up with a table and two chairs, representing the interviewer's desk in an office. Interviewees should be ready for the interview with their portfolios and résumés and consider shaking hands with the interviewer when entering the room in the mock interview. The interviewer is seated on one side of the table. The interviewer completes the interview by thanking the designer for applying and deciding whether to have the interviewee return for a second interview; if the applicant is to return, the interviewer gives the applicant instructions as to what type of additional presentation to prepare for the next interview.

7. The applicant responds to the interviewer, adapting the answers prepared in anticipation of the interview to the interviewer's actual questions. The applicant should also use the invitation to pose questions to emphasize any qualifications that make him or her especially qualified and to cover any important points not yet discussed. The applicant leaves, expressing thanks to the interviewer and interest in the position and shaking hands.

8. After the role-play session, the interviewer makes a list of the pros and cons of hiring this designer for the position and decides whether the designer should be hired.

9. The designer makes a list of pros and cons of working with for the design house and assesses the likelihood of being offered the job. The designer can also write down a list of pros and cons for accepting or declining a potential a job offer based on the interview.

10. The interviewer and designer share their findings.

11. The pair change roles and start a new interview for the second company they have researched, following Steps 6 through 10.

12. The class meets as a group and shares what each pair learned from the role-play. Following are some examples of points for discussion:

▶ Share some of your individual pro-and-con findings from Steps 8 and 9, and discuss where there might have been a misunderstanding or misinterpretation of one party by the other. This can be a valuable tool in learning to read other people's social cues in a hiring situation.

▶ Did any of the interviewers pose unanticipated questions? If so, how did the applicant respond?

▶ Was either partner thrown off by any questions, gestures, or inferences by the other? Share those instances with the class and see whether either member of the pair was reading the wrong cues from the other party.

▶ How did the interviewers and applicants deal with portfolio presentations that were not an obvious match for the job?

▶ How well did the applicant sell his or her qualifications? What would you suggest for the applicant to do in the next interview to improve?

WHAT TO EXPECT IN AN INTERVIEW SITUATION

Although every interview scenario is different, you should be aware of some basic modes of the interview process. Each interviewer may or may not practice some of these actions, as each interview is based upon the two people interacting in a room at a given time. There will be spontaneous reactions and chemistry between two people in a work environment. You or your interviewer may be having a bad day, and the experience could be a bust, not because your portfolio and market insight are off base, but because it is simply a bad day.

Keep in mind that there are many variables to your being offered a position. You may not get the job based solely upon your portfolio and the personality and experience you present. There may be outside forces that decide for the interviewer who the right candidate is. These might include the influence of executives within the organization or a friend of the decision maker to hire a relative as a favor. No matter how talented or well prepared for the interview you are, another applicant may be better suited for the position. You might even be overqualified. The point is, if you don't get the job, you may never know why. Some interviewers will give you feedback on your portfolio or experience when you get a letter or phone call saying you weren't hired for the job. Some interviewers will give you feedback on your portfolio presentation on-site, which is always helpful. You can make changes to your book that might change your future.

You can use each interview as a learning experience by looking for repeat patterns from your interviews. If you feel your portfolio presentation needs tweaking, you can redesign your portfolio presentation based on the feedback you received. Find an experienced friend or instructor to guide you through some suggestions for changes if necessary.

The interviewer will most likely ask you sit in a chair opposite his or her desk or drafting table. Other setups can be standing at a patternmaking or grading table in the design room, sitting at a large table in a conference room, or meeting an interviewer "on the fly" at an airport, diner, coffee shop, restaurant, taxi, or limo. Because designers and corporate executives are busy and have unpredictable schedules, your appointment may suddenly need to change venues, or this may be the only time the interviewer can squeeze in a 20-minute meeting. It shouldn't be a reflection upon your importance to the interviewer. The demands on designers' time can be grueling as they try to fit in as many applicants as possible in a small window of time, in addition to completing their daily design tasks.

Have a copy of your résumé ready to hand to your interviewer in the highly likely event that you're asked for it, and keep your portfolio close at hand so that you can show it when the interviewer wants to look at it.

Most interviews begin with a brief overview of you résumé bullet points and experience. Be prepared to discuss what your work experience is *after* the interviewer asks you questions. Remember that the interviewer is leading the conversation and will ask you whether you have any questions after asking his or her questions for you.

Be prepared for a request to "tell me a little about yourself." This can catch you off guard if you aren't prepared for such informality, so preplan a basic remark that describes your design ambitions and lifestyle.

When the interviewer asks to see your book, present it on the table, facing the interviewer directly in front of him or her. Unzip the case and open to the first page. Then let interviewer turn the pages at his or her own pace, not yours.

During the review of your book, the interviewer may have questions like the following regarding the general impressions of your collection:

+ How did you come up with your ideas?
+ What trends do you think are important going forward?
+ Where do you get your influences or gather your information?
+ For whom did you design the collection(s)?
+ How do you shop the retail market?
+ May I see your sketchbook to see your design process?

Generally speaking, the interviewer may ask you any of these questions:

+ What are your greatest strength and weakest asset?
+ How well do you work with other designers?
+ Can you multitask?
+ Can you put together technical information for tech packs?
+ Are you able to travel domestically and/or internationally?
+ Do you have a passport for travel?
+ Why do you want to work for this company?
+ Why are you the best person for this position?
+ What do you know about this company?
+ Where do you see yourself in 5 or 10 years?
+ Why did you leave a job that is listed on your résumé?
+ How do you handle pressure on the job?
+ If we were to hire you, how soon can you start work?

As the designer being interviewed, when the interviewer asks whether you have any questions, it is appropriate to ask the following:

+ What is your time frame for hiring someone; is it right away?
+ What is the typical day like in the position?
+ Will I be working directly with you on a day-to-day basis or with another designer?
+ Whom would I report to?
+ How many designers are in the department?
+ Where do you do your production?
+ Do you have a design sample room? Are there pattern makers, drapers, and sample-makers on staff?
+ What are the work hours?
+ What are the opportunities for advancement for employees who have been here for more than a year?
+ Should I expect to hear back from you regarding the interview? Should I call your office in a certain number of days, or will I hear from you?

The interviewer will answer your questions and may take you on a tour of the design studio. Take your cue from the interviewer about when the meeting is ready to end. This is when to say thank you and express your interest in the next step.

Don't spend time beating on a wall, hoping to transform it into a door.

COCO CHANEL

INTERVIEW FOLLOW-UP

Congratulations! You've completed your first designer interview. Each time you interview for a job, you should get more relaxed and confident with yourself and the process. Just remember everyone is a little nervous or tentative during interviews, and the interviewer most times wants to put you a little at ease, to get to know you a little better in order to make an educated decision about the hire.

Immediately after the interview, prepare a hard copy of a thank you letter. If you know the interviewer is traveling and won't be in the office for weeks, you can send an e-mail thank you letter in addition to a hard copy letter sent to the office.

After the second or third interview, no matter how redundant it may sound, it is always good to send a follow-up thank you letter. Include in the letter any presentations that you made, and the names of any staff member that you had the opportunity to meet. Use correct spellings of the individuals' names by asking them for their business cards during your meeting with them. Send follow-up letters individually to the designers, executives of the company, and human resources interviewers if you were also interviewed with them. All these people will appreciate a letter in the mail thanking them for their time.

INDUSTRY PROFESSIONALS' PORTFOLIO REVIEWS

Read through the following interviews for some insight into how your portfolio can be viewed from different professional perspectives. Each interviewer will look for something different for the same type of position.

I guess you just fall into things when you're supposed to.

STEPHEN SPROUSE

You can create a simple personal letterhead on the computer. Give your full contact information.

When you are at the interview, be sure to get the exact mailing address and spelling of the interviewer(s) name(s).

Allow an extra line space between the date and the interviewer's address.

Leave an extra line space between paragraphs.

Choose letter paper that matches your résumé paper. Include a copy of the résumé along with your letter, and/or an optional leave-behind 8½" x 11" synopsis design page. Plan a matching business-size envelope in the same paper stock as the letter and résumé.

Choose a simple font, like Times New Roman, for the letterhead. You can choose one font for the letterhead, and another font for the body of the letter if you like. Use 10- or 12-point font size for the letter, with the exception of your name, which you can optionally size to 14 or 16 point. Center your contact information on the top of the page.

Center the body of your letter on the page from the top to bottom margin. Approximate placement of the date can be 7–10 lines down from the letterhead, depending upon the length of your letter. The letter should be two to three short paragraphs of work, not any longer than shown here.

Leave a line space between the address and the salutation. Address the interviewer by his or her family name unless you are invited to use the person's given name.

Begin the body of the letter an extra line space below the salutation. Single-space the body of the letter.

Send the thank you right away. As soon as your interview is over, send out the thank you letter in the mail. The interviewer will be very impressed by your business acumen.

Notice that the opening paragraph focuses on "you" rather than "me." Keep the sentences short, focused on the interviewer's talents and workplace.

Remind the interviewer of why you are a good fit for the position. Touch upon some of the skill sets you have that are right for the job description.

It is customary to close the letter with "Sincerely". Leave 3–4 spaces between your name and the closing so you can sign the letter.

Close with a show of appreciation and interest.

Type "enclosure" or "enclosures" underneath your name if you are including, for example, your résumé or a leave-behind piece.

Jane Doe

742 East 79th Street
Apartment 4G
New York, NY 10017
Phone 212.555.5555
Email janedoe@yahoo.com

May 25, 2012

Mr. John Smith
John Smith Designs, Inc.
8407 Broadway, Suite 616
New York, NY 10016

Dear Mr. Smith:

Thank you for taking the time to meet with me today regarding the position of assistant designer with your firm. It was a pleasure to speak to you about your design background, and how you work on a day-to-day basis.

I am very excited about being considered for the position. I hope my practical knowledge of Gerber Technology can be an asset to your production needs. I enjoy working with Gerber software, and I am confident I could assist you in the process of bringing forward new product with your team of associates.

Thank you again for your time, and I look forward to hearing from you. Please feel free to call me or e-mail me should you have any further questions.

Sincerely,

Jane Doe
enclosure(s)

A sample of a follow-up letter after the first interview.

BIOGRAPHY

Formerly vice president of two major national apparel companies, Danskin and Capezio, Peter Morrone has had a distinguished career requiring design, administrative, and fiscal responsibility. A remarkable parallel career in academia includes positions as Professor Emeritus and Chairman, Fashion Department, School of the Arts, Virginia Commonwealth University; and Instructor, Parsons School of Design and Fashion Institute of Technology in New York. Extensive travel to Paris, Milan, London, Tokyo, Hong Kong, and Canada gives him a perspective of the global marketplace. His recognition and credibility have been enhanced by his TV appearances, videos, and articles in trade publications.

INTERVIEW

Question: When you interview a candidate for a design position, what strikes you that this is a designer with potential?

PM: In addition to the materials that are presented, which help me to evaluate the interviewee's sense of style, color, proportion, etc., it is always the personality traits that are revealed via the verbal interaction. His or her enthusiasm, passion for fashion, confidence, and—most important—the expressed desire to work for your company are the deciding factors. Personality means a lot—it goes beyond the portfolio. It's about the person themselves; who they really are. The portfolios are not the end-all but the way the person comes across. I know when it is real. Body language and eye contact are also, as they indicate a certain amount of poise and confidence.

Q: How do you garner the level of practical knowledge the designer has from looking at illustrations, not the 3D product during an interview?

PM: Practical knowledge is displayed by including fabric swatches in some of their garment illustrations. A fabrics swatch shows that the candidate has taken the next step in the creative process. The potential employee should bring up the content and cost of the fabric used, e.g., "I am thinking of a wool gabardine for this style but it could be just as effective in a wool/polyester blend for a better price point." The same applies to intricate details that the candidate mentions that could be simplified to reduce cost. Of course all of this is revealed in leading questions that I may ask in order to determine their practical knowledge of production.

Q: What do you look for in a portfolio to get a sense of the designer's market knowledge?

PM: Desire, with a real interest in the job and the company. Today it is easy to do research before you get there, which means retail shopping, the Internet, catalogues, etc. Know what the latest looks are and how they affect my company's offerings. Imagine how impressed I would be if the candidate tells me about my latest group that they have seen in Macy's, what they thought of it, and perhaps have the confidence to talk about some improvements.

Q: How do you assess whether the designer will be a good fit with your work style, environment, and design team?

PM: Here is my inspiration. As director of design at Danskin, one of my responsibilities was to be a liaison to one of our licensees, the Jim Henson

Organization, as we were producing Muppet character apparel for children. On one occasion I was working with one of their creative directors, when a package was put on his desk containing a résumé and a handmade puppet. The puppet was a miniature version of the creative director, complete with eyeglasses. He immediately said to his associate, "Hire this person!" and the candidate got the job. Why? Evidently the candidate did research on the company to the point of getting a photo of the creative director.

How does this translate to our business? The proposed interviewee should take the time to study all they can about the look and the merchandising concepts of my label before the interview and present me with one to two pages or one board especially made for my company. It should feature the company's colors, logo, and styles. This approach is valid in any category of business they are interested in: dresses, sportswear, accessories, etc. This shows the interviewer that you took the time, are serious, and that you really want to work for the label. It's the clincher!

BIOGRAPHY

Margee Minier's international design career spans 30-plus years. In the mid-1970s, she designed eveningwear for Albert Capraro; costumes for Geoffrey Holder; and contemporary missy dresses and sportswear for Carillon Fashions, Orsini Sportswear, Act I, Rue Jolie, Rap Session, and Sweet Talk; traveling to Paris to attend couture fashion shows and sketching emerging street and boutique trends. She then became the international fashion advisor for the Wool Bureau and Saks Fifth Avenue.

In 1979, Ms. Minier moved to Paris and became a member of the Chambre Syndicale de la Couture Parisienne, where she wrote and illustrated fashion trend reports from Paris and London and organized fashion shows for the

Kimono design by Margee Minier

Salon de Prêt-a-Porter Féminin. She created advanced color spectrums and fiber/ fabric trends for the Wool Bureau and promoted Paris trends for worldwide distribution. Her clients included Yves Saint Laurent, Givenchy, Pierre Cardin, and Emmanuel Ungaro. She spent 6 weeks in China and Hong Kong lecturing and promoting Paris fashion and the versatile properties of wool. She also taught fashion design at the Eliza Couture School of Fashion Design in Taiwan.

In 1984, Ms. Minier moved to Tahiti and opened a boutique exclusively selling her couture fashions, hand-painted kimonos, and evening bag designs for an international clientele.

In 1987, she started a family and moved to Connecticut and converted a horse barn into her design studio, Atelier Margétoile. For the past 20 years, she has created uniquely wearable art pieces for private clientele in France, New York, New England, and Tahiti. She creates collage bags, jewelry, découpage art, and window treatments and teaches fashion design and French.

Ms. Minier created a method of teaching French to children using culture through the arts, music, impressionism, fashion, make-up, jewelry, science, and history.

INTERVIEW

Question: What do you look for in a portfolio when you review a designer's work?

MM: A young designer's portfolio should have fresh, new ideas which are innovative and unique. The styles should be relevant to the current market and reflect the ability to design styles that will fit in and enhance the look of the firm interviewing them. The illustrations should show the designer's degree of understanding of patternmaking, draping, and technical skills. This is evident if the style lines are clearly sketched and in proportions which correspond to the dimensions of the body form they are designed for versus a wildly illustrated fantasy design. The book should show that he or she is an ideal candidate for the position they are being interviewed for.

Q: What was the one best thing you learned from your first employer about your portfolio presentation and job search?

MM: I learned that I should believe in my portfolio and also believe in myself. I must exude self-confidence and not leave an impression that I am anxious to get the job. I should portray the message that I am capable and talented and will be an asset to their firm. It's important to research the firm before the interview. The interview should not be about me: it should be about what I can do for them. In addition, during the initial interview process, I should wait for a question to be asked before answering it. I learned to listen and to tune in to what I felt they were seeking, rather than just talk about me. I learned you need to show them that you can adapt your style to their look and clientele. A young designer, even if he or she has put some of their fantasy ideas into their portfolio, should be careful not to give the impression that they want to change the world but rather that they can go with the flow of the firm, work cooperatively with others and fit in.

Q: What do you think should be included in a designer's portfolio presentation?

MM: Based upon my experience, I've seen a shift or reversal which has occurred over time as a result of a woman's role in society. In the seventies and eighties, as she gained ground in a man's world, I saw a new woman that emerged—more women began working, moving into a higher income bracket, and finding they had more money to spend on clothes. This sophistication resulted in the emergence of a new class of women interested in designer fashion. Women no longer let designers dictate what they would wear or things like the length of their skirts or where their waistline should fall. Women's new attitudes changed the industry. Therefore, a young designer's portfolio should reflect this fast-paced world; and reflect it in a subtle way. The illustrations should not look like the student labored over them. They should have smooth quick lines—although the designs are well-thought out. They should look spontaneous, not bogged down with details, and should show originality. The rendering should be simple and partial, these are not museum paintings or for an art gallery. There should be both harmonies. This would translate into variations on a theme portrayed in a multi-figure illustration with dramatic looks using opposites, such as a long and a short skirt, a wide and narrow pant, both straight and full lines. There should be a variety of proportions. The opening pages of the book should be of illustrations which reflect the look and style of the company before showing illustrations which depict designs relating to other areas of the industry. Ultimately, a diverse portfolio will show the interviewer that you are open and flexible and that you have the ability to create diversity in your collections from season to season.

BIOGRAPHY

For 21 years until his retirement in 2005, Cyprus-born designer Christos Yiannakou created couture wedding gowns known for their romantic, classic, and unique qualities for his own label and company, Christos Inc. The bridal collection is now under the creative direction of the designer Amsale Aberra. Christos's bridal design career spans 45 years, including 24 years as a bridal designer for two bridal houses prior to owning his own company. *Brides* magazine awarded Christos Designer of the Year in 1969, a Hall of Fame Award in 1996, and a 2006 Lifetime Achievement Award.

Christos Yiannakou, couture wedding gown designer

INTERVIEW

Question: Did you always know you wanted to be a designer?

CY: No. I came to this country in 1952 not knowing anyone, except for my aunt. I worked for five years doing any kind of work. One of my bosses noticed my illustrations I was sketching on my lunch hour, and he took me to enroll in a fashion design school.

Q: What was your first job in the industry? Can you describe the interview?

CY: My first job was not in bridal. I worked one year as a textile designer, because that was the job that was offered to me after winning first and second awards at the culmination of my design school years. I didn't know anything about textiles, but I learned very fast. I knew this was not what I wanted to do the rest of my life. I worked for two years after that in freelance jobs. I put an ad in *WWD* as a designer looking for work, and a bridal company called me. He and the buyers liked my work, and hired me as an assistant designer, but I never met his designer for almost a year. I finished the line on my own, and I became the designer. My boss took a chance with me. With wedding gowns, I had no idea where to start. If you have talent, you can do it.

Q: What would you advise a designer to put in their portfolio to make the book distinctive?

CY: Don't just show one type of work. You won't know who will be interested in your book. I always showed wedding gowns, evening gowns, cocktail dresses, and bridesmaid's dresses in my book, so I would have the chance to get a job in bridal or something else. A designer is a designer. He or she should be able to design anything. I would advise a designer not to leave their portfolio with anyone so they can copy your work. This happened to me; soon after I left my book with an interviewer, I saw my designs in the newspaper.

Q: What do you look for in a portfolio when you review a designer's work?

CY: Sketches; anyone can do. You don't know if they are some else's work. Don't just say you are a designer and you want to sketch. Show me you are eager and ready to work; this is what it comes down to. You need to know clothing construction, and if you don't, I need to hire someone else to interpret your work. You need to know how to tell a pattern maker and production people how to make something, or else it won't be your design. My advice is that you don't push yourself to think you are the greatest. Lower yourself, prove yourself, see if you can make your ideas happen over and over again, work around the clock to accomplish what you want to do. If you have a talent, don't give up. Be sure of yourself that you are good at design, and prove it to someone else.

BIOGRAPHY

Amsale Aberra's career as a couture bridal and evening wear designer happened by necessity. While planning her 1985 nuptials to film executive Neil Brown, Amsale scoured the stores to find a simple, refined wedding dress. She found little in the way of clean, sophisticated gowns, and discovered an untapped niche in the bridal market—elegant and understated dresses.

"Everything was so overdone and with too much ornamentation," says Amsale, who was sure that her taste in gowns was shared by many other brides-to-be. Amsale placed a classified advertisement for custom-made gowns for other brides-to-be who shared her taste, and so, with a few responses, a sketchpad full of designs, and a small team of couture sewers, Amsale started her business out of her New York City loft apartment. Since then, the name Amsale (pronounced Ahm-sah'-leh) has become synonymous with the "forever modern" wedding dress. Her collections are designed for brides who desire a fashionable, sophisticated, and timeless look.

Amsale Aberra, bridal and evening wear designer, at a show of her bridal designs. *(Courtesy of WWD/Steve Eichner)*

Amsale's love of fashion began when she was a young girl growing up in Ethiopia. However, Amsale never considered becoming a designer: "In Ethiopia, there were no fashion designers. I never knew that designing beautiful clothes was a profession to which one could aspire."

Amsale convinced her parents to allow her to leave Ethiopia in order to study commercial art in New England. While she was in school, a revolution broke out in her native country, which forced Amsale to stay in the United States to support herself and complete her undergraduate education at the University of Massachusetts, Boston, through a number of odd jobs. With limited financial resources, Amsale admits, "I would design and sew my own clothes because I couldn't afford to buy new things. That's when I first thought of becoming a fashion designer."

Amsale left Boston, enrolled in New York's Fashion Institute of Technology, and began her career as a design assistant for Harvé Benard upon graduation. Two years later, Amsale launched her custom bridal gown business with her "forever modern" approach to design.

She extends that viewpoint of individuality to her collection of chic and refined gowns for the bridal party, and in the Amsale Evening collection of couture evening wear—both lines a natural progression from the modern styles of her bridal collection. Amsale's ball gowns, cocktail dresses, and evening suits have been featured on the fashion and party pages of all the top fashion magazines and worn by celebrities and socialites including Halle Berry, Julia Roberts, Selma Blair, Salma Hayek, Lucy Liu, Heather Graham, Kim Basinger, Deborah Norville, Vivica A. Fox, Vanessa Williams, Lisa Kudrow, Heidi Klum, and Katherine Heigl. Producers turn to Amsale when they need beautiful designs for films and television programs; her gowns have been featured on *The Oprah Winfrey Show*, *Grey's Anatomy*, and *27 Dresses*.

Amsale's bridal designs are found nationwide at the finest boutiques and specialty retailers, such as Bergdorf Goodman, Saks Fifth Avenue, and Neiman Marcus. Her Madison Avenue boutique, which opened in September 2001, has fulfilled Amsale's desire to present her designs in a setting that reflected her "forever modern" vision. The boutique offers a full range of designs from all of the brands within the Amsale Design Group, including Amsale, Amsale Bridesmaids, Christos, and Kenneth Pool. The Kenneth Pool line is designed by Project Runway alum Austin Scarlett, Amsale is the Creative Director for the Amsale and Christos lines.

INTERVIEW

Question: Do you remember your first interview for your first job in the industry, and what apparel did you represent in your portfolio?
AA: I was a sportswear major in school. My teachers recommended I put together more of a general interview portfolio.

Q: What do you look for in a designer's portfolio during an interview?
AA: My advice for students is really two things: Firstly, be passionate and committed in the interview, and that should show in your work. Your work will show me that you were able to follow instructions from your professors or from your school projects. Secondly, your portfolio designs should have a strong point of view. If you understand my design aesthetic with a strong point of view, your entire book will show me that. You will be the right fit for me if your design aesthetic is very clean. If the designer is incredibly elaborate in their aesthetic, then this is not the right place; and they would be better off at another company. By showing me consistency throughout their work, I can judge if their point of view would be right for me, or if they would be better at another company that shares their aesthetic; better that than try to change them.

Q: What work should be included in a designer's portfolio?
AA: A school portfolio can be diverse like a project. You can show me you can follow a project with your interpretation, execution, and versatility. This gives me more to work with if I hire them than if they stuck to one vision or collection. It doesn't need to be a bridal portfolio to meet with me for an interview. I can look at an evening wear portfolio and know you would be good for bridal if it is the right aesthetic.

Q: How should a designer prepare for an interview?
AA: No matter the specialization, the designer should want to be into my work. Look at my website, give me a feeling about my company and my aesthetic in your collection. It can be sportswear, but they should want to design or learn about bridal design.

Q: What is your best advice for a young designer looking for a first job?
AA: Be passionate, do your homework about the company, get your foot in the door, don't worry about the money, do everything possible to get into the company, tell your interviewer you are a hard worker (and follow through with hard work), be able to take instruction so they can relieve me of the things I trust them with; they can assist and learn. Senior designers want to hear from an interviewee that they would die to have this job! Back up the passion with a strong portfolio and commitment; that is the best combination.

BIOGRAPHY

Bissie Clover is a senior apparel executive with extensive experience in the wholesale, retail, and manufacturing arenas. She brings to the table a set of skills that encompass the disciplines of design, product development, merchandising, sourcing, and sales presentation in both the private label and wholesale sectors. This experience provides her the unique capability of understanding the process from concept to consumer, and with that, the importance of every step in the process. Her true passion lies in the design and development of the product and in recognizing and nurturing creative genius.

She has held management positions in such companies as Reebok, Spalding, Liz Claiborne, Express, Pringle of Scotland, and Ellesse.

Career highlights include utilizing communication and presentation skills as a guest speaker at a career workshop for the Harvard Business School and as a guest host on QVC television network; conceptualizing, designing, and launching a high-tech apparel system of clothing; outfitting a team to ascend Mount Everest; and organizing a New York gala event for the U.S. retail community to meet Princess Diana, who was appearing as an ambassador for British trade. She is currently designing a women's tennis collection for PureLime, a premier Scandinavian women's fitness brand, which has begun distributing product in the U.S. market.

INTERVIEW

Question: When you interview a candidate for a fashion designer position, what strikes you as a sure sign that this is a designer with potential?
BC: If, in an instant, you can see the pure creativity jumping off the portfolio pages. The elements of design, color, and layout combine to create a magical impact that feeds your creative appetite. You just *know*.

Q: How do you garner the level of practical knowledge the designer has from looking at illustrations, not the 3D product during an interview?
BC: The details in the sketches are the true measure of practical knowledge. While a conceptual illustration can take your breath away, the garment must make its way from the portfolio page to a consumer's closet. Details in the illustration show the designer's understanding of garment construction.

Q: What do you look for in a portfolio to get a sense of the designer's market knowledge?
BC: I look for the representation of current market trends . . . silhouettes, colors, prints . . . and how these have been incorporated and reinterpreted in the portfolio.

Bissie Clover, Senior Apparel Executive

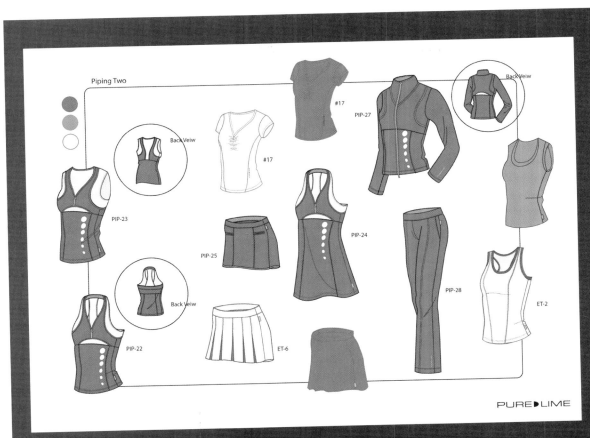

Tennis designs in flat sketch presentations

Q: How do you assess whether the designer will be a good fit with your work style, environment, and design team?

BC: To be honest, chemistry is always a very important factor that cannot be underestimated. An easy, fluid conversation is the first sign of a good fit . . . sharing creative ideas back and forth, experiencing the candidate's passion and commitment. But beyond that, a frank conversation describing the work ethic and environment is important. Creativity will only thrive in a nurturing environment, so the pitfalls and pressures of the current corporate environment should be shared with the candidate.

Questions then should be asked about how they would cope with the requirements.

Q: If you had to advise a young designer going on an interview, what would you advise them to think about or prepare; either in material form or mentally?

BC: Mental preparation is as important as portfolio preparation. Here's a tip: be prepared for anything, stay cool and calm, and remember, you can't control the interview. Be genuine and enthusiastic. You are who you are, your work is what it is . . . if it works, it works.

BIOGRAPHY

Cheryl Zarcone is Department Administrator, Global Sourcing, for Casual Male Retail Group in Canton, Massachusetts. Cheryl is an apparel design technician with extensive experience in women's wear, menswear, big and tall menswear, and children's wear. As supervisor of the technical department of Reebok, International, she oversaw the day-to-day operation of the department staff while training entry-level spec technicians and created a Tech Manual for new employees. She held positions in product development for Bradlees. She got her start working for College Town/Panther group as a technician and also managed the costing/import departments. She worked for several years in retail upon her graduation with her degree in fashion design from Mount Ida College. Cheryl loves fashion and the technical design aspect of the fit of the garments.

Cheryl Zarcone, Department Administrator, Global Sourcing in the studio preparing for a technical fit session with her staff

INTERVIEW

Question: What materials do you expect a technical designer to present to you in an interview?

CZ: They must have an updated résumé, including any internships they may have had in college, groups or committees they were involved in. You want to see that they are well-rounded individuals. They should bring a design portfolio, a garment they have constructed with the pattern also, to show they have patternmaking knowledge.

Q: If a technical designer has a design portfolio, do you review that in the interview?

CZ: Yes, we are always interested to see what they are capable of doing. The portfolio should have the first sketch, design inspiration (fabric, swatches, and colors), and a photo of final garment.

Q: What strengths and skills do you look for in a technical designer?

CZ: Patternmaking is a must; you must have knowledge of garment construction and how to grade a pattern, and turn that into a graded spec sheet for production.

Q: Do you assemble tech packs solely on the computer, or do you also log measurements by hand?

CZ: Tech packs are currently always created on the computer. Most companies have the Gerber system or a PLM system that has grading templates to format and create a spec. When measuring garments, we handwrite sample measurements and then input the changes into the computer program. Tech packs are the bible of garment construction from beginning to end. It has a top sheet with all pertinent information, trim/fabric page, detailed construction page, label page, and graded spec sheet.

Q: Can you describe a typical workday of a technical designer?
CZ: You must always prioritize your day according to your fit schedule and deadlines. Read all e-mails first, to make sure the factories have all their questions answered. Certain samples must be fit first. If garments are ready to cut in production, you must have a final fit. Other samples, such as TOP (top of production) samples, are just measured and reviewed (not fit). Make sure you send all information out to the factories at the end of the day, as timing is everything.

BIOGRAPHY

"Fear no art, battle boredom." These are more than just phrases. They are the artistic philosophy that is the key to the success of the Jamie Sadock founder and designer, Jamie Sadock. Fourteen years ago, Jamie founded her company, and her success has been nothing less than spectacular. Jamie Sadock's ability to create elegant concepts using unusual colors and design mixes puts her company far above the rest. Composed of both men's and women's resortwear, the range offers a variety of categories from performance golf to a complete collection of resort sportswear.

Yet she hasn't stopped here. Realizing that there was a total and frantic demand for more products created with her artistic foundation. Jamie Sadock has recently developed additional categories including "comfort footwear" and an accessories/purse division that premiered to accolades at the recent PGA (Professional Golf Association) Show.

CFDA designer Jamie Sadock

INTERVIEW

Question: Can you describe your first design job interview and portfolio presentation?

JS: My first job interview (at age 20) was somewhat strange. I was in college in Pittsburgh finishing my degree in psychology and English Literature. My father was in the apparel business with an office in New York. Someone in his office knew about my artistic side and set up an interview for me for an assistant design position. I went and thought I looked very fashionable in a suit and my hair pulled tightly up. The president of the company interviewed me, and halfway through, asked me to take my hair down. I wondered why that would influence his decision to hire me. It was strange. That was many years ago. Today's young woman would have less naïveté and just walk out.

During that interview, I only had my presentation of my art to show my creativity, my organization of it, and my color sense. I did get the job.

Q: In the first few year of working in the industry, how did you update the contents of your portfolio to be ready for interviews?

JS: If the company got media coverage on my designs, I added that to my portfolio. If I was going to an interview, I studied the company and did a group that I thought would make sense to be accepted into their collection. This included swatches of fabric and color as well as the sketch.

Q: What do you look for in a portfolio and in the person when you interview someone for an assistant designer? Are there any one or a few things that give you an indicator that this person is right for the job?

JS: In a portfolio, the first thing I look at is the résumé. If someone has job hopped and been at a different company every 6 or 8 months, or moved every year, I throw it away. I put a lot of time into training someone and it's truly a waste if they move on from job to job just to increase their salary.

After that, if the résumé looks good, then I look for creativity. I look for:

- ▶ Color sense.
- ▶ Taste level.
- ▶ Sense of balance.
- ▶ Organization.
- ▶ Attention to detail of the presentation.
- ▶ Attention to detail in the designs.
- ▶ Sketching ability.
- ▶ Computer ability (we give the potential candidate a test on the computer right then and there).
- ▶ Communication skills.
- ▶ A sense of thoroughness and accuracy.
- ▶ Their demeanor: Are the calm? Hyper? How will they handle the stress that is rife in any successful business?
- ▶ Are they management material in the long run?
- ▶ What makes them tick? What makes them frustrated? What is it about others that brings them to the edge?

I find that until the candidate has the ability to actually prove themselves on the job, their claims of experiences as well as being thorough and accurate are moot.

Q: Do you have any portfolio content and/or interview advice for the today's fashion design college graduate hoping to enter the industry?
JS: Be honest about your experience and skill level. Don't hope for the money; get the real experience. Never say, "It's not my job," and take any and all projects that get thrown your way that you can handle, and handle it well.

While you are on the job, review your work three times for errors or improvement; be timely with getting the job done accurately. Don't become moody and inconsistent as your co-workers won't want to approach you. Bring new ideas forth to your employer, even if they're not viable; it will show that you're thinking. Be in tandem and a step ahead of your supervisors and anticipate their needs. Work towards being able to do your job and more without having to be spoon-fed. Become indispensable. Avoid mediocrity, and therefore you will rise within the company. If you're good, you'll end up as a very lucky person and loving what you do! I am a lucky girl!

BIOGRAPHY

A design luminary for more than 30 years, Joseph Abboud is renowned for his innate ability to design classic clothing and build brands that reflect the true American man. Joseph Abboud is currently president and chief creative officer of HMX's portfolio of brands. Abboud leads the creative direction for brands including Hickey Freeman, Hart Schaffner Marx, Coppley, Bobby Jones, Exclusively Misook, Simply Blue (Christopher Blue Denim, Worn Men's and Women's), and Monarchy Collection.

The Abboud family was a working-class Christian Lebanese family that started out in the South End of Boston and later moved to the Roslindale section of Boston. Abboud's mother, Lila, was a seamstress. On a trip to Australia, Abboud discovered that his great-grandfather had owned Australia's largest men's tailored-clothing company.

Abboud started in the fashion industry as a 16-year-old, working part-time at Louis Boston. Abboud stated, "Louis Boston was a huge part of my career. I really landed in a world of very glamorous style, beautiful clothes, just the world of what international fashion was about. If this had never happened, then the rest of it wouldn't have happened."

Abboud joined Ralph Lauren in 1981, eventually becoming associate director of menswear design. He launched his own label in 1986. In 1991 Abboud worked with fashion director Peter Speliopoulos. Abboud was the first designer to win the CFDA Award as Best Menswear Designer 2 years in a row.

Many of Abboud's famous friends are also his customers, including American trumpeter and composer Wynton Marsalis, author and former TV news anchor Tom Brokaw, and former Boston Red Sox shortstop Nomar Garciaparra.

Abboud wrote *Threads: My Life Behind the Seams in the High Stakes World of Fashion*, in which he thoroughly describes the fashion industry from designing and selling clothes to naming colors.

INTERVIEW

Question: What do you look for in a designer's portfolio when you are interviewing?

JA: A lot of times it comes down to touch, feel, and emotion. I spend a long time looking for insight into who the young designer is. A lot of times a designer will work to have the best portfolio for an interview and design something, for instance, that Polo/Ralph Lauren might like. I don't prescribe that way of thinking. The collections shouldn't be wild and crazy but should show me how smart the designer is. I'm looking to the designer's plan of attack and how they would tackle problems. I want the designer to show me who they are in the clothing they design; which will also reveal their intellect, interesting concepts, and approach to

CFDA Award-winning designer Joseph Abboud with a sampling of his menswear design. (Courtesy of WWD/ George Chinsee)

real clothes, and not way-out concepts. Show me what you can bring to the team.

Q: What is the worst mistake a designer can make in their presentation to you?

JA: Not knowing who they are interviewing with. Not being prepared for the company. While the portfolio should reflect the designer's DNA, and the designer should know what they represent, if they aren't prepared and don't know a lot about the company, it comes out in the interview. The designer has to do their homework: What does the customer want, and what is happening with the retailer? It is a two-way street; the designer has to be right for the job, and this has to be the company that the designer most wants to go to. The designer should speak articulately and be a good salesman in a professional way.

Q: What should the designer include in the portfolio?

JA: The designer has to include a color palette and the connection to the thought process, what you thought from the color and how it evolves into the creative process. What does it tell me about the designer's comprehensive thought process? I need to read this in their collection presentation; what colors you derive from your original concepts.

Q: Can you tell us about your worst interview with a designer and your best experience interviewing a designer?

JA: A designer should try to be very aware of the situation and all levels of life. It is not about "I" or "me" as opposed to what services you can bring to a company. You have to take a subordinate position to the company during the interview and in the job. Present to the interviewer that you can provide a great service to them. I'm looking for someone that is not egocentric. The worst interview a designer can have with me is one in which they are not listening, and it's all about them. I look at the portfolio and how the designer answers to creative questions. Can they articulate their visions? If they have a different idea than my taste and direction, I don't care about that; it is the sophistication of the answers, which show me that the designer is smart and flexible as I interact with them on their thought process.

Q: Do you look through the designer journal in an interview?

JA: That is a little too personal for me; it is a slight intrusion from me to them. I don't need to see their journal; the artsy part is kind of nice, but it's really how it is applied in their portfolio.

Q: How was your first interview for your first job as a designer in the industry?

JA: My first interview just kind of happened. As I was working in sales for Louis of Boston, without realizing it, I was designing sweaters. I became a Sherlock Holmes, looking for ideas that would work for the consumer on the Louis of Boston selling floor. I would go to manufacturers and ask questions as we began developing sweater programs: fully fashioned, argyles, Fair Isles, etc. By asking the manufacturers what they can do, you become a better designer by being a buyer and a merchant of their production capabilities. By doing so, you are actually creating. It was my retail sales job at Polo/Ralph Lauren that was my entry into design. Ralph asked me to join his company in design based upon my work at retail. Life happens differently for all of us. I never had to create a portfolio.

BIOGRAPHY

Carole D'Arconte is a prominent color and trend merchandiser with extensive product development expertise in the woven and knit textile markets and the manufacturing and retail environments. Her focus has been primarily in the menswear, women's wear, and children's trend and design areas, as well as in the accessories and makeup markets.

She was president of COLOR PORTFOLIO, INC., a full service trend and communication marketing company for over 25 years, when she successfully sold her business in 2001. COLOR PORTFOLIO offered private trend presentations to the apparel, accessory, and home markets, providing directional color recommendations, lifestyle merchandising, and textile design input. Since then, she was instrumental in helping create colorEDGE, a digital color management system for the manufacturing and textile markets. She continues to consult to leading retailers and

manufacturers on trend and styling ideas under her new company name, Carole D'Arconte LLC.

Carole studied at the Fashion Institute of Technology and received its Mortimer C. Ritter Award for Achievement and the Alumni Star Salute Award. She continues to maintain active roles in The Fashion Group, Round Table of Fashion Executives, The Fashion News Workshop, Color Marketing Group, The Retail Marketing Group, The Business Connection, and The National Arts Club. Her many articles and quotes have been seen in the *New York Times*, *USA Today*, the *Los Angeles Times*, Gannett Newspapers, *Women's Wear Daily*, and *America's Textile and Apparel Industry Magazine*, to name a few.

INTERVIEW

Question: Can you summarize the process of how your formulate forecast color palettes?
CD: The formula that works for me is to evaluate what the current best-selling colors are in the line, edit out the weak colors, and balance with the basics. Once these shades are determined, then it is easier to fill in with fashion colors and to determine whether the fashion color will be used as a base color or an accent.

Q: Can you advise designers for their college-level and entry-level portfolios as to how to best show color on the page? Would you show yarns or fabric swatches with the Pantone color match-ups?
CD: Since we are living in a very visual world, it is important to show each color with as many viable visuals as possible. Yarns and/or swatches are part of the visual story, but today it is imperative to be able to translate that color digitally so that any mill globally can understand immediately what color is being offered. The easiest way to support

Carole D'Arconte, color and trend merchandiser

COLOR: Featured Shade Groups: Daffodil Yellow, Jade Green, Coral, Peri Blue

elsy

Trend and style forecasting board presentation

the color story, for a new professional, is with Pantone and/or SCOTDIC color matches and their respective numbers. Most large mills and retailers have digital systems in place and require their teams to use in-house systems.

Q: What was your first design job in the industry, and can you describe your portfolio presentation and the interview?
CD: My first job in the industry was as an assistant color coordinator for a button house. My portfolio showed sketches and photos of garments I designed with swatches of the fabrics used and examples of the accessories. My job was to call textile companies and evaluate what colors they were introducing in their textile line that season and then to recommend the colors to be used in the button design that would coordinate with those textiles.

Q: What color sources should a designer exhaust to develop color for a season?
CD: A designer must be *aware*—of hot movies, plays, sitcoms, museum shows, runway, the political and financial climate of the day—also trends in home fashion—people often wear colors they live with and vice versa.

Q: Can you advise designers as to how to edit color choices for a design collection? How many colors for a collection should a designer show in a portfolio?
CD: The most successful colors selected are often colors that wear well with black. Colors should be considered as shades that can be worn with a black basic piece that's already in the customer's wardrobe or as a replacement for black. This is because black is still the most prevalent color in people's wardrobes. Most manufacturers don't want more than six base colors in a line, if that many. Black plus two additional colors per style is probably sufficient.

EPILOGUE

OBJECTIVES

✛ Understand the steps for preparing a portfolio (see Chapters 1, and 2)

✛ Decide on the market direction of the portfolio (see Chapters 3, 4, and 5)

✛ Assemble the Portfolio Project portfolio (see Chapter 6)

✛ Revise the Portfolio Project portfolio to meet changing needs (see Chapters 7, and 8)

✛ Prepare for job interviews with the completed portfolio (see Chapter 9)

This summary will help you check your completed portfolio package for any changes, additions, or deletions you may want to make, today and in your future career, whether you are extending your education or applying for a promotion or new job. The portfolio should be updated on an on-going basis. The process never stops! You should always tweak and change it to support your career goals and to be ready for interviewing on a moment's notice. Your latest work should be added to the portfolio on a weekly basis, and it should be reviewed once a month, adding new designs and deleting those that are no longer relevant.

As you add and delete designs and press releases, check that the sequencing and page turning effects of "wowing" your audience are intact.

UNDERSTANDING AND PREPARING THE PORTFOLIO: CHAPTERS 1 AND 2

Chapters 1, 2, and 3 helped you prepare to create your portfolio. Review the items below for reminders and tips on how to check your current and future portfolios for applying these methods to your book.

CHAPTER 1 ILLUMINATES THE DESIGNER

The portfolio is a selling tool and a foot in the door to a design position. A dynamic portfolio presentation will set you apart from other design candidates for positions in the industry. Portfolios have evolved over the last century; starting with fewer figures on the page, progressing to complex multi-figure pages with dimensional backgrounds and type. The portfolio consists of the portfolio case and the materials outlined in detail in Chapter 1, and summarized below. Check through your work to see that it meets these criteria. Determine the purpose of your portfolio based upon your audience.

+ Materials: Portfolios consist of set materials, with approximately 3–4 collections shown with 17-21 pages per collection. The physical components include the case, label, résumé, and sleeves, and the case may also house your sketchbook, leave-behind piece, business card, and electronic presentation. The pages for each collection include a title page, mood/ concept pages, color pages, textile pages, illustration pages, flats pages, and CAD pages,
+ Sketchbook: An important visual message about your design process to show during interviews.

You set up a temporary portfolio of student work to use as a learning tool for imagining your ideal portfolio. Following the set-up techniques of reviewing the work on a large tabletop, formally mounting and storing the illustrated fashion plates, you've preserved the images for years to come, either in the temporary portfolio or in a permanent archival storage box.

The work is critiqued and assessed for your layout abilities, progress over a course of time, your strengths and weaknesses, your rendering skill level, and your ability to meet a deadline for completion. You define the general design category(ies) of apparel for your final portfolio, and you purchase the portfolio case that matches your design aesthetic and your work style. The following exercises can be used time and again for building your temporary portfolio, your portfolio project, and revised portfolios throughout your design career.

+ *Objective critique* A critical review of your work without bias or prejudice. Concern yourself with the realities of your artwork rather than your thoughts as an artist.
+ *Layout critique* Branding of your story through sequencing and story-telling.
+ *Portfolio page sequencing* The order in which you arrange the pages within a collection, and the order in which you present multiple collections in your portfolio.

- *Critique over time* Tracking your performance over a period of time with a critical analysis of your work without bias or prejudice
- *Skills assessment* By assessing your strengths and weaknesses and your rendering skill level, you can add strength to your portfolio presentation. By setting realistic goals to meet your deadlines, you can be ready for any design project.

CHAPTER 2 MANIFESTS THE ILLUMINATED: CREATING AN IDEA STORAGE BANK

Suggested levels of structured research and set-up techniques are intended to help you bridle your creative skills. The design of the conceptual portfolio layout is conceived during the apparel collection design. The design process is reviewed, the compile/edit/finalize format is introduced. Guides to help organize the research of retail shopping, forecast/color services, textile/print markets, fashion shows, trade shows, and outside influences are presented.

The concept of "hitting a mark" of your client's design needs is discussed. The groundwork for the Portfolio Project relies upon formulating the concepts, passing them through the designer filter, and bringing the line forward into a portfolio presentation.

DECIDING ON THE MARKET DIRECTION OF THE PORTFOLIO: CHAPTERS 3, 4, AND 5

Chapters 3, 4, and 5 helped you decide on the market direction of the portfolio. Review the items below for reminders and tips on how to check your current and future portfolios for applying these methods to your book.

CHAPTER 3 LAUNCHES THE DESIGN PROCESS AND APPAREL LINE BUILDING

Decide on the basic direction of your portfolio plan by reviewing channels of distribution, retail apparel categories, generalized and specialized markets, idealizing the portfolio and completing a designer grid.

Identification of the target consumer, designer taste, price range, age groups, and size ranges are reviewed. Your motivation and skill level are layered into the decision-making process.

CHAPTER 4 MARKETS THE DESIGN COLLECTIONS WITH A FOCUS

The portfolio is presented in visual examples for the level of focus of the viewer and the consumer base. Gender categories, mixed gender possibilities, children's wear, size range options, generalized sportswear portfolios, and key categories of apparel are visually represented.

Fashion figure body-types and attitudes are important understructures of the illustrated garments. The Look Book and Leave-Behind-Piece are portfolio options.

CHAPTER 5 BRANCHES THE DIRECTION FOR THE CHOICES PORTFOLIO COLLECTION

The areas of specialized portfolios are visually defined. The client's needs for performance and function are paramount driving forces. How the garment works on the body, functional color palettes and hardware, durability of fabrics, and illustration and layout considerations are developed. The designer is challenged to develop innovative products to compete in an evolving market.

DOING THE PORTFOLIO PROJECT: CHAPTERS 6, 7, AND 8

Chapters 6, 7, and 8 walked you through the completion of the Portfolio Project. Review the terms below for reminders and tips on how to check your current and future portfolios for applying these methods to your book.

CHAPTER 6 CREATES THE PORTFOLIO

The Portfolio Project is a step-by-step process that can be approached in a linear fashion, a circular progression, with feedback, with a branching path technique, and/or by the natural pathway approach. There is no one way to approach line-building, and a combination of these approaches is encouraged.

The three basic steps of line building are spelled out and explained for mood, color, textiles, and silhouette/flats segments. The basic concept of organizing the portfolio process using the designer grid is put into action in steps of conceptualizing, editing, and finalizing.

The segments and steps are linked by previously outlined extensive market research, design, layout, number of pages per collection, page sequencing, and number of collections to be shown in the portfolio. Presentation materials are outlined and explained for each segment of portfolio line development. Photographs demonstrate how to put materials onto the page.

CHAPTER 7 ADAPTS THE FINAL PORTFOLIO TO DIFFERENT PURPOSES

Check through your idealized portfolio goals to see if they are actualized, consider optional refinements of layout details, consider page turners and sequencing techniques, review branding the apparel, consider past collections to be included in the presentation, and keep yourself fluid through the refinement process and throughout your career.

Consider the brand image for the portfolio collection and advisability of including fashion show photographs as part of image building.

CHAPTER 8 GIVES GUIDELINES FOR AN ELECTRONIC PORTFOLIO

Review your final presentations of digital or web-based portfolios. The CD-ROM, DVD, flash drive, or Web-based portfolio is detailed. The chapter outlines how to approach the visual image so the end result is exciting and engaging.

+ Portable devices for portfolio images include CD-ROM, DVD, or USB flash drive.
+ Multimedia programs for the portable devices may be in the form of PowerPoint presentations, Adobe Director presentations, or Adobe Flash presentations.

+ Web-based portfolios are created to showcase the designer's work. Web-page program choices include Adobe Dreamweaver, Adobe Acrobat, Adobe Photoshop, Corel Painter, Adobe Illustrator, Corel Draw, Quark Express, and Adobe InDesign.

Review basic digital and Web-based terminology; make the best decision for an electronic program that you can learn and grow with as you develop your electronic portfolio. Review color terms: for a balance of color harmony for the electronic presentation.

CHAPTER 9 WALKS YOU THROUGH INTERVIEWING WITH THE COMPLETE PORTFOLIO

Consider how you will present your portfolio in interviews to balance your expectations as a potential employee with the employer's expectations. Prepare for the interview by researching the companies you want to work for and make adjustments to your portfolio pages prior to each interview to impress the interviewer with your market knowledge and desire to work for his or her firm.

An imaginary interview scenario is discussed, and industry leaders' insights are helpful for planning how to approach an interview. You are encouraged to pay attention to the following:

+ Job descriptions that are advertised or that you learn about from you school's placement office or other sources. Employer expectations regarding the specific set of skills, design aesthetic, personality, and work-style that are reflected in the employer's interpretation of the job description.
+ Your own expectations of the specific set of design responsibilities, position level within the company hierarchy, pay scale, benefits package, corporate policies, and opportunities for advancement and career growth.

Mock interviews with a classmate or friend are a good way to practice for the real interview.

The chapter also advises you on preparing a follow-up letter after the interview(s) to thank the interviewer(s) for meeting with you and to list your reasons for believing you are a good candidate for the job.

CONCLUSION

You've worked hard to accomplish your best portfolio. It will be a constant task to update your visual design communication presentations throughout your career. The work should reflect who you are and how you have grown as a designer at the time of each presentation.

You can reference *Fashion Design Portfolios* throughout your career to make your portfolio an effective tool for selling your capabilities as a designer.

APPENDIX A

TREND RESEARCH FOR THE ZEITGEIST

Keep an ongoing observational eye on the world around you, and seek out sources to keep you informed and "in the moment." With the Internet, you can easily stay on top of current trends and access information about them virtually instantly. Remember, the library and past research is just as important to observe and take notes on. Add all observations to your sketchbook or a journal for ideas.

+ Magazines: Not just fashion magazines, but broaden your visual field by exploring art, photography, architecture, travel, home design, gaming, sports, graphic design, and industrial design magazines. A good place to search is your school or local library as well as a leisurely read at the local bookstore in the magazine section, which is broken down into subject categories.
+ E-zines.
+ Entertainment reports: Television, Internet, and magazines.
+ Current theater productions: Broadway, off- and off-off-Broadway plays, local theater companies.
+ Current cinema: Categories such as drama, documentaries, short films, foreign films, action/adventure, children's films, and science fiction.
+ Historical documentaries.
+ Art museums and commercial art galleries.
+ History museums.
+ Science museums.
+ The stock market and how it effect consumer buying and day-to-day activities.

+ Current news: Read newspapers such as the *New York Times*, the *Los Angeles Times*, the *Miami Herald*, the *Herald Tribune*, the *Wall Street Journal*, and the *Chicago-Sun Times*. Search for the Sunday magazine and style sections for reports on current trends. Watch broadcast and cable television or Internet streams for local news, world news, and news magazine shows.
+ Television specials: The Oscars, the Emmies, The VHI awards, the Grammies, and so on.
+ Music: All genres.
+ Poetry and fiction.
+ Seasonal changes.
+ Textiles and industrial design research.
+ The life sciences, ecological trends, pollution controls, GPS system updates, hybrid vehicles, fuel options, and so on.
+ Auto, trucks, trains, airplanes, and so on, for design and functional feature updates.
+ Professional sporting events, such as international soccer, the NHL, the MLB, the NBA, the PGA and the LPGA.
+ Special sporting events: The X Games, the Olympics, the United States Figure Skating Championships and the World Figure Skating Championships, the Triple Crown of horseracing (the Kentucky Derby, the Preakness, and the Belmont Stakes), the Superbowl, the World Series, the World Cup, NASCAR, the US Tennis Open, and worldwide tennis tournaments.
+ Hip restaurants and nightclubs and trendy bars.
+ Trendy foods.

APPENDIX B

FASHION RESEARCH SOURCES

Websites

The Fashion Center New York City:
  www.fashioncenter.com

InfoMat: www.infomat.com

First View: www.firstview.com

Elle: www.elle.com

Condé Nast websites:
  Women's Wear Daily www.wwd.com
  Style.com www.style.com
  Brides www.brides.com
  W Magazine www.wmagazine.com
  Lucky www.luckymag.com
  Vogue www.vogue.com
  Teen Vogue www.teenvogue.com

Fashion 4-11: www.fashion-411.com

Fashion Live: www.fashionlive.com

Fashion Network: www.fashionshowroom.com

Glam.com: www.glam.com

FIT's sustainable design website:
  www.fitnyc.libguides.com/sustainable_design

Color Matching Systems

A vital tool for designers in the apparel industry for selecting and specifying color used in the manufacture of textiles and fashion. Pantone and SCOTDIC offer color forecasting services in addition to their color matching systems.

MUNSELL COLOR SYSTEM

www.munsellstore.com

ColorAccuracy.com

1765 Taylor Drive

North Brunswick, NJ 08902

(732) 301-2625

(866) 690-3952

PANTONE COLOR INSTITUTE

www.pantone.com

590 Commerce Boulevard

Carlstadt, NJ 07072

(201) 896-0242

SCOTDIC COLOURS LTD.

www.scotdic.com

488 Seventh Ave., 3K

New York, NY 10018

(845) 361-4119

Magazines

CONSUMER FASHION MAGAZINES AND TRADE NEWSPAPERS

Allure

Another Man

Collezioni

Collezioni Close-up, which offers a broad range of specializations

Collezioni Edge

Collezioni Internazionale di Pret-a-Porter

Collezioni Trends

Details

Ebony

Elle (American and French)

Esquire

GQ

Gap Press Collections Haute Couture

Glamour

Harper's Bazaar: American, British, Chinese, Spanish, and Italian editions

I-D Magazine

InStyle

Interview
Lucky
Marie Claire
Men's Vogue
New York Magazine fashion issues
The New York Times style magazine
O, the Oprah Magazine
People
Real Simple
Rolling Stone
Self
Seventeen
Style.com Print
L'Uomo Vogue
Vanity Fair
Vibe
Vogue: American, British, Brazilian, Chinese,
    Indian, French, Italian editions
W
Women's Wear Daily (WWD)
WWD The Magazine
Wired

SPECIALIZED MAGAZINES
Accessories
BBW (Big Beautiful Woman)
Bambini Collezioni
Black Book: Progressive Urban Culture
Brides: American and British editions
Collezioni Baby
Collezioni Accessories

Collezioni Bambini
Collezioni Beachwear
Collezioni Sposa
Collezioni Uomo
Costume
The Costume Designer
Costume Society Newsletter
Martha Stewart Brides
Sports Illustrated
Teen Vogue
Vogue Bambini
Vogue Sposa

INTERIOR DESIGN MAGAZINES
Apartamento
Apartment Life
Architectural Design
Architectural Digest
Casa Vogue
Elle Décor
Martha Stewart Living
Metropolitan Home

FINE ARTS AND CRAFT MAGAZINES
Artforum
ARTNews
Fiberarts
Metalsmith

APPENDIX C

PORTFOLIO WEBSITES

Current designers' portfolios can be viewed on the following websites:

www.coroflot.com

www.styleportfolios.com

www.newschool.edu/parsons Follow the links from the home page to student work, and filter by program to Fashion Design (AAS) and Fashion Design (BFA).

www.drexel.edu

www.fitnyc.edu

www.mylifetime.com/shows/project.runway

APPENDIX D
ART SUPPLIES TO TRY

Here is an annotated list of art supplies to add to your tool box as you experiment with various media.

Markers

Markers are used for creating a quick style that is most often used for fashion illustrators and designers to capture their work "in the moment." Markers dry quickly and work well on a smooth surface, such as magic marker paper or layout paper. They are sold individually or in sets. They can come in different-sized nibs, with brush nibs, or with dual tips. The dual-tip markers give you one to three different nibs on each marker to use in broad strokes or in tight fine lines.

There is a separate category listed for fine and ultra fine tip markers for outlines and garment details.

Some markers are water-based, and others are based with solvents, which can be toxic. It is always advisable to work in a well-ventilated room when using markers. One marker that can be a designer's favorite to work with is called the "colorless blender." This marker is a colorless solvent that when applied to the page or to a marker color on the page blends the colors together, much like water added to watercolor paint.

When you are shopping for markers, bring your fabric swatches and color standards with you, along with a sample sheet of the paper on which you are going to render. Test the colors of the markers on the paper. Let them dry for a few minutes. See if they match the standard of your fabrics and/or colors. Remember: *Always* snap the cap back on very tightly, as the marker will dry out if not sealed properly. If you find the color marker that works, reach for a marker at the back of the shelf, test it again, and purchase that one. It is more likely that the marker at the back of the stock was less tested and has more solvent left in the tube, meaning it is wetter and it will have more shelf life. You can layer colors over one another to achieve your color standard and/or use the colorless blender to match your colors.

CATEGORIES OF MARKERS

Archival markers contain pigments instead of dyes and are acid-free. They are good for working on photographs.

Brush markers are pigmented or watercolor. They can be used like a painter's brush for effect.

Calligraphy markers are good for a brush-like effect.

Design and layout markers have the widest range of colors and are the most popular for fashion designers' work. These are permanent markers and can't be washed off with water. They are not lightfast and need to be protected by the polypropylene sleeves in the portfolio to keep their color from fading.

Fabric markers are preferred if you want to take a swatch of fabric and add color, pattern, or texture to it for presentation in your portfolio.

Highlighters can be used for neon bright colors.

Marking pencils and china markers can be used for outlines and details.

Metallic ink markers for hardware and metalized fabric effects.

Paint markers are very opaque and can add drama to the page.

Permanent markers are very opaque.

Water-based markers are very translucent and blendable.

BRANDS OF MARKERS

Design and layout markers Chartpak, Copic, Letraset, AD Design, Pantone, Prismacolor, Letraset Tria.

Pigmented-ink markers Faber-Castell PITT Artist and Brush Pens, Prismacolor Premier Archival Markers, Sakura Pigma Brush.

Watercolor brush markers Bienfang, Carn d'Ache Fibralo, Crayola, Le Plue, Marvy, Pentel, Staedtler Mars.

Highlighters Crayola, Dixon, Sharper, Staedtler.

Metallic-ink markers Elmer's, Faber-Castell, Pentel, Pilot, Prang, Sharpie, Staedtler.

Brush-tip markers Le Plume, Pentel Metallic, Prang.

Dual-tip markers Artline Twin Nib, Copic, Graphic Art, Le Plume, Sakura, Sharpie, Zig Memory.

Fine and ultra-fine tip markers Artline, Bic, Copic, Pelikan, Sharpie, Staedtler.

Pencils

Pencils (in any variety listed here) are used in fashion illustration for laying down the first sketch in a journal or as the first outline of a figure on a fashion plate. They are also used by some designers to render a fashion plate fully, although markers are recommended as the medium of choice for portfolio layouts. Graphite pencils, colored pencils, charcoal pencils, carbon pencils, pigmented sketching pencils, water-color pencils, and oil color pencils all combine well with markers (if rendered properly) in a fashion presentation.

Graphite drawing pencils can be put down as the first outline to follow as a guide for the final illustration. When markers touch the outline, they can smudge the lead and muddy the color. With practice, the pencil outline can be avoided with the marker nib to keep the marker colors pure on the page.

Graphite pencils can be "stick" or wood pencils, or mechanical pencils. Mechanical pencils come in different sizes, which are listed as follows.

Graphite leads come in a variety of grades, which run from 9H to 2H for a light line on the page. H, F, and HB are close to a grade of a #2 pencil. B and 2B through 8B become softer and will leave a darker pencil line on the page the higher the number gets. H indicates a *hard* pencil. B indicates the *blackness* of the pencil's marker and has a softer lead. HB is *hard* and *black*. The standard grades run differently from one manufacturer to another, so it is best to try different brands and to test the pencils in the store before purchasing. While it is helpful to purchase a set of pencils, consider trying pencils by purchasing them after testing them in the store one at a time, to see which brands and which grades work best for you.

Paints

Watercolor paints, acrylic, and gouache are the choices of paints for designers. Brushes are made specifically for each medium and should be purchased accordingly. Brushes come in a range of tiny heads to wide fan-shaped heads. Most art supply stores display brushes sold in sets or as individual purchases. Shop carefully to select brushes that match your medium, and buy a range of brushes sold individually. As you experiment

Categories and Brands of Pencils

Category	Brands	Description
Graphite pencils	Cretacolor, Derwent, Faber-Castell, General's, Prismacolor, Sanford, Staedtler, Tombow	See above.
Mechanical pencils	Alvin, Koh-I-Noor, Paper Mate, Pentel, Staedtler, Zebra	Fitted for removable leads in a variety of sizes, and each pencil can only use one size. Designer sizes and refills are 0.3 mm, 0.5 mm, 0.7 mm, and 0.9 mm.
Carbon pencils	Alvin, Koh-I-Noor, Paper Mate, Pentel, Staedtler, Zebra	Can be used for a smudgy look.
Water-soluble graphite pencils	Caran dAche, Derwent, Graphitint, General's	Soft and smooth, can be blended to create soft hues. Add water and the color becomes more vibrant—nice for special effects.
Pastel pencils	Conté, Cretacolor, Derwent, Faber-Castell, General's Koh-i-Noor, Stabilo	Larger diameter pencils for toning and precise lines,
Watercolor pencils	Caran d'Ache, Cretacolor, Derwent, Faber-Castell, Prismacolor	Can be rendered dry or combined with water for varying degrees of a wash of color.
Oil-based pencils	Caran d'Ache, Cretacolor, Derwent, Faber-Castell, Prismacolor	Like a creamy crayon in a pencil, providing smooth control on the paper; not waxy.

with brushes, you will find the right combination of brushes that work for you.

Following are reliable paint brands for the three categories favored by fashion designers:

Watercolor Chroma, DaVinci, Grumbacher, Rembrandt, Winsor & Newton

Acrylic Amsterdam, Chroma, Golden, Liquitex, Winsor & Newton

Gouache Caran dAche, Holbein, Pelikan, Winsor & Newton

Papers

Designers render fashion plates on a range of different papers. While some designers are purists and will render markers only on marker paper and watercolors on watercolor paper, just about any paper can be used for any medium, depending on the artist's hand, technique, personal preference, and expected final outcome. It's best to experiment with different types of surfaces and papers to see which works best for you.

Understanding some basic terminology of paper effects can help you in your decision-making process.

+ Sizing can be a natural or artificial solution added to paper, the pulp, or the surface during the making of the paper. Sizing regulates the type of absorbency the paper will have when wet or dry media are added to it. The package description label on the pad provides information about sizing. The more sizing added, the less moisture is absorbed into the paper when media are added. Surface-sized paper will give watercolors a crisp edge, and pencil can be erased. Most watercolor papers are well-sized. Papers that lack sizing or have very little sizing added will absorb water and will give your colors a fuzzy, dull look. It is almost impossible to erase pencil from the surface.
+ Cold-pressed, rough, laid, or sanded papers have texture. They can give watercolor an added surface-interest.

+ Very smooth papers are hot pressed and can be great for fine details.
+ Archival paper is acid-free and has a neutral pH. It is 100 percent cotton or cotton rag. It won't deteriorate.
+ Newsprint, craft paper, and construction paper will deteriorate over time and are not archival.

PAPER CATEGORIES

Sketching paper can be used for final fashion plates or rough sketches, and comes in light weight and heavy weight.

Marker paper is usually translucent in quality, with a smooth, perfect surface for quick strokes of color.

Watercolor paper is textured and comes in different weights.

Bristol Board has a smooth finish, fine for any medium.

Pastel paper has a soft feel with a tooth. Black is the usual color; but other dark colors are available in a pad.

Charcoal paper (light colored paper with a slight texture). It works well with pastels, pencils, and any media where the designer wants to render on a textured surface.

Vellum paper is a high-grade, highly transparent paper that accepts most media.

Tracing paper is a transparent paper. Generally used only for tracing one's own drawings and making corrections in layers of pages. It is not generally used for final portfolio illustrations. The closest paper in feeling to tracing paper is vellum paper, which is heavier and more suited for a final rendering.

Acrylic paper is a heavyweight, textured paper that is perfect for acrylic paint and wet paints.

Mixed media paper has a surface that allows wet media to perform on a dry-media surface and can accept different types of media on the page in a creative mix or blend, such as watercolor, acrylic, pen and ink, pencils, markers, pastels, and so on.

BRANDS OF PAPER

The following companies make various categories of paper described on pages 363–364:

Bee Paper
Borden and Riley
Cachet
Canson
Fabiano
Hahnemuhle
Reeves
Sennelier
Stonehenge
Strathmore

Other Categories of Art Supplies to Research and Explore

Consider adding some of the following to your tool kit.

Adhesives, adhesives sheets, and *sprays* work with adhesives that are archival and won't change the surface or colors of your medium or paper.

Airbrush paints and *inks* can be expensive. To decide whether to invest in an airbrush tool or kit, experiment with airbrush techniques by using a stippling method of dipping a toothbrush in paint and scratching your finger over the surface aimed toward the page. See how well you like the airbrush effect.

Anatomical models can help you develop different gestures and poses.

Brushes produce many effects. Test different types in the stores or experiment with friends' brushes. Some types of brushes include acrylic, synthetic and sable (black and red) bristle, foam, quill, squirrel, and watercolor. Among the many brush shapes are fan and flat.

Pastels, chalks, and charcoals can produce a variety of effects. Finish work with a spray fixative so the medium won't spread or blur when inserted into a portfolio sleeve.

Colored papers can be used for different background effects.

Dry pigments can be used for intense effects. Experiment to decide whether they work well for your illustration style.

Gel ink pens are effective for whimsical and metallic colors and for pure white applications.

Inks can give your illustrations a soft watercolor effect or intense saturation of color.

Metallic powders can be added to different mediums for varied effects.

Makeup (eyeliner, mascara, eye shadow, blush, and so on) can be very effectively used on the page for dramatic effects.

APPENDIX E

ART SUPPLY SOURCES

Listed here are major online art supply sources for you perusal. For local art supply stores that are closest to your college, dormitory, apartment, or home, use the Google search engine, and type in "art supply stores," and your city. This will give you a list of stores within a close proximity to your locale. Your college bookstore usually is the most convenient shop for getting art supplies. Depending on the college, the prices for this convenience may be higher than if you research competitive pricing and purchase the items online. Remember to add shipping to the cost when you are doing price comparisons. Online shopping usually requires a longer lead time to allow for the package to get to you, usually 5 to 7 business days. AC Moore and Michaels stores and websites cater mostly to the crafts consumer; and they feature a much narrower selection of fine

artist's materials. Broaden your search to include some of the classic art supply stores listed below for your portfolio case and all of your art supplies.

+ A.C. Moore   www.acmoore.com
+ Art Supplies Online
  www.artsuppliesonline.com
+ Dick Blick Art Materials   www.dickblick.com
+ Cheap Joe's Art Stuff   www.cheapjoes.com
+ Jerry's Artarama   www.jerrysartarama.com
+ Klo Portfolios   www.kloportfolios.com
  /fashion-design-portfolio-presentation-books/
+ Michaels   www.michaels.com
+ MisterArt.com   www.misterart.com
+ Pearl Paint   www.pearlpaint.com
+ Rex Art   www.rexart.com
+ Utrecht Art Supplies   www.utrechtart.com

APPENDIX F

TRADE SHOWS OF INTEREST TO FASHION DESIGNERS

Here is a sample of important trade shows in the fashion industry. For more trade show listings, visit the websites that follow. When planning to attend a show, you should access dates, times, and venues from these websites because the trade show market varies from year to year. Also check requirements and fees for admission and note the list of exhibitors and schedule of events.

Major Trade Shows

Bread and Butter   Progressive, innovative fashion apparel brands.
www.breadandbutter.com

Direction by Indigo   Prints.
www.indigo-salon.com

Interfiliere   Leading trade show for lingerie and beachwear fabrics.
www.interfiliere.com

Interstoff Asia   Tradeshow for textiles, yarns, and fibers.
www.interstoff.messefrankfurt.com

ISPO   Activewear apparel, and sporting goods merchandise.
www.ispo.com

MAGIC   Men's, Women's, and Children's apparel and manufacturing sources, as well as textiles and prints at Sourcing at MAGIC.
www.sourcingatmagic.com

Maison & Objet   International trade show for the home.
www.maison-objet.com

Pitti Bimbo   Clothing and accessories for children and teenagers, and maternity.
www.pittimmagine.com

Pitti Filati   The leading trade fair showcasing yarns for the knitting industry.
www.pittimmagine.com

Premiere Vision–New York   Textiles.
www.premierevision–newyork.com

Premiere Vision–Paris   Textiles
www.premierevision.com

Printsource   Prints and surface design.
www.printsourcenewyork.com

Unica   International Textile Fair.
www.milanounica.it

Who's Next and Premiere Classe   Trend-setting international apparel show.
www.whosnext.com

WSA Global marketplace for footwear and accessory buyers.
www.wsashow.com

Websites Listing Trade Shows
www.aboutsources.com
www.expodatabase.com
www.biztradeshows.com
www.weconnectfashion.com
www.eventseye.com

APPENDIX G

RESEARCHING AN APPAREL MARKET

To become really informed about a company or a demographic group, follow this list of some key areas to look into. Using Google or other search engines to search the topic can lead you to information that will help you to design your line appropriately.

+ Market profile
+ Market size
+ Market share
+ Market growth
+ Market structure
+ Segmentation

+ Competition
+ Trends
+ Market demand
+ Demographics
+ Price points
+ Service
+ Brand loyalty
+ Expansion plans
+ Retail distribution and product distribution
+ Advertising and promotions
+ Socioeconomic data

Source: www.infomat.com/research

APPENDIX H

FASHION FORECAST SERVICES

Many forecast services have international headquarters and/or satellite offices throughout the world. If the service has global offices, the New York address is listed for consistency. Refer to the website for regional office locations.

**THE COLOR ASSOCIATION
OF THE UNITED STATES**
www.colorassociation.com
33 Whitehall Street, Suite M3
New York, NY 10004
(212) 947-7774

INTERNATIONAL COLOUR AUTHORITY
www.colourforecasting.org
Colour Academy Ltd
PO Box 6356
London W1A 2WA

THE DONEGER GROUP
www.doneger.com
463 Seventh Avenue
New York, NY 10018
(212) 564-1266

DIRECTIVES WEST
www.directiveswest.com
110 E. 9th Street, Suite A229
Los Angeles, CA 90079
(213) 627-5921

TOBE
www.tobereport.com
463 Seventh Avenue, 2nd Floor
New York, NY 10018
(212) 867-8677

MARGIT PUBLICATIONS
www.mpnews.com
463 Seventh Avenue, 3rd Floor
New York, NY 10018
(212) 564-1266

THE COLOR MARKETING GROUP (CMG)
CMG's major focus is to identify the direction of color and design trends.
www.colormarketing.org
1908 Mount Vernon Avenue
Alexandria, VA 22301, USA
(703) 329-8500

HUEPOINT
www.huepoint.com
39 West 37th Street, 18th Floor
New York, NY 10018
(212) 921-2025

COLOR PORTFOLIO, INC.
www.colorportfolio.com
OPR—Overseas Publishers Rep
247 West 38th Street 12th Floor
New York, NY 10018
Tel: (212) 564-3954, (972) 447-9599,
toll free: (866) 876-8884

COLOR BY DESIGN OPTIONS
www.design-options.com
110 East 9th Street, Suite B769
Los Angeles, CA 90079
(213) 622-9094

PROMOSTYL
www.promostyl.com
853 Broadway, Suite 803
New York, NY 10003
(212) 228-8001

ESP TRENDLAB
www.esptrendlab.com
A division of Ellen Sideri Partnership Inc.
12 West 37th Street
New York, NY 10018
(212) 629-9200

FASHION SNOOPS
www.fashionsnoops.com
39 West 38th Street
New York, NY 10018
(212) 768-8804

PECLERS PARIS
www.peclersparis.com
114 Fifth Avenue
New York, NY 10011
(212) 228-1173

STYLE SIGHT
www.stylesight.com
25 West 39th Street
14th Floor
New York, NY 10018
(212) 675-8877

STYLELENS
www.stylelens.com
8581 Santa Monica Boulevard
West Hollywood, CA 90069
(310) 360-0954

TREND UNION, USA
www.trendunion.com
Edelkoort Inc.
Emmanuelle Linard
The Firehouse
604 East 11th street
New York NY 10009
(212) 420-7622

TRENDSTOP.COM
www.trendstop.com
28-39 The Quadrant
135 Salusbury Road
London NW6 6RJ
UK
+44 (0)870 788 6888

TRENDZINE FASHION INFORMATION
www.fashioninformation.com
Gainsborough House
81 Oxford Street
London
W1D 2EU
United Kingdom

WORLD GLOBAL STYLE NETWORK WGSN
www.wgsn.com
Greater London House
Hampstead Road
London NW1 7EJ

APPENDIX I

FASHION ILLUSTRATION REFERENCES FOR INSPIRATION

Following are lists of fashion illustrators to research and study for style and illustration technique. Use your local and school library to search archives of fashion illustration books and periodicals to gather more information. Online research can also be a tremendous time saver. Many current and contemporary fashion illustrators have a Facebook page (www.facebook.com), where you can see current displays of their work.

Some Current Professional Illustrators

Ruben Alterio
Alvaro
Carlos Aponte
Gennaro Avallone
Nick Backes
Christian (Bébé) Bérard
François Berthoud
René Bouché
Steven Broadway
Stefano Canulli
Zack Carr
James Childs
Michael Cooper
David Croland
Bil Donovan
Tod Draz
Rodger Duncan
Richard Ely
Eric (Carl Eric Erickson)
Joe Eula
Paul Fisher
Robert Fontanelli

René Gruau
Fred Greenhill
Robert and Bertha Herrmann
Glenn Hilario
Grizelda Holderness
Jim Howard
Katharine Sturges Knight
John Lagatta
Esther Larson
Pierre Le Tan
J. C. Leyendecker
Hélène Majera
Mats (Gustafson)
Lorenzo Mattotti
Lawrence Mynott
Nadja (Flower)
Chuck Nitzberg
Mel Odom
Alvin J. Pimsler
Robert W. Richards
Michael Roberts
Hippolyte Romain
Karen Santry
George Stavrinos
Paul Thek
Ruben Toledo
Hélène Tran
Marcel Vertès
Tony Viramontes
Michael Vollbracht
Jane Bixby Weller
Judy Francis Zankel
Zoltan (Halasz)

Illustrators for *Women's Wear Daily*

The following illustrators, whose work has appeared in *Women's Wear Daily,* can be researched through the book *WWD Illustrated: 1960s–1990s* by Michele Wesen Bryant, published by Fairchild Publications in 2004. They are listed by decades, which are worth noting and researching.

Analiese
Pedro Barrios
Kenneth Paul Block
Charles Boone
Stephen Cervantes
Julianne Engelman
Jack Geisinger
Sandra Leichman
Antonio Lopez
Dorothy Lovarro
Deborah Marquit
Steven Meisel
Robert Melendez
Kichisaburo Ogawa
Robert Passantino
Catherine Clayton Purnell
Joel Resnicoff
Richard Rosenfeld
Steven Stipelman
Richard Thornton
Glen Tunstull
Robert Young

Manga Illustration Style

Manga styles can be studied and added to basic fashion illustration techniques. Here are some sources from Dick Blick Art supplies, www.dickblick.com, to get started:

+ Basic Anatomy for the Manga Artist: Everything You Need to Start Drawing Authentic Manga Characters
+ Gothic Lolitas: How to Draw Manga Step by Step
+ How to Draw Manga
+ Kids Draw Manga Series
+ Kids Draw: Big Book of Everything Manga
+ Let's Draw Manga: Ninja and Samurai
+ The Manga Artist's Workbook: Chibis
+ Manga Chibis: How to Draw Manga Step by Step
+ Manga for the Beginner
+ Manga for the Beginner: Chibis
+ Manga Madness
+ Manga Mania: Chibi and Furry Characters
+ Manga Mania: Magical Girls and Friends
+ Manga Mania: Occult and Horror
+ Manga Mania: Shonen
+ Manga Mania: Shoujo
+ Manga Pro Superstar Workshop
+ Massive Manga: The Complete Reference to Drawing Manga
+ Mega Manga
+ Shonen Art Studio
+ Watson Guptill Comic and Manga Books

GLOSSARY

Accessory The term used to categorize items that are worn or used for a fashionable effect with an outfit: millinery, belts, handbags, luggage, leashes, jewelry, socks, gloves, hosiery, shoes, eyeglasses, scarves, neckties, and shawls. (Chapter 1)

Apparel channel of distribution A course of transmission in which a line of apparel is sold. (Chapter 3)

Apparel retail distribution categories A range of consumer spending venues, ranging from luxury to budget. (Chapter 3)

Attitudinized fashion figures Focused body type(s) and gestural-posed fashion figures which reflect the basic attitude of the customer. (Chapter 4)

Brand packaging Developing a brand or enhancing a brand's image with a consistent visual image, layout, design aesthetic, logo, texture, colors or silhouette message. (Chapter 2)

Buyer The person responsible for choosing and buying the goods for a retail store. (Chapter 1)

Collection editing Critical thinking to cull down the collection presentation for the portfolio. (Chapter 6)

Color forecast service A company that predicts color palettes for particular markets within the fashion industry. The timeline for prediction and reporting available can be for the current market through the future 18 months in-store placement. (Chapter 2)

Concept building Brainstorming ideas and collecting research from trends, media, retail, color, fabric, apparel silhouettes and all walks of life to be used as a starting base of designing the portfolio collection. (Chapter 6)

Croquis A drawing template of the human figure which is placed under a drawing surface (paper or computer) to quicken the process of designing garments or accessories and/or to standardize the scale of the figures and garments on the illustrated page. (Chapter 1)

Designer Filter A metaphor for the process of screening through trend and market information for the aesthetic message you want to bring forward. (Chapter 2)

Designer grid A basic platform for creating a design line through the process of concept building, editing, and finalization. (Chapter 3)

Eco/green apparel Clothing manufactured using fabrics and construction techniques set forth by guidelines currently being established by the garment and fiber industries and world trade. (Chapter 5)

Entry-level design job A designer's first job in the industry. (Chapter 1)

Fashion forecast service A company that predicts trends for particular markets within the fashion industry; including concepts, color, mood influences, retail and apparel silhouettes. The timeline for prediction and reporting available can be for the current market through the future 18 months in-store placement. (Chapter 2)

Fashion illustrator A trained commercial artist who renders fashion garments and accessories for a designer or design house and who generally is not educated as a fashion designer. (Chapter 1)

Fashion market specialization Design work concentrated on a special branch of apparel or accessories. (Chapter 3)

Fashion plates An illustrated, stylized fashion figure(s), drawn and rendered on paper or computer by a designer or illustrator, wearing the designer's garment(s) and/or accessory(ies) with an attitude of the designer's muse or end-consumer. The term can also be a reference to a stylish man or woman who dresses with chic style and panache from head to toe; hence looking perfectly like an illustrated, idealized fashion figure. (Chapter 1)

Fashion trade shows A show that is open to the trade only, held at a large convention center, small or large hotel room, or manufacturer's showroom to showcase manufacturer's products which pertain to the marketing and production of garments (for example, textiles, trims items, display mannequins). (Chapter 2)

Fiber bureau A corporate office for public relations and development of new and existing fibers for textile manufacturers which have trend services and fabric resources for designers within the industry. (Chapter 2)

Finalization editing Committing the images to the portfolio age after making changes. (Chapter 6)

Fit model A male or female person with standard body measurements established by a designer, company, or manufacturer of apparel. He or she is a model for the designer to try on sample garments from the factory to see whether the garments fit according to the designer's specifications. (Chapter 4)

Flat drawings A technical, graphic line drawing of a garment or accessory that depicts how the garment looks laying on a flat surface without indication of a body inside of it. (Chapter 1).

Fluid portfolio building On-going, never-ending update to the fashion designer's portfolio throughout his/her career. (Chapter 7)

Forums for trend, color, and textiles Areas designated at fashion, color, trend, and textile trade shows that feature intense interactive exhibits for designers to touch, feel, and research information. (Chapter 3)

Hanger appeal How a garment or accessory looks on a hanger or a display case in a retail environment. Used as a gauge for a product's ability to sell at retail. (Chapter 1)

Idealized portfolio The visual image of the portfolio you want to create. (Chapter 3)

Inclusion choices for the portfolio book In-class collection illustrations, past work from former jobs, fashion show photographs, press coverage, and awards. (Chapter 7)

Internship An assistant job within a corporation that is usually short-term and is unpaid. A paid internship is the same as an internship, with the exception of a salary. (Chapter 1)

Junior sizes Women's clothing sizes, that run in odd numbers, 1 through 11. (Chapter 4)

Key categories Focused areas of apparel design for a specific end use. (Chapter 4)

Knockoff To produce an inexpensive, sometimes illegal copy of a well-known product. (Chapter 1)

Leave-behind-piece A printed page, folder, CD/ROM, DVD, or flash drive promotional representation of the portfolio images given to an interviewer to keep. (Chapter 4)

Look book A seasoned designer's portfolio of press releases, photographs, illustrations, and schematic drawings of their successful product placements on customers, models, celebrities, retail ads, fashion shows, entertainment, sporting, political and/or everyday events. (Chapter 4)

Mass merchant A retailer that appears in many areas of the country or world that carries large amounts of merchandise; for example, Sears, Walmart, JCPenney, Target, and Kmart. (Chapter 2)

Merchandiser The position within a manufacturing company or design house that oversees product placement and position in the retail market. He or she helps to meld the creative process of the design staff with the corporate sales, buying, distribution, production, and marketing teams. The merchandiser may also be an employee of a retail store, helping to bridge the corporate buying, production, development, and selling of apparel/accessories. (Chapter 1)

Misses Sizes Women's clothing sizes that run in even numbers, 0 through 22. (Chapter 4)

Multi-media programs Computer-based programs for presentation purposes, such as PowerPoint presentations, Adobe Director presentations, or Adobe Flash presentations. (Chapter 8)

Page sequencing The order in which you place your illustration collections in your portfolio. (Chapter 7)

Plus sizes Women's clothing sizes that range in even numbers Plus-size 14 through 32, and 1x , 2x, and 3x. (Chapter 4)

Portable device CD-ROM, DVD, or USB flash drive used to store portfolio images. (Chapter 8)

Price point The price for a garment that is based upon the quality of the material goods, trim costs, design, construction, the perceived value of the goods, and retail venue. (Chapter 3)

Prototype A first full-size model of a garment/accessory to test or review the essential features, function and aesthetics prior to completing a final product. A test sample, drawing, rendering or sketch to see how it will work before you make the final product. (Chapter 1)

Retail distribution The set of stores and/or Web sites that the designer is designing for. (Chapter 1)

RTW (ready-to-wear) Clothing that is offered for sale in a standard size and completely finished, as opposed to clothing made to the customer's specifications or requirements. (Chapter 1)

Samplehand The sewing machine operator in a designer's studio that produces the first samples of a garment or accessory. (Chapter 1)

Size Range The set numbers assigned to the fit of apparel for a given market. (Chapter 3)

Specialized portfolios Detailed design collections in a portfolio which focus upon the practical, applied functional details customized to the client's needs; such as accessories, bridal, haute couture, etc. (Chapter 5)

Specs (specifications) The exact measurements of each panel or patterned section of a garment or when measured on a fully constructed, flat surface. (Chapter 1)

Thumbnail A rough fashion sketch drawn quickly without precision or thought to detail to capture an idea or design on the page. (Chapter 1)

T-shirt blanks T-shirts without graphic prints added to them, which can be purchased in a full range of colors. (Chapter 5)

Web-based portfolios A website created by the designer to showcase his or her designs. (Chapter 8)

INDEX